For Angel

On your 15th birthday 😊
I am so glad that you have
made a commitment to purity!
It is so worth it. I thought
this book would help you as you
strive to live your single years
for Christ and looking forward
to the wonderful adventure of a
Godly marriage.

With much Love
Rachael♡

SO MUCH MORE

SO MUCH MORE

*The Remarkable Influence of Visionary
Daughters on the Kingdom of God*

By Anna Sofia Botkin *and*
Elizabeth Botkin

THE VISION FORUM, INC.
San Antonio, Texas

"Where there is no vision, the people perish." (Proverbs 29:18)

The Vision Forum, Inc.
4719 Blanco Rd., San Antonio, Texas 78212
www.visionforum.com

Visit www.visionarydaughters.com for more.

ISBN-10 0-9755263-8-3
ISBN-13 978-0-9755263-8-5

Detail of "Caller Herrin", circa nineteenth century,
by Sir John Everett Millais (1829-1896, b. England).
Oil on canvas, 43 ½ x 31 in., private collection,
Agnew's, London, United Kingdom.

Design by Jeremy Fisher

Printed in the United States of America

DEDICATION

To our heavenly Father
who chose to make us the daughters of our earthly father,

And to our earthly father
who taught us about our heavenly Father.

TABLE OF CONTENTS

TABLE OF CONTENTS

ACKNOWLEDGMENTS

We are so thankful to God for our dear parents, whose sacrifices on our behalf made this book possible. Their godly examples inspired us. Their love of Scripture instructed and challenged us. Their library of books and other resources has opened up to us a world we are thankful to live in.

We have come to value those things they appreciate, from good literature to good theology to good friends like Doug and Beall Phillips, who for years have courageously stood up for the best ideas represented in this book. We thank the Board of Directors of Vision Forum for having the courage to publish such a controversial book by such young authors. We are also indebted to Mrs. M.L. Chancey, who read a draft of this book and provided careful and wise counsel. We thank our friend Genevieve Smith, whose story inspired this book, and who provided encouragement to us when the writing was hard going. Special thanks are due our heroines who contributed not only personal stories but many helpful observations.

Last but not least, we are deeply grateful for our five brothers, who have helped give us a vivid understanding of the created differences between men and women, and of why they need each other.

CHAPTER ONE

DAUGHTERS OF THE ETERNAL FATHER

WHO SHOULD READ THIS BOOK

"The world is a mess, and it's our fault." This is one of the most important things our father has taught us over the years. It sounds hard, but sometimes we need to hear hard truths. God has given principles for all people to live by. Christians are supposed to know exactly what these principles are and live by them, setting the example and upholding the standard. Yet Christians can be some of the most careless and ungrateful and forgetful people. We Christians can be responsible for leading the culture either away from God's design or toward it. Our father has taught us to confess our errors and admit our mistakes. Christians truly have been a part of the problem, because we have been careless with the standard.

We are faced with the challenge in life, Dad has told us, of either living the way everyone else does, or of being different, faithful to God's design. We've discovered that being faithful to God's design is not possible if we have neglected to "study it out" from Scripture. We attempt to examine this design in this book. Where the design differs from the world, we have to think differently, act differently, and even dislike the world.[1] This is the really hard part.

God doesn't call us to "find our place in the world" but to wage war with a worldly culture that has declared war on God's design. This is why our father has inspired us to be as different as we need to be in order to be obedient to God's design.

This book is not another Christian-teenage-girl "survival guide." This book explains how Christian girls can wage war with the world and win. We aren't going to tell you how to be swept into a horrendously perverse culture while still hanging on to the teeny little shred of purity that the world allows you to have. We'd rather focus on how young women can rise above their God-hating culture and change it for the better.

Who we are

We are Anna Sofia and Elizabeth Botkin, the only daughters of Geoffrey and Victoria Botkin. We wrote the bulk of this book during a fascinating two-year period of our lives. We started when we were 17 and 15, respectively.

Our use of the first person plural is an important component of this book. "We" are writing about shared experiences and shared

---

1 When we say "world" we refer to culture that is not in submission to God, and the people in enmity with God. Enmity means ill will, hatred, and hostility. The Bible's commands about our relationship to the world are clear: "Love not the world, neither the things that are in the world. If any man love the world, the love of the Father is not in him. For all that is in the world, the lust of the flesh, and the lust of the eyes, and the pride of life, is not of the Father, but is of the world. And the world passeth away, and the lust thereof: but he that doeth the will of God abideth for ever" (1 John 2:15-17). "Ye adulterers and adulteresses, know ye not that the friendship of the world is enmity with God? whosoever therefore will be a friend of the world is the enemy of God" (James 4:4).

conclusions. We have challenged one another and examined one another as we collected our observations, our research, and our theological convictions. This collaboration has helped us dig more deeply into each controversy.

We're not authorities. We're teenagers. We write this book as a candid examination of our times and the issues facing us, from the perspective of two young girls. We believe many of our interesting experiences give us a unique vantage point in society. Before we go further, we must honor and thank our heavenly Father for ordaining a family life for us that has been full of blessings. We have an earthly father who loves us enough to protect us and challenge us. He and our wonderful mother have shown us what marriage and family life can be like when the purpose of marriage is rediscovered, and how the home can be a place of adventure.

We, along with five energetic brothers, have enjoyed great adventure. We have enjoyed the privileges of academic freedom, exposure to many modern cultures, exposure to diverse people and remarkable leaders. We have also been exposed to the experience of growing up "different." We are not strangers to controversy.

The adventure that most directly influences this book is what went on around our large, lively dinner table. Since the days of our earliest memories, our successive dining rooms in different states and countries have seen many regular visitors. People like to be around our table. They like to be around our parents. They like to listen to our father talk about important theological discoveries and issues. Because university students have been some of the most regular and numerous visitors, we two girls grew up listening to, and then conversing with, some very interesting people, learning about the weighty issues facing them. When we were little girls, our first real friends outside our family circle were young college girls, often

Christians, who were hundreds of miles from their homes and who were made welcome in our home.

As we grew older, we became acquainted with problems and predicaments that tortured so many of these young ladies. Broken homes. The desire to have families. Futile, politically-correct college courses. The need for protection. Confusion about the meaning of "true love." Disinterested fathers. Confused mothers. The longing for spiritual guidance. An irrelevant Church. The need for security and stability. It is no wonder so many of these girls felt orphaned, unloved, and without hope for the future. What they all seemed to want more than anything else was truth, safety, purpose, and *faithful male companionship and protection.*

Today's young women have good reason to be even more confused and painfully frustrated than those we met in the 1990s. Society has deteriorated, and they know it. Most of our friends take a look at the world facing them and become pessimistic to unbearable proportions. Let's face it: it's a cruel, vicious world out there for a girl. There are the general problems most Christians recognize: skyrocketing crime rates, divorce rates, promiscuity and infidelity, the abortion culture, the redefining of "marriage"… but perceptive young women can see that there are greater, deeper problems facing them directly.

Many girls are spiritually and emotionally abandoned by parents during their "day care" years. After high school graduation, they are left to fend for themselves in a dog-eat-dog world. Feminism promised that women in a feminist society would live on a utopian playground, enjoying liberation and equality. What we see instead is women being exploited by men to an extreme never before seen on such a wide scale in the West.[2] Most of our friends have an inner longing to be loved and protected, but most of the men they have ever known are either cowards or predators. All these girls know is what they see around them, and it makes them cynical about their families, their parents, their future husbands, and their future children. Many of them are confused about what womanhood is all about and don't know where to look for godly, feminine role models.

The answers girls need

Today girls come to our home for the same reasons they always have: to experience the safety and happiness of a solid family environment and to see if the family might provide answers to some of their most pressing questions. They come to learn from the godly example of our wonderful mother and to take refuge under the strong spiritual leadership and guidance of our incredible father. Today we interact with these young women as peers. This book is a cursory summary of the questions they are asking and the answers we have been trying to cautiously provide them. This is the main reason the book follows a question-and-answer format.

We fully acknowledge that we're somewhat young to be coming to such strong conclusions. We also understand that we may handle these issues more wisely after our teenage years. But we see a need to write this book now.

---

2   The "West" is the term we use to identify the societies created by the influence of Christianity as it spread across Europe, influencing the Reformation of the 16th century and then the colonial outposts of Great Britain in the 17th through19th centuries. The nations of the West have been understood to be those in Western Europe, North America, and the British Commonwealth countries. The term "Christendom" is sometimes used to refer to the same nations, but during a period in history in which Christianity was flourishing. Today Christianity is being replaced by a rival faith known as statism.

Young women make many decisions during the teen years that dramatically affect their futures. We know many who are struggling hard with the painful frustrations of life in an anti-family, feminized world. We believe the ideas in this book will help them now. We also believe the ideas in this book will stimulate further scholarly examination of topics that should not be neglected by adults. We introduce many topics with the aim of getting them into the public debate.

How should this book be used?

Maybe a warning is needed. Don't read this book at all (I would rephrase: "You won't like this book…") if you have a bad attitude toward your father and if you are trying to keep your distance from him. Many girls enjoy having "space" away from their fathers. That space is dangerous.

This book is about protection. We know a number of girls whose fathers are so passive they don't provide their daughters with any kind of guidance, direction, discipline, or correction. We know girls who like it this way. One of these girls said, "I sure hope my dad never picks up any of these ideas about interfering with my life or what I want!"

That girl is afraid to lose a measure of childish independence. She is afraid of fatherly input and protection. If you don't want this from your father, then you don't have the heart for this book. If you are not willing to give your heart to your father, this book will put you at odds with the scriptural mandate you will find here. Besides, if you leave the book lying around, your father might find it and get fatherly ideas. However, this is not a book for fathers. Even though there are many things we might like to say to fathers, it is simply not a part of God's design that we do the saying. In Appendix A, we have asked our own father if he would volunteer some advice to men, which he agreed to do.

If you decide to read this book, read it like a Berean.[3] Check what we say against Scripture. If it is hard going, read slowly, in small doses. We wrote this book to be read from beginning to end, as the questions get progressively tougher. We have tried to address each of the main issues that weigh on the minds and consciences of young women in the 14-24 age bracket. Thus, the book is organized into seventeen main topics, including careerism, college, courtship, and other controversial subjects. Perhaps the most spiritually foundational chapter in the book is Chapter Four, about your duty of submission. Please pray for a responsive heart before you read it.

How radical are the ideas in this book?

Many of these ideas will be very uncomfortable to readers, at first. Those readers who finish the whole book will begin to see more comfort in the ideas than threat. In the course of our research, we discovered that a lot of our "radical" and "new" ideas used to be held by practically all Americans. The lifestyle and worldview we present is not merely theoretical. It was lived before, when women were much happier. It is being lived again today by brave young women who are determined to follow the wise course for womanhood, lovingly designed by God Himself, whatever the cost. As we were writing this book, we were delighted to find that a biblical understanding of the father-daughter relationship is spreading farther and faster than we dared to imagine. Fourteen other daughters, mostly from the United States, have contributed their own stories to this book.

---

3   "And the brethren immediately sent away Paul and Silas by night unto Berea: who coming thither went into the synagogue of the Jews. These were more noble than those in Thessalonica, in that they received the word with all readiness of mind, and searched the Scriptures daily, whether those things were so." (Acts 17:10)

Many of the answers and solutions we, and they, have found
will seem incredibly extreme and drastic. We believe that in a day of
extreme apostasy and judgment, *extreme measures are exactly what is
called for*, and that *a drastic step in the opposite direction is exactly what
we need to take.*

21st Century heroines of the faith

This is a book by young women for other young women. Let us
introduce you to the fourteen young women you will get to know
in its pages. Sometimes we refer to them as *The Young Heroines of the
Underground Feminist Resistance Movement*, because they have dealt
so courageously with the destructive influence of feminism.

We're certain they would rather be known simply as daughters
who have turned their hearts to their fathers. In so doing, they are
rediscovering the benefits and blessings God intended girls to have.
In so doing, of course, they are repairing the feminist mistake made
by millions of their fellow women.

They have chosen femininity over feminism. In becoming ladies,
they have become heroines at a time when militant feminism has
created an horrendous culture of intimidation that makes purity,
gentleness, and biblical womanhood very uncool.

Their ages range from mid-teens to mid-twenties. They are not
the only heroines out there. There are tens of thousands of young
women with similar frustrations, similar decisions, similar results,
and similar stories to tell. The most common theme in every story
is repentance. Each young lady faced a challenge to obey something
in the revealed word of God. These girls realized where they were
wrong and turned to a new direction—changing their ways of
thinking, and their actions.

Today they are at peace with God and their circumstances, though they all must continually contend with a predominantly feminist culture. They must also endure the disapproval of many people who call their zealous obedience to Scripture "legalism."[4]

Genevieve was raised to be an independent, high-powered career woman. From a young age, she diligently pursued academic excellence and made it her goal to achieve political recognition and power. She developed the idea that by gaining personal power and authority in her nation, she could accomplish God's will for her life and His will for her nation. Like so many other women of her day, she lived as though independence was a virtue, believing that competing with men was good for her and that having a career was more important than having a family. By God's grace, her eyes were opened, and she discovered that she had been lied to and was being exploited. She involved her father in her remarkable recovery.

Sarah was also raised with a feminist mindset. Though she wanted to use the abilities God had given her to impact the culture for Christ, she didn't think that could be accomplished through simply being a daughter and a sister. So she listened to the world's advice for her methods and desired to train for a career as a lawyer and judge. Through her study of Scripture, she realized that the very way she was trying to please the Lord was displeasing to Him. She asked for her father's help in the changes she made in her life. In receiving that help, she enjoys a new relationship with her father and family that has been an example to all who know them.

---

4 None of these heroines are legalistic; none come from legalistic homes. We define legalism as the fleshly pursuit of man's moralism in hopes of earning salvation. Joyful obedience, on the other hand, to all of God's precepts, is the response of the grateful believer who has been saved by grace through faith.

Rebekah greatly disliked being a girl. She was at times angry and bitter toward God for not making her a boy. She consoled herself by indulging in every boyish pursuit she could and gloated over anything that she thought made her superior to boys. She tried to be "tough" and "strong," resenting any male assistance or courtesy that she considered patronizing or insulting. When she repented of her anger, rebellion, and bitterness toward a loving heavenly Father, she became willing to learn what God wanted to say about women. Now Rebekah can truly say, "While pursuing femininity, I have found more strength, especially in character, than I ever did in pursuing feminism."

Amber worried about her life's purpose. As her high school graduation neared, many doors of opportunity opened up for her, but she knew none of them was a cause worth giving her life for. After years of seeking God's design for single young women, she and her father finally found it.

Amy was 23 years old and ready to start a life on her own, when suddenly her mother was diagnosed with cancer and died seven months later. Before she died, Amy's mother asked Amy to take care of her nine younger brothers and sisters, the youngest just a year old. Amy's struggles in coping with this devastating turn of events, and adjusting to her new role of surrogate mother and lady-of-the-house, have required strength and grace she never could have found in feminist solutions. She also found that she needed her father even more than he needed her.

Hannah never wanted to go off to college or to enter the corporate world. But her father gave her no other direction for her life after graduation, and in her heart she began to resent him for this. As a result, she did not truly honor her father, who did not fully have her heart. When the Lord revealed to her father His plan for daughters, He also revealed to Hannah the bitterness that had begun to grow in her heart against her father. By His grace, He turned their hearts toward each other, giving Hannah contentment and trust in her father's guidance, provision, and protection.

Erica wanted to use her life to serve God, so at age nineteen she jumped into full-time "ministry" 300 miles away from home. Over time, God worked in her heart and convinced her that her goals were not His goals. Erica then gave up her own priorities and began seriously seeking God's will to find out where He really wanted her, instead of where the world said He wanted her.

Fiona was intelligent and had a fiercely independent spirit—the key ingredients to being a successful woman by our generation's standards. At age eighteen she left home to pursue higher education and launched herself into a life of independence. She describes it as a life of grief and depression. After five years of unhappiness, becoming increasingly distressed that she didn't know how God wanted her to use her life, Fiona repented.

Ruth was brought up in a Christian home and was consistently taught Ephesians 6:1-3 which says, "Children, obey your parents in the Lord: for this is right. Honor thy father and mother; which is the first commandment with promise; that it may be well with thee, and thou mayest live long on the earth." However, like all girls Ruth has struggled with honor and obedience. Though she loved her parents, she realized she could be honoring them and serving them more than she was. She has now put her heart into delighting them and making their lives comfortable, and she shares many of the things she has learned in her journey.

Amber Dawn has faced the challenges of patience and contentment. Through her personal study of Scripture and her loving relationship with her father, she discovered the priceless beauty of contentment in all things and the great value of the time spent with her father before marriage.

Jennie was a promising scholar whose parents wanted to see her distinguish herself in academics. So, after she won a full college scholarship, she was packed off to begin her "higher education." It was obvious that Jennie had many talents that deserved to be developed, yet after studying only a short time, she began to be disillusioned with the whole experience everyone had raved about as being beneficial. Through genuine humility she found a more biblical approach to higher education. Jennie is now a happy wife and a mother of seven children.

Kelly, the oldest of four children, never understood just how influential a sister's life is to younger siblings. Not having embraced God's design for sisters, she wasn't fulfilling her role of encourager, mentor, and friend. Kelly began to find more joy and fulfillment for her life when she asked herself the questions: "How would God's Word define the role of older sister?" and "What does God ask of a daughter and sister?" From those questions she began a journey to understand, through the sufficiency of Scripture, what the Lord has prepared for her to do.

Crystal was brought up with a vision for how she wanted to conduct business: in the same way that the Proverbs 31 woman did. However, she struggled with the feminist mentality even while seeking this goal. She began to realize that even in a seemingly harmless situation, selfish, feminist thoughts could take root in her heart, and she had to cry out to God to help her overcome them. Now He has shown her what it truly is to have works worthy of "praising her in the gates."

Sarah Irene tried to prevent her parents' divorce but found herself powerless to do so, and she was then angry with God when it happened. Diving into a life of rebellion, she went to live with a passive father so that she could do anything she wanted. When she finally repented, she found herself without protection or guidance.

As you can see, none of our heroines come from ideal circumstances. The answers and solutions we have found are not primarily for girls with perfect families or good situations. These ideas are for girls who want to obey God's design for women no matter *what* their circumstances.

The stories of these young ladies represent feminine heroism. Their stories are stories of repentance, forgiveness, and God's blessings. These girls will be commended and remembered for the courage they have shown in discarding lies and embracing God's truth, for daring to be women in a culture that condemns real womanhood and denies the power of godly femininity. We are proud to take our stand beside them.

Feminists will say we're weak, but after struggling with feminism ourselves, we realize that being a woman of God will take more of our strength than trying to be anything else. It will require the courage and conviction of a martyr. This is not a book for the weak-hearted or peer-dependant.

CHAPTER TWO

DAUGHTERS, FATHERS, AND THE CRISIS

WHAT DAUGHTERS HAVE BEEN MISSING

*Does my relationship with my father
really influence my future?*

In this generation, girls are facing a lot of problems. In fact, this year young women are facing a lot more problems than they did a century ago. Some of these are novel problems invented by modern times. We know more than we wish to know about the problems troubling young women, because ever since we were little girls young women have been coming to our home to get a taste of functional family life and pour out their troubled hearts.

They are facing all kinds of complications, conundrums, cynicism, and confusion over where they're headed in life. They struggle with a proper idea of femininity and masculinity, a healthy view of authority and submission, a sense of direction and priority, the concept of protection and security, and an elementary understanding of what it means to be daughters of God.

We've found that these girls all have one more thing in common: they are missing a functional, confiding, loving relationship with their fathers.

Oh sure, they have happy, casual buddy relationships with their dads, but this is not a substitute for a strong, biblical relationship that edifies, inspires, and strengthens both the father and the daughter.

Is their missing relationship with their fathers the root of all their other problems? No, not the only root. But we believe, after years of studying both God's Word and modern times, that *the forgotten principles of fatherly protection and daughterly honor are the missing dynamic girls need in leading fruitful, stable, happy lives which will give honor to God.* We do not believe that the father-daughter relationship is somehow more important or special than the mother-daughter relationship, or the father-son relationship, nor do we mean to breathe into this relationship a kind of super-special, mystical quality never seen in the Bible. But we do believe the father-daughter relationship is being more ignored and abused than other relationships in this generation, with disastrous and heartbreaking repercussions. Girls are hurting from the absence of strong, biblical relationships with their fathers, and repairing those relationships should be a priority for the young women of our generation.

Isn't developing a good relationship with God a higher priority?

Of course. "He that loveth father or mother more than me is not worthy of me: and he that loveth son or daughter more than me is not worthy of me" (Matthew 10:37). This doesn't lessen the importance of your relationship with your father in any way. In fact, having a loving relationship with your father is one of the ways you show your love for God.

The fact that God describes himself as a Father to us shows us that the position of earthly father is like *an earthly reflection of God*. To understand God's nature as our "Father," we need to understand what a father is for and how we are supposed to relate to our fathers. This is why it's so important to God that we show our fathers *love, honor, and obedience*. Matthew 25:40 tells us that doing well by others is how we do well by Him. God reckons it as love to Him when we love our neighbors, and He reckons it as honor and service to Him when we honor and serve those whom He gives us as His representatives.

The virtues we learn by being good daughters to our fathers on earth help us in being good daughters to the King, preparing us for this life and the life to come. Being protected by our fathers teaches us how to be protected, loved, and cherished, and teaches the responsibilities that go with this blessing—how to be faithful, how to be trusting, and how to have a yielded heart. Learning how to relate this way to our earthly fathers will teach us to relate this way to our Heavenly Father.

So is my father supposed to be more than my friend?

Our fathers are supposed to be dear, trusted confidantes and friends, but God has given them a charge to be much more than this. They are to be our knights in shining armor, our protectors, our guardians, and they are even supposed to represent God to us. This means that our dads have the tremendous responsibility of being accurate reflections of God's authority, as well as providers of the security and love that God created us, as women, to need. There is something no girl can honestly deny—that she has a need, built into her from the beginning, for male affection, love, and protection.

Girls who don't get these things from their fathers generally go looking for them in other places. This leads to trouble and the most common (and most stupid) mistakes women make.

Why do I have an innate need for male affection, love, and protection?

Because that's how God created women. We will not be able to understand our own needs and desires and strengths, and how we ought to relate to our fathers, until we understand the original relationship God created between men and women.

We would not exist but for men; man was our source. We read in Genesis that God created man in His image, saw that it was not good for man to be alone, and so took a rib from him and fashioned it into a woman. Man was formed from dust, but woman had her origin and being *from* man and *for* man.

But man was incomplete without her. It is the two of them *together* that reflect the image and glory of God. It is only when woman is, in effect, restored to man's side, that the two are fully complete. And it is because we were created from the rib of man that we have an innate desire to be restored to the side of man.

This is a great mystery. Most people don't even care to understand this. Some find this idea very offensive and hard to accept. But until we can understand the relationship between mankind and womankind as God created them, understanding the way we can together reflect the image and glory of God, we can't fully understand what it really means to be women or how we can best serve God as women.

Gloria Steinem, founding editor of *Ms. Magazine* and one of the mothers of the feminist movement, stated, "A woman without a man is like a fish without a bicycle."[1]

Even many women who have rejected more extreme feminism feel this way. Even independent women who acknowledge men's usefulness and who plan to get married or be somehow involved with men "someday" are held captive to the idea that men are optional and can be put off until later. Many women feel they are too busy doing their important work to involve any male input and involvement in their lives. To these women, men are just a distraction.

But God created men to be more than just optional lifestyle accessories. He created women to be dependent on them, in a good way.

1 Corinthians 11:11,12 tells us, "Nevertheless neither is the man without the woman, neither the woman without the man, in the Lord. For as the woman is of the man, even so is the man also by the woman; but all things of God."

Ms. Steinem's statement was not only absurd; it was blasphemous.[2] This is because the relationship between men and women parallels the relationship between Christ and the Church (Ephesians 5:23). It's the equivalent of saying, "The Church without Christ is like a fish without a bicycle."

God is the one who created us and decided whom we will need. Women *do* need men, in the same way that the Church needs Christ. To deny this is to blaspheme.

---

1 *The Oxford Dictionary of Modern Quotations* by Tony Augarde (Oxford University Press, Oxford and New York, 1992).

2 Blasphemy is defined in the *Webster's 1828 Dictionary* as "…an injury offered to God, by denying that which is due and belonging to Him, or attributing to Him that which is not agreeable to His nature."

Are men and women equally important?

Of course men and women are equal in God's eyes. Galatians 3:28 says "There is neither Jew nor Greek, there is neither slave nor free, there is neither male nor female; for you are all one in Christ Jesus." We are fellow heirs according to the promise. Our souls are of equal worth to God. We are individually accountable before God for our actions.

But this doesn't mean our earthly purposes and functions are the same. Equal doesn't mean identical. God gives us different abilities and different jobs, according to His plan for order. And men and women *are different*. God created them to be different. He called them and their differences "good."

What are the different roles God gave to men and women?

God saw that it was not good for Adam to be alone and said, "I will make a helper suitable for him." Being companions and helpers is more than just a job God gave us. It's what we were actually created *for*. It's what we were designed and specially equipped to be. In fact, it's an intrinsic and inextricable part of our natures to be helpers to men. It's not something we can get away from, even by choice.

In the same way, men were created to lead, and this is not something they can get away from, even by choice. Now, they can choose to lead badly, or they can choose to let women lead them (which is the same as leading badly). Even men who don't look like they're leading at all have made an active decision *not* to lead properly.

Women can help men lead badly. They do this by taking advantage of men's weakness to put themselves in charge.

In the Garden of Eden, Eve let herself be deceived by the serpent, and Adam didn't protect her from the deception. He then followed her lead, even though he knew it was wrong. Interestingly enough, "...in Adam all die,"[3]—not in Eve! Adam is rightly blamed for the sin they both committed because he could not escape his responsibility as leader any more than Eve could escape from her role as his helper.

Have there ever been any women who found complete "liberation" from men?

Women who think they have are merely deceived. Complete independence from man would go against the very order of God's creation. Every woman's life is built around men and men's role and leadership in some way. This is true for the parasitical women who live like leeches off men and whose lives revolve around attracting men, and for the die-hard feminists who dedicate their lives to proving that they don't need men, and for the godly, virtuous women who understand that submitting to God means joyfully submitting to the authority He has placed over them. *Women have really only two ways of relating to men: helping them lead poorly, for Satan's glory, or helping them lead well, for God's glory.*

Women who don't know this usually—unwittingly—spend their lives helping the wrong men. Women who do recognize this fact structure their lives and priorities around making the most of their innate purpose and abilities, carefully choosing what causes they will support and what men they will help. They are more fruitful in serving God, because they accept the purpose He created them for, thus making wise decisions.

Take a look back in history for a moment, at all the women we think of as being "independent" of men. You will discover something

---

3   "For as in Adam all die, even so in Christ shall all be made alive." (1 Corinthians 15:22)

fascinating. Take Betty Friedan, America's premier feminist. Even *she* couldn't escape from her own inherent nature as helpmeet. She spent her whole professional life advancing the agenda of Karl Marx and his disciples. The modern feminist movement was designed by these men, as we will show in Chapter 6.

Though some of the women they recruited to their cause didn't realize it—women who genuinely thought they were breaking away from men, casting off the shackles of submission, promoting freedom and independence, and paving the way for a better tomorrow for women—they were merely serving these men's primary goals.[4] They were really just unknowingly making the same choice Eve made at the very beginning: to help men lead badly for Satan's glory.

Understanding these fundamentals of manhood and womanhood is what daughters need to start setting their relationships with their fathers back onto a more biblical course.

---

4 "Women's lib is a 'ladies' auxiliary of the radical left. The hard core embraces Marxism, although Gloria Steinem will admit only to being socialist. Prime purposes of feminism are to establish a lesbian-socialist republic and to dismantle the family unit." ("The Declaration of Feminism" or "The Document," quoted on www.fathersforlife.org.)

CHAPTER THREE

FATHERS, DAUGHTERS, AND PROTECTION

WHAT OUR FATHERS DO FOR US

Exactly how do fathers fit into God's design?

Because the Bible doesn't give a huge amount of instruction exclusively to fathers and daughters, most of what we have to work from are the passages setting the patterns for men and women in general. God has given men three very specific and important duties regarding women.

Even before the fall, there was an order—a hierarchy of authority—established by God. This order states that man is the *authority* over the woman and is supposed to *lead* her. "But I would have you know, that the head of every man is Christ; and the head of the woman is the man; and the head of Christ is God" (1 Corinthians 11:3). Why does Paul write to Timothy, "But I suffer not a woman to teach, nor to usurp authority over the man, but to be in silence"? "For Adam was first formed, then Eve" (1 Timothy 2:12,13). The reason for her submission to him is not a result of the fall, or of our now sinful natures. It was God's plan for humanity from the beginning.

So man's first responsibility to woman is to *lead* her in the same way that Christ leads the Church. He is her spiritual head and covering.

Secondly, because of Adam and Eve's disobedience in the garden, God cursed them both. The curse given to each of them was different. Adam's curse was, "...cursed is the ground for thy sake; in sorrow shalt thou eat of it all the days of thy life; Thorns also and thistles shall it bring forth to thee; and thou shalt eat the herb of the field; In the sweat of thy face shalt thou eat bread, till thou return unto the ground; for out of it wast thou taken: for dust thou art, and unto dust shalt thou return" (Genesis 3:17b-19).

Adam's curse pertained to the difficulty he would have providing for his family. This is the man's duty. 1 Timothy 5:8 says, "But if any provide not for his own, and specially for those of his own house, he hath denied the faith, and is worse than an infidel."

Never in Scripture are women given the responsibility to provide for their families. This is a job specifically given to men, to the extent that if they fail in this responsibility, they are worse than unbelievers.

Thirdly, husbands and fathers are supposed to *protect* their wives and daughters.

One of the passages that directly speaks to the father's duty to protect his daughter is in Numbers 30:

> If a man vow a vow unto the Lord, or swear an oath to bind his soul with a bond; he shall not break his word, he shall do according to all that proceedeth out of his mouth. If a woman also vow a vow unto the Lord, and bind herself by a bond, being in her father's house in her youth; And her father hear her vow, and her bond wherewith she hath bound her soul, and her father shall hold his peace at her; then all her vows shall stand, and every bond wherewith she hath bound her soul shall stand. But

> if her father disallow her in the day that he heareth; not any of
> her vows, or of her bonds wherewith she hath bound her soul,
> shall stand: and the Lord shall forgive her, because her father
> disallowed her. (Numbers 30:2-5)

If a man makes a rash vow, the Lord holds him accountable,
and he has no way out of it. However, God in His mercy granted
daughters a go-between, or mediator. Her father can protect her
from her foolishness, and the Lord shall forgive her. Because the
consequences for making a rash vow could be dire, this is why a
daughter's special exemption from obligation is a sign of particular
mercy from God—and why her father's protection is such a blessing.

Men are also supposed to protect women's lives, as shown in
Ephesians 5:25: "Husbands, love your wives, even as Christ also
loved the church, and gave himself for it."

It's interesting to see that there is even a distinction in the kind of
love that men and women are to bear to one another. In the original
Greek, the word "love" used here is *agape*. Carolyn Mahaney, in her
book *Feminine Appeal*, explains, "The Greek word *agape* refers to a
self-sacrificing love. It's a love that gives to others even if nothing
is given back."[1] In contrast, whenever women are instructed to
love their husbands, the word agape is not used. Women are to
have *phileo* love for their husbands. *Phileo* love refers rather to a
tender, affectionate, brotherly love. It is men who are commanded
specifically to show sacrificial love and be, as Christ was, "the Saviour
of the body" ("body" referring to the wife, see Ephesians 5:23).

> "So ought men to love their wives as their own bodies. He that
> loveth his wife loveth himself. For no man ever yet hated his

---

1 Carolyn Mahaney, *Feminine Appeal: Seven Virtues of a Godly Wife and Mother*
(Wheaton, Illinois: Crossway Books, 2004), p. 33.

own flesh; but nourisheth and cherisheth it, even as the Lord the church:" (Ephesians 5:28,29)

Aren't all Christians, both men and women, supposed to be willing to lay down their lives for each other?

Yes, all Christians are supposed to die for one another in various ways. But the Bible does have specific, different instructions for men and women on this subject! Certainly, women are supposed to make sacrifices, even lay down their lives, for others, but never in Scripture does God issue a command for women to die for men. He does lay it down as a command for men, though.

When God commanded Israel to go to war, the qualification of someone "able to go forth to war" was first to be a male twenty years old or upward (Numbers 1:2,3). The Christian principle (and the historic tradition) is always that *men* are the ones who go out to defend hearth and home, women, and children. The standard laws of warfare in Deuteronomy 20 command Israelite soldiers to kill all the enemy males, but to spare the enemy women and children.[2] Even in war, men have a duty to domestic life and those things that ensure the future.

As Jennie Chancey, editor of BeautifulWomanhood.org, explains in her article "When Mamma Wears Combat Boots":

> In the Christian faith, the Groom dies for the Bride [Christ dies for His Church]. The strong lays down his life for the weak. Women and children are of vast importance in God's economy, because children nurtured and diligently trained are the future of the Church, the community, and the world.

---

2   Sometimes there were different instructions for specific enemies, whose customs and culture were under a comprehensive death sentence.

...God has given the unique role of childbearing and nurturing to women, and He has given the work of providing for and defending the family to men...We cannot get away from the fact that women were designed to bear children. Men will never be able to have babies. God has given that precious privilege to women only. And because of this unique role, women must be protected and defended at all costs if a society is to survive.

...A society that does not protect its young (and the ones who bear the young) is a society that has forgotten why it exists. We are not placed here to live lives of middle class complacency, content with our Big Macs and our technological gadgets. We are here to pass along the wisdom of generations to the ones who will grow up behind us and take over for us when we are gone. We are here to disciple our children and to infuse them with a long-term vision for their children's children.

...Allan Carlson writes, "The strong and normal human instinct is to protect infants, toddlers, and their mothers. Indeed, their well-being and security form the central purposes of every healthy nation. From the smallest tribe to the greatest empire, the human rule has been that all others must sacrifice, and even die, to protect the mothers of the young, for they are a people's future."[3]

Women are, by all means, called to make sacrifices for others and give their lives for the Christian faith. How? A true woman of God will spend her life serving God with every aspect of her being, glorifying Him by following His pattern for the family. A woman who is willing to lay down her life for others will devote her life to her family, to her husband and children.

---

3   Mrs. M. L. Chancey, "When Mamma Wears Combat Boots," www.visionforum.org, April 14, 2003 (quoting "Mothers at War: The American Way?" by Allan Carlson).

Women deserve a special status among humankind: the status of the cherished, the nourished, the protected, and the honored. Does this make men expendable? Hardly…But when the enemy comes to kill our children and hurt their mothers, God appoints men to stand up and shield those entrusted to their care. Without such protection, the next generation cannot survive.[4]

Has our society always been as ignorant of these principles as it is today?

There was a time in American history when the culture was predominantly Christian and even non-Christians understood Christian principles, such as protection and respect of women. In everyday life men showed women honor and deference in such simple acts as removing their hats when greeting women, giving their seats to them, and refraining from swearing around them. They also made greater sacrifices. It was expected of every man to lay down his life for a woman if the need ever arose. One well-known example of this is the story of the *Titanic*, in the year 1912. When it became obvious that the *Titanic* was going down and there were not enough lifeboats for everyone on board, the Captain's orders were not unfamiliar to the passengers: "Women and children first!" Sacrifice unto death is never an easy sacrifice, but the men of that generation, meaning every male aged 13 and up, were raised to consider it their honor and privilege to die in order to preserve the lives of the women and children. It would have been shameful and cowardly for a man to get into a lifeboat, and the men of the *Titanic* knew it. It didn't stop some of them from behaving as cowards, but the overwhelming majority of the men on that ship understood duty.

---

4   Ibid.

This act of selfless chivalry on the men's part was nothing new or extraordinary. It was the normal thing, expected of every man.

The principle of gentlemanly conduct was based on the analogy of Christ laying down His life for the Church, and of men considering others as more important than themselves.

Why do men no longer show women this kind of honor?

A hundred years ago, even non-Christian men understood the need to protect women. Today, even most Christian men don't understand this. In the past century, the whole attitude of men toward women and women toward men has changed astonishingly. We are often told by "experts" that these gender role and mentality changes are for the better, yet we see only more and more wretchedness between men and women the further we stray from God's design, which He laid down in His lovingkindness for our own good and happiness.

When we were young our father taught us to study the Bible, then interpret the depressing signs of the times that we see around us *in terms of God's covenant with man.* If we obey Him, He blesses us. If we disobey Him, we subject ourselves to His judgment and loving chastisement. Because of international departure from God's law, every Western nation is under God's promised judgment. For some nations, the chastisement is more severe than for others.

When we understand this, it clears up a lot of confusion or depression we may feel when we look around and notice that our society is really sick. The more observant and biblically literate we become, the more our eyes are opened to understand current times—and, in fact, the whole course of history—in terms of nations' obedience and disobedience and God's consequent blessings and curses.

We were brought up in a part of the world where women were respected and courtesies toward them were observed. When we were aged 13 and 11, our family moved to one of the more secularized British Commonwealth nations. In this strange new culture we were suddenly confronted with fashionable European socialism, Fabian feminism, and trendy androgyny.[5] It was anti-patriarchal, anti-male, anti-marriage, and anti-family, as every Western nation is rapidly becoming. Emerging from our familiar American surroundings, we could see the magnitude of God's judgments, which are striking not only the British Empire, but all of the West.

With a freshness of perspective only foreigners can bring to a different culture, we saw that women for the most part are not respected; they are viewed as prey, as objects to exploit and discard. Husbands have become eager to abdicate their responsibilities and have ceased to lead their wives. The men in this nation are thus forcing the women to take on the burdens of responsibility and leadership in addition to motherhood. Daughters are not protected but sent away from home when quite young. On graduation, they must fend for themselves, often finding themselves in very dangerous and compromising situations and under oppressive debt from school loans. The best marriages these daughters tend to hope for are the 50-50 arrangements of dual careers, separate hobbies, separate bank accounts, 1.2 children, long-term mortgages, high taxes, and divorces after 6.5 years when they find themselves on their own again. But of course, they were really on their own all along.

Today, at the beginning of the 21st century, young Christian women find themselves in a world where real men are rare—men who

5   Androgyny refers to the sharing of both male and female characteristics simultaneously.

understand God's order, and who practice gentlemanly behavior to women. And why? Because this is just one of the ways God presses His lawsuit against an entire nation—or in this case, several nations—of rebels. This is just one of the fruits of our disobedience. The particular transgression was a two-sided one. Following in the example of Adam, men ceased to exercise godly leadership and retreated from responsibility, and, following in the example of Eve, women charged forward to seize authority they were not meant to bear.

What can we do to restore a biblical view of manhood and womanhood?

First, we need to repent. We are all sinners. We all tend to rebel. Even young women rebel. We rebel because it is part of our deep-rooted sin nature. We direct our rebellion at God through our rebellion to men. This means that *all women are rebellious feminists at heart*. Without God's help it is impossible to overcome our stubborn rebellion. Before we can expect any fruitful results in our society, we must first work toward results in our own hearts, starting with repentance and humility, asking God to help us fight our flesh.

Second, we need to study the Word. Understanding and applying truth is hard, especially when it challenges or destroys something we have believed and practiced for a long time. A true servant of Christ will have a hunger for truth—that truth which can be only found in His Word. So a true woman will be known for her practice of studying God's Word with the intent of being edified, challenged, and sanctified. It alone can tell us what womanhood is all about.

Third, each of us must become true women. Our feminine influence is powerful, and we want to encourage the men in our society to be men by being biblical women ourselves. If we ever want men to fulfill their duty to us, we have to fulfill our duty to them.

After years of studying the decline of our world, God's requirements for righteous conduct, and how He is pressing His lawsuit against our disobedient nation, we believe that the way daughters are treating their fathers is one of today's biggest issues. One of the reasons our society is in moral shambles is because dishonoring sons and daughters are invoking God's curses on the land. They're not only bringing destruction and misery upon themselves…but also upon their nations, as God warned in Malachi 4:6: "…[turn] the heart of the children to their fathers, lest I come and *smite the land with a curse*."

CHAPTER FOUR

DAUGHTERS, FATHERS, AND DUTY

WHY YOUR DADDY NEEDS YOU

What does God want me to do for my father?

Again, we'll start with God's commands to men and women in general. There is one scriptural command for women that stands out. Today it stands out like a lightning rod in our society. This is *submission*.

Before we get into submission, we should let the reader know that we are fully aware that "submission" is seen as a dirty word to our generation, especially when connected with pejoratives like "hyper-patriarchal tyranny."[1] The Church at large is made very uncomfortable by these passages, because they seem to violate our fallen sense of what's "right" and "fair." The few Christians who

---

1 It's a shame the word "patriarchy" has been so maligned and misconstrued. Tyranny and abuse are foreign to biblical patriarchy, which actually refers to masculine, multi-generational responsibility and leadership in a home or culture. Biblical patriarchy takes the character of Christ and His sacrifice; men lay down their lives for those under their care.

recognize that this command does actually appear in the Bible and therefore needs to be obeyed, tend to be ashamed and apologetic of the fact. Why is this? What is there in God's pattern for authority and submission that is not wonderful, wise, loving, and perfect? We should rejoice in it and make the most of it!

Ephesians 5:22 commands, "Wives, submit yourselves unto your own husbands, as unto the Lord." Various forms of this command are repeated in numerous places throughout the New Testament. An interesting point to note is that *all* women are not to be in submission to *all* men. Wives must be in submission to their *own* husbands, and daughters must submit to their fathers. If all women had to submit to all men, it would put women in a very vulnerable position, but God's design gives each woman, whether married or unmarried, a protective head to whom she must submit.[2] As we have said before, a woman's life will always be tied into a man's life, whether she is married or not. This is a basic feature of womanhood, and women are to be dependent on men's protection and leadership. This is how God created it to be.

According to the laws of the vows in Numbers 30, an unmarried girl is under the authority of her father, just as a wife is under the authority of her husband.[3]

2　Submission, according to the *Webster's 1828 Dictionary*: "1) The act of submitting; the act of yielding to power or authority; surrender of the person and power to the control or government of another. 4) Obedience; compliance with the commands or laws of a superior. (Submission of children to their parents is an indispensable duty.) 5) Resignation; a yielding of one's will to the will or appointment of a superior without murmuring. (Entire and cheerful submission to the will of God is a Christian duty of prime excellence.)"

3　"These are the statutes, which the Lord commanded Moses, between a man and his wife, between the father and his daughter, being yet in her youth in her father's house" (Numbers 30:16). The only women exempt from this were the widows and

In addition to being able, as we mentioned earlier, to annul his daughter's vow, a father has the authority to guide his daughter concerning marriage (1 Corinthians 7:36-38). God has placed our fathers in a position of authority over us, and to disobey them is to disobey God, unless the two come in direct conflict with one another. A father does *not* have the authority to make his daughter commit sin, because his authority is limited—he can't overrule God's commands or usurp God's authority. A daughter has a duty to disobey her father in such circumstances.

What does true submission look like?

One of our heroines of the faith, **Ruth**, says:

> One of the ways I show submission to my father is by asking his opinion—Daddy is my God-given authority. I want to honor him by knowing his thoughts and views so that I can properly represent him and be able to understand and articulate what I believe. He enjoys answering my questions and helping me to search the Scriptures. If he, for instance, has a preference in colors that I wear, I seek to honor him by finding that out and dressing in a way that would please him. By asking what he thinks, and then taking the advice he might have to offer, I am indicating that I am delighted to know what his wishes are and glad to follow them. As children we can learn so much from our parents by their words and their examples. This reminds me of John 5:19 where Jesus said, "Verily, verily, I say unto you, The Son can do nothing of himself, but what he seeth the Father do: for what things soever he doeth, these also doeth the Son likewise."

---

the divorced women (v. 9), who in many cases either remarried or moved back under their fathers' authority. See the examples in Leviticus 22:13 and the book of Ruth.

Actively seeking our fathers' authority and guidance and instruction can be difficult, especially when the things our fathers want for us are not what *we* want. But this is the pattern God lays down, and our obedience is rewarded with blessings.

God means for our parents to be a blessing to us, and their instruction and wisdom we are supposed to cherish as being just that: a blessing. These verses are just a few which tell us how precious our parents' instructions are:

> "They will be a garland to grace your head and a chain to adorn your neck." (Proverbs 1:9)

> "[T]hey will prolong your life many years and bring you prosperity...Then you will win favor and a good name in the sight of God and man." (Proverbs 3:2-4)

> "[T]hey will be life for you, an ornament to grace your neck. Then you will go on your way in safety, and your foot will not stumble; when you lie down, you will not be afraid; when you lie down, your sleep will be sweet." (Proverbs 3:22-24)

Proverbs 2:1, 5 says, "My son, if thou wilt receive my words, and hide my commandments with thee; ...Then shalt thou understand the fear of the Lord, and find the knowledge of God."

Another of our young heroines, **Kelly**, struggled with the day-to-day application of this principle. She tells us,

> Out of all the members in my family, I am probably the most opinionated and strong-willed. My mother and siblings have never had quite as hard a time loving and embracing the wishes of my father as I have. Although they don't always understand, they're more willing to accept the direction of my father without complaint. I, on the other hand have a tendency towards

questioning what he says. "Why?" I want to know. "Why is what you say right? What if I don't hold the same conviction you hold in this area? Why do you have to make choices that will make our family so different from everybody else? Why?" (Sound familiar?)

There are many, many things I appreciate and admire in my father, but one of the things that has meant the very most to me is the way he responds to my selfish questions. "I know this doesn't make any sense to you," he would often say. "But because I feel so strongly in this area, so convicted by the Lord, I'm asking you to trust me. I know it won't be easy, but I need the support of my family in this. I'm sorry it's painful, but I love you."

I would obey, but not for the best of reasons. I wasn't sure of very many things, but this I knew: If I claimed to be a believer in the Lord Jesus Christ, then I had no choice but to obey the commands of my father; and so I would find myself saying: "Lord, I don't understand this at all! My flesh is not willing, and so I need your help. Give me a heart that trusts in you even when I don't understand."

Because I was faithful in obeying, even when I didn't understand, God blessed me with a change of heart. Not only do I obey and honor the commands of my father and mother, the convictions they hold are convictions I hold now! My heart was melted, and God convicted me in those same areas my father had conviction in.

Only by the grace of God can I say that the commands of my father and the laws of my mother are in my mind and in my heart all the time. When I sleep, they comfort me, and when I'm awake, they speak with me. They do so because God promised they would—if I would trust in them.

Does there come a time when a smart, capable girl who's been raised right no longer needs her father's instruction?

Unfortunately, some girls have been told by their fathers, who in turn have been told by their corrupt culture, that it's a sign of maturity for a girl to stop looking for her father's instruction and start relying chiefly on her own judgment. If a girl's judgment is well grounded in an understanding of her father's will, she may not need to ask for his advice often. But a truly smart, mature girl will recognize that her father's wisdom and experience are a blessing and a lamp to her. The proverbs that extol the glory of our parents' instruction never indicate that it's just for little children and that girls with "good heads on their shoulders" don't need it. Now, when a girl marries, her father's authority is transferred to her husband, and she is no longer obligated to obey her father. But in the same way that it's good for us to read the Bible, no matter how many verses and principles we already know, it is healthy—humbling to us and honoring to our parents—to show them that we will always seek the blessings of their wisdom.

What kind of attitude does God want me to have toward my father?

God has a lot to say on the subject of how women are to view and relate to those in authority over them. In most biblical instruction directed at women, we are commanded to *reverence or respect* the authorities over us: "…and let the wife see that she reverence her husband" (Ephesians 5:33). This same kind of respect is required for sons and daughters to their parents: "Honor your father and mother, which is the first commandment with a promise: that it may be well with you and you may live long on the earth" (Ephesians 6:1).

Genuine honor begins with personal humility before God and an acceptance of who He is, who you are, and who your father is. We manifest this love of God's order by cultivating a deep reverence for our fathers as the authorities God has placed over us.

If a girl has a deep, abiding inner reverence for her father, she will value every good thing about him. She will want to understand him, what he does, and why. Some daughters see a few faults in their fathers, resolve to find these faults despicable and unbearable, and never see anything but these faults.

An honoring daughter will study her father closely, looking to identify his virtues and emulate them. She will train into herself a great appreciation for the good, admirable things about her father and think the most exalted thoughts of them. When she sees his faults—which she inevitably will—she will be understanding of them and pray that he can overcome them.

Honor is more than just a feeling or sentiment; it's something you practice daily. We must treat our fathers and speak to our fathers with great respect.

Confiding in our fathers (and, of course, our mothers) is another way we can show them honor. When we let our fathers know our hearts—our struggles, our weaknesses, our hopes and dreams—it encourages them to pay closer attention to the instruction and guidance they give us. Our fathers can better protect us if they know our weaknesses and struggles and can better lead us when they know what direction we want to be going.

How can I show my father love?

Proverbs 23:26 suggests, in paraphrased form, that daughters must give fathers their hearts: "...and let your eyes observe my ways."

We show our fathers that we love them by giving them our hearts. A girl turns her heart to her father by caring about what he loves, learning about what is important to him, desiring and seeking his counsel and approval, caring more for his opinion than that of her peers, serving him, helping him, sharing his vision, letting him know her heart.

Hannah tells us of the consequences of turning her heart to her father:

> I am rich to have such a father as mine. I listen to my father pray weekly for my sisters and me—that we would be established in marriage, that our marriages would be Christ-honoring, and blessed with many children. This does a wonderful thing in the heart of a girl, when she knows how treasured she is by her father, when she knows that her life was not created in vain, but has a significant purpose to which she was called. It gives a girl hope and it gives a girl vision.
>
> But it was not until I understood my mission as a daughter of the King of kings that I understood my mission as a daughter of the king of my home. I know my place and glory in my duties, for I know that only when I am faithful to perform my duties will my father rise higher in his. It is such a blessing to be the daughter of my father, and even more so to know and to share his life vision.
>
> Do you seek to be obedient to Christ by giving your heart to the one whom Christ has placed over you? I thought I loved my father before, but it was for selfish reasons. He was just my dad. But now he is my father, my friend, my guardian, my priest, and my knight in shining armor. I give glory to God for my dad, and for his willingness to search the Scriptures and embrace the biblical vision. May we all seek to revive this biblical vision.

Kelly illustrates the position of a daughter who has turned her heart to her father:

As I observe the convictions and the passions for the things of God in my earthly father, I begin to make myself available more, in helping him, walking beside him in his ministry, asking for ways I can help him and pray for him. I want to know more about what he believes. I want to know why he believes the things he does. As I come to understand more and more each day the kind of "unit" that a family is supposed to be, I find myself wanting to be involved more. The beautiful thing is, that as I begin supporting my father in his God-given ministry, I find that his convictions are becoming my convictions, his passions, my passions.

Rebekah tells us:

One of the consequences of adopting a feministic spirit is an independent spirit, the lasting effects of which I am still overcoming by God's grace. As a result, I at one time rejected the protection and shelter of my father (which I am now grateful for and enjoy), because of my independent, rebellious nature and the inability in my mind to reconcile submission with strength. Oh, what strength the Lord has granted unto me—especially in my character—in yielding to my father, asking him to forgive me for rejecting for so long his effort to fulfill his role. Finally, I have found my true calling and mission in life: to be a godly woman and fulfill all that it included for the glory of God. This means, while I am yet unmarried, as a daughter I am my father's helper. It is my duty as a girl and as a daughter to seek out what pleases him, and what makes him strong in his vision, so that I too can embrace his vision and make his passions my passions. My position as a daughter is to be feminine and content with whatever my father does, and in being feminine, I can help my father in his masculinity and can give him confidence by being confident in whatever he says or does. I had to turn my heart, and I still do, daily, to my father. It wasn't a one-time thing. I have to continually search out my heart and make sure there is no discontentment or bitterness in it. I have found untold delight and joy and pleasure in doing this, in being a young woman and in being my father's daughter, in completing the tasks that the Lord has given me.

Is every girl called to be her father's helper?

As we stated before, every woman is, by nature, a man's helper. You are a helper, no matter what your age or marital status. The choice before you and every other young woman isn't "to help or not to help?" It's *whom* to help. Can you imagine a man more deserving of your devotion and assistance, someone whom you love and trust more than your own father? You may not immediately see how much your father needs your help and just how much you can help him, because the very importance of a "helpmeet" has been long forgotten.

Our friend **Ruth** makes an important point:

I realize that it is most likely God's will for me to be married someday, and I desire and have the responsibility to be prepared, as much as possible, for this role as God sees fit. I want to be a true helpmeet to my husband, and what an excellent opportunity I have to practice this with my own father!

As **Amber** realized:

How is one to prepare for being a suitable helpmeet, if your entire life up until marriage has been filled with a me-first mentality? It is nearly impossible to learn selfless service if we have not learned to practice it prior to marriage.

The greatest source of contentment I have found is in the fact that whether I ever marry or not I have found my true calling: that of serving the one I am under with joy and enthusiasm. Whether God calls me to marriage or to singleness, I have found a cause worth giving my life for. If I have not learned the vital principle of serving the one I am under, what right do I have to marry a godly man?—for in the truest sense I have proven myself not worthy of one.

Sarah says:

As I began to understand that my calling was not somewhere out there waiting for me to "find it," but my calling was to help my dad fulfill his calling, it gave me a whole new perspective on life and my purpose as a daughter.

Why is being a good helpmeet so important that we have to devote so much time to it?

Because man, for all his abilities to lead and conquer cultures, cannot do this without woman's help. In order for a man to lead, he needs a helper. Whether a man leads badly or well can depend upon his helper. Women can have a huge amount of influence over men. If we are good helpers, we can actually further the vision of our men and encourage them to greater heights of biblical manhood. When we build them up, we can be their greatest assets in becoming masculine warriors for Christ. They need us as much as we need them.

According to Reverend William Einwechter, "The Hebrew word 'help' (*ezer*) [used in 'help meet'] comes from two roots: the first meaning to rescue or save, and the second meaning to be strong. It indicates one who is able (has what it takes) to come to the aid of someone who is in need."[4]

What were women originally supposed to help their husbands do?

We read in Genesis that Eve was created to help Adam with a mission.

> So God created man in his own image, in the image of God created he him; And God blessed them, and God said unto them, *Be fruitful, and multiply*, and *replenish the earth*, and *subdue* it: and *have dominion* over the fish of the sea, and over the fowl of the air, and over every living thing that moveth upon the earth. (Genesis 1:27,28, emphases added)

Theologians call this the "Dominion Mandate," the command to us to take dominion over the earth, filling and subduing it. This command is repeated in a different form as Jesus's last command as a man on earth: "All power is given unto me in heaven and in earth. Go ye therefore, and *teach all nations, baptizing* them in the name of the Father, and of the Son, and of the Holy Ghost: *teaching them to observe all things whatsoever I have commanded you*: and, lo, I am with you alway, even unto the end of the world" (Matthew 28:18-20, emphases added).

The theme of these commands is the same. All the earth is now under Christ's authority. The job of Christians is to teach all the nations and peoples to obey God, to bring all the earth into complete subjection to Christ. This means that Christians have to do more than just *evangelize* all the nations, but *teach* them all to

---

4   Rev. William Einwechter, vice-president of the National Reform Association and Editor of *The Christian Statesman*, "Exegetical Defense of the Woman as Keeper at Home," www.visionforum.org, February 9, 2004.

observe *all* that God commands and to live in complete, perfect conformity to His pattern for mankind. And we're not only to convert natives and savages to this, but also kings, fashion designers, film makers, newspaper reporters, businessmen—all mankind! And most of all, our own families.[5]

The Dominion Mandate and Great Commission were given to men and women equally, but the way we both fulfill our tasks is different, according to the distinctions in how we were created and the roles we were given at the beginning. R.C. Sproul, Jr., summarizes the calling of a man:

I see my life in terms of challenge, quest, warfare and adventure. That's what men do. This reflects the outward call of the dominion task. Men go into the jungle and turn it into a garden. Men are by nature conquerors, which is why it makes such perfect sense that Jesus calls us to this task. In Him we are more than conquerors. The difference is that we do this for Him, rather than for ourselves. Dominion is all about conquest; that's what we're made for. Men live for a cause, and this is the cause, the crusade to which we have been called—to make manifest the reign of Jesus Christ.[6]

---

5   "Behold, I have taught you statutes and judgments, even as the Lord my God commanded me, that ye should do so in the land whither ye go to possess it. Keep therefore and do them; for this is your wisdom and your understanding in the sight of the nations, which shall hear all these statutes, and say, Surely this great nation is a wise and understanding people. For what nation is there so great, who hath God so nigh unto them, as the Lord our God is in all things that we call upon him for? And what nation is there so great, that hath statutes and judgments so righteous as all this law, which I set before you this day? Only take heed to thyself, and keep thy soul diligently, lest thou forget the things which thine eyes have seen, and lest they depart from thy heart all the days of thy life: but teach them thy sons, and thy sons' sons..." (Deuteronomy 4:5-9)

6   R.C. Sproul, Jr., *Bound for Glory: God's Promise for Your Family* (Wheaton, Illinois: Crossway Books, a division of Good News Publishers, 2003), p. 41.

And in this great, glorious task, women are the indispensable helpers and supporters of their men.

What does being a good helpmeet involve?

The most beautiful and complete illustration of a perfect helpmeet is the Proverbs 31 woman. Though there are differences between how a daughter helps her father and a wife helps her husband, this illustration shows us just how much a good helpmeet can do.

Though the Proverbs 31 woman devoted herself and her abilities to helping her husband and his ministry, this does not mean she was his slave. The wife is a fellow laborer in the work of the gospel, equal in essence, although subordinate in function.

A good wife can *make her husband successful.*

Proverbs 31:23 says, "Her husband is known in the gates, when he sitteth among the elders of the land."

The Proverbs 31 woman's husband was distinguished among the wisest men of the land. The connotation (considering that the passage is in praise of the woman's abilities as helpmeet) is that she was in a large way responsible for his success and honor.

God meant for women to be honored and respected. However, this respect was not to be gained in the same way as for men. It is said, "Behind every great man there is a great woman." In times past, people would see a great man and know that much of his greatness and success was due to his wife, and she would be honored and praised accordingly. Because women are not praised for being good wives and furthering their husbands in our society, it is little wonder that women don't think of that as being a praise-worthy thing and seek praise and glory elsewhere. No wonder our society is so short of real men! If our men aren't successful, it largely means that their women have not made them successful. They need our help.

How can I make my father successful?

A godly young woman will seek to discover her father's vision and goal and life work, and will embrace it as her own. She will devote herself to his ministry, to make it as fruitful as possible. A father is most fruitful when he has the help of his children (in addition to his wife, his helpmeet), and a daughter is most fruitful when she is making her father successful in this way.

As **Rebekah** puts it:

> A true young woman channels her abilities into supporting and building up her father or husband, enabling him to fulfill his God-ordained role.
>
> I cannot describe the satisfaction I have experienced in doing God's will and completing the tasks, both specific and general, that He has given to me. What delight, joy, and pleasure I have found in being a young woman and being my father's daughter. For the greater part of my life I had no idea of the importance of our God-ordained mission as women. What responsibilities are attached to our work!
>
> Our faithfulness as daughters and wives to welcome our responsibilities and do our duties will better enable our fathers and husbands to more fully and easily carry out their God-ordained missions in life.

Can a helper assist her man in his business?

Yes! In fact, a good wife can *further her husband's estate.*[7] She helps him manage matters of finance and enlarges his wealth and property. She doesn't just work and earn money for herself, but for her household. She is a prudent businesswoman and acts as a careful steward of her family's wealth. As a result, "The heart of her husband doth safely trust in her, so that he shall have no need of spoil" (Proverbs 31:11). A good wife can make her husband rich.

How can I further my father's estate?

A good daughter can further her father's estate and increase his wealth and holdings by caring for his estate, "looking well to the ways of her household" (Proverbs 31:27). You can help your father by helping his helpmeet (your mother), leaving her more free to help her husband in other ways.

A girl can also help increase her father's wealth by helping him manage and conserve his wealth. Your father is a steward of the financial assets God has given him, and he could use your help in his stewardship. This doesn't mean taking over the management of your dad's money. It means being prudent and wise when spending it. It means helping him conserve the money God has given him by being conscientiously frugal.

Ruth talks about gratitude, service, and love toward her father:

> We have a friend who used to ask us, very kindly, but pointedly, "Do you get your father's slippers for him?" (to which the answer is no, only because he doesn't wear slippers!) and other such

---

7 "Estate" used to be a common expression, referring to a man's sphere of dominion and influence, holdings, headquarters, legacy.

questions. His point was, "Are you helping your father even in small things which he might never ask help with?" Those are things that will simply make his life more comfortable and pleasurable, things that will simply bring joy to his heart and make him more free to accomplish the work that God has given him.

This has made me stop and consider, what exactly am I doing, consciously, with the specific goal of helping my father? How many times have I actually asked him, "What may I do to help you?"

My father is responsible before the Lord for the guidance of his family. His heart is relieved and encouraged when he can trust in his household, when he knows that our hearts are with him, that his wishes are obeyed, that his decisions are submitted to cheerfully, and that his family is praying for him and supporting him as he seeks guidance from the Lord.

Helping my father has been a fun adventure and one that I am constantly growing in and learning from. Since I am a young woman, and since I am preparing to be a keeper at home, most of my time is spent serving my mother in various ways as I learn from her and help her with daily tasks. This is a blessing to my father and my mother as I become more submissive, responsible, capable, and dependable.

There are so many ways in which I can be a blessing to my father. Of course, his greatest joy is to know that his children walk in truth (3 John 4). Sometimes the best way that we can be an encouragement to him is to pray for him. Some fathers have jobs where their situation makes it impossible for their families to offer much physical help. I would urge them in times like this to spend extra time praying for their father. In my case, I can help my father with his job, and it is easy to see how I can assist him in that area. I have been able to help him with many of the small but time-consuming tasks, making his load lighter.

Another aspect of this is finding out what particular ministry opportunities he might have a vision for. I might ask myself, for instance, if he has a ministry to co-workers. How can I help him in this area? We have enjoyed sending freshly-baked delicacies with Daddy to work, which is a pleasure to him and a project that enhances our creativity as well.

Sometimes Daddy offers our help to a family who is in need. It might not be possible for him to take off from work every occasion that he would like to minister to a friend, but maybe he can send his family to help them in their need. We have had opportunities to help families move, assist a struggling family as they homeschool their children, stay with children while their father helps with the birth of a child, etc. Our adventures have been endless as we have been, in a sense, ambassadors for Daddy whether he can be present or not. Ultimately, we are serving the Lord as we joyfully serve others to His glory and as we are faithful to Daddy's guidance and headship over us.

Daddy has encouraged us to help the elderly in their need. For example, several years ago, we had an elderly lady at our church who came by herself to the meetings. Daddy asked my sister and me to sit with her (which we did nearly every Sunday) and do little things like hold her hymnal for her. We walked her to her car every week. I can't tell you how delighted she was! This was his idea, and we might never have thought of it, but it brought delight to both my family and this sweet elderly woman. For years, another elderly woman, who had never married, lived across the street from us. Daddy and Mama had a desire to help this dear lady, and we went over to her house almost daily to chat with her, mow her lawn, or take care of some little errand that she could no longer manage. She became like a grandmother to us, and we were blessed to know her!

These are all just a few ways in which I have been able to help my father. Every father might have different needs or a different vision, and other daughters might have a thousand other ways that are appropriate for them as they help their father. I pray that whether we serve directly or indirectly, whether it is recognized or behind the scenes, that all will be done to the glory of God with joy and gratitude to Him as our Creator, Savior, and Sovereign Lord.

CHAPTER FIVE

DAUGHTERS, FATHERS, AND DIFFICULTIES

DAUGHTERS WITH LESS-THAN-PERFECT FATHERS

What if I have a less-than-perfect father?

All fathers are less than perfect. So are all daughters. We can't wait for our fathers to be perfect before we become the perfect daughters. We must begin finding ways to honor and value our fathers where they are, as God's law commands us. Even the worst father is worthy of respect from his daughter, simply because he is her father. Even if his daughter could find nothing to respect him for personally, she can and should respect his position as father. If nothing else, a daughter must be grateful to her father—for giving her life; if he has fed and clothed her; if he has ever done anything kind for her—because gratitude is the beginning of honor.

However, we believe that most fathers, if not criminally wicked,[1] do have at least some admirable qualities somewhere. Be quick to see

---

1 We understand there are some fathers who are abusive, exploitive, and engaged in ongoing criminal activity, as defined by Scripture. In such cases, girls can only

these qualities. When you think of your father, you shouldn't think of his weaknesses that spring to your mind, but of how much you love and appreciate his good qualities. When you speak of him to others, you shouldn't talk about his mistakes, but of the good things he's done. When you speak to him, instead of criticizing and nagging him for his faults, you should tell him how much you admire his strengths. For example, if your father is the slowest, laziest man on earth, perhaps he's slow about getting angry. There's an asset! You could appreciate him and thank him for not getting mad and impatient with you.

You don't have to respect his weaknesses, but you should be sensitive to them. We are all weak.

Is there any way I can help my father overcome his weaknesses?

Even though we are under the authority of our fathers, yes, we do have a kind of feminine power and influence which we can use to help our fathers become stronger, more masculine leaders.

True women have a kind of power that our society knows nothing about. Daughters, when trying to pursue femininity, can have a huge effect on their fathers and families. 1 Peter 3:1 commands, "Likewise, ye wives, be in subjection to your own husbands; that, if any obey not the word, they also may without the word be won by the conversation of the wives; while they behold your chaste conversation coupled with fear." When husbands are struggling with obedience to God, it is in a wife's ability to "win" her husband over by her respectful behavior. In

---

help their fathers long-distance by praying for them after being geographically separated from them. If church officers are unwilling to intervene in such circumstances on behalf of the victim(s), direct state intervention may be necessary.

many cases, even the most stubborn men, when they observe their wives submitting humbly to *them*, will feel ashamed and repentant, and their consciences will compel them to submit again to God. A woman, even without speaking a word, can have such an effect on her husband simply through her submissive femininity as to encourage repentance! Can this principle work in the same way between fathers and daughters? We have personally seen daughters who have had this effect on their fathers simply by demonstrating chaste and respectful behavior. We're not prepared to say there is a precise scriptural parallel and that fathers can be "won," but we have certainly seen fathers be strongly influenced.

A good start to your influence is to pray for your father, but in addition to this, you should ask your father what he would like you to pray for him. This shows your father that you are serious about helping him and that you are dedicated to seeing him become the kind of man he should be. It also gets him thinking about his faults and how to overcome them. Also ask him if he would pray for your character, and be humble enough to tell him what faults in particular you need help with. This will nurture your emotional and spiritual bond with each other.

Your manner is vitally important when speaking to your father, regardless of how mature or immature he might be. When **Amy** lost her mother to cancer, she was confronted with the importance of strong relationships and good communication with her family. It was a struggle for her to adapt, and she shares some insights she learned.

> Mum was the good one at communicating and Dad wasn't, so we usually talked to Mum about everything. Communication is now an area of weakness that we are having to work on strengthening. I am realizing that I must do my part to make this happen. I can't

wait around for someone (such as a mother), to ask what's wrong, or ask if there is anything I want to talk about. I need to go out of my comfort zone and instigate communication sometimes.

Remember to keep a reverent spirit when speaking. Balaams's donkey could appeal and be heard, simply because he had nothing in the past that Balaam could accuse him of. He basically said "Haven't I done everything you asked me to, and been your faithful donkey so far?" Balaam had to agree, and he listened. If we have been disrespectful, selfish, lazy, disobedient, etc, in the past, (and didn't put it right), our dads are going to be less likely to hear us. They must see and know that we trust them, obey them, honor them, and want to make them successful. Also, in the case of appeals, or concerns, once the problem has been respectfully and prayerfully expressed, we need to leave it to God and our fathers. Nagging and constantly complaining are not signs of trust and surrendering all to the Lord. No matter what things may happen to weaken your family, God is fully able to work it out for good, as He promised in Romans 8:28.

How can I help my father with his mission and vision if he doesn't have either?

How do you know he doesn't? One of our friends was discouraged because her father's vision extended only as far as bringing home the bacon, and he didn't have a mission she could help with. We encouraged her to go to him and ask him if he had ever had a secret, long-buried desire to help people, make something of himself, or passionately pursue a life-work that was bigger than a paycheck. She was astonished when he told her that he had always really wanted to have a ministry to street kids. Why hadn't he pursued this? Because he had never had anyone to help him make his dream a reality.

This is where a father needs his daughter. It may be up to you to initiate and discover the mission you can work on together. If your father never considered anything like this, you could sit down together and come up with a "dream ministry," something that you and he could work on together with the whole family.

How can I encourage my indifferent father to protect me?

Many girls have lamented to us that their fathers are not involved in their lives and refuse to offer guidance. In some cases, the reason fathers become afraid to "interfere" or "intrude" in their daughters' lives is because their leadership and guidance have been pushed away in the past. If this is your story, repentance is called for. But it's not enough to merely repent in your heart and then expect your father to automatically reciprocate; you need to confess your error and ask him to forgive you, and then you will need to show him very decidedly that you *have* repented, that you have given him your heart, and now *seek* his guidance. You may already know that you should never resist your father's authority, but how often do you invite your father's instruction and counsel to take an even more active role in telling you what he wants you to do?

Before you can accuse your father of being unprotective, ask yourself: do you make it clear to him that you are a woman of virtue, worthy of his special protection? If your behavior was more gentle, feminine, respectful, and lovely, would he be more inclined to feel protective of you?

If a father continues to be indifferent, you could appeal to him with Scripture, showing him that God has ordained him to be the authority in your life. Pray that God will work in his heart to take you back into his protection and will renew in him a spirit of manliness so that he will want to truly lead his daughter and his family.

How good a relationship can we have with fathers who aren't Christians?

Even though a non-Christian father will not be able to be a conscientious spiritual leader, he is still your protective authority, and God can lead you through him. But the case may be that your father needs you more than you need him.

1 Peter 3:1 says, "Likewise, ye wives, be in subjection to your own husbands; that, if any obey not the word, they also may without the word be won by the conversation of the wives; while they behold your chaste conversation coupled with fear."

The principle of this verse may be applicable to fathers and daughters, as we have suggested. Many girls want to be missionaries. Who could they possibly wish to see reconciled to God more than their own families and their own fathers? And who could better minister to a blind man than his own daughter?

Your very behavior can evangelize your father. Show him what an amazing power has effected such a change in you. Accurately represent the saving and sanctifying grace of God. No, we can't save our fathers; it's ultimately up to God's grace to do that. But the least we can do is present the gospel to them, not just the verbal explanation of the gospel, but the part that consists of the fruits in a believer's life. Show your father and your family the amazing power of the Holy Spirit to create a "new heart" in you! Display to them the fruit of the Spirit: love, joy, peace, patience, kindness, goodness, faithfulness, gentleness, and self-control (Galatians 5:22, 23). To what extent are you "salt and light" in your home?

When might it become necessary for me to disobey my father in some things, and how can I do this in a biblical way?

Our first duty is always to God and not man. Because all earthly authority is limited, there are biblical grounds for disobedience to an authority who's trying to play God. If an authority commands you to do something God has commanded you not to do, or if an authority commands you not to do something God has commanded you to do, you have a moral duty to "obey God and not man" (Acts 5:29). You will need to study Scripture carefully to know what God's commands really are and what would constitute disobedience to Him. We also need to be able to discern the difference between God's real commands and the interpretations of our own imaginations. We must not assume that God is leading us through our hearts and passions, which are "deceitful above all things, and desperately wicked" (Jeremiah 17:9, see also Ezekiel 13:2-9,17), but only through His infallible Word.[2]

A good illustration of necessary disobedience is the story of Daniel and King Nebuchadnezzar. This story also shows a proper relationship between a non-Christian authority and a Christian subordinate. Daniel was a good servant who served his pagan king with appropriate respect. He treated the king faithfully and loyally, as the one God had placed in a position of authority. When the King commanded Daniel to break the first commandment, Daniel had to humbly and respectfully give his reasons why he could not obey. This was not enough to change the mind of the king, who became furious and demanded that Daniel be put to death. But because of Daniel's obedience to God above all, God chose to save his life.

---

2   2 Timothy 3:14-17.

Joseph is another example of a good and faithful subordinate. He was a slave under the authority of a religious[3] pharoah. But his respectful conduct toward his master was pleasing to God. Even in his state of subordination, Joseph had a sanctifying influence on the household, and God blessed the whole house because of Joseph's presence there.

When it comes time to disobey an authority, there is a respectful and godly way to do this.

A story in the Bible that illustrates this way is the story of David and Saul. Saul wasn't just *any* bad authority; he was hateful, had a terrible temper, and was spiteful, jealous, cruel, and unreasonable to the point of being almost insane—and he was trying to kill David, his son-in-law. The way David dealt with this hateful authority puts most of us to shame. David was never angry at Saul, never talked back to him, never spoke badly or disrespectfully of him to others, and showed him only respect, love, honor, and kindness. He did have to resist Saul's wishes and often had to flee from Saul's anger. He had to plead humbly with Saul and entreat him, but he continued to acknowledge him as "My lord, the king," the one in authority.

What should a girl do if her father no longer wants to be her authority figure?

This is such a complex problem we should not offer any specific advice. Each situation should be dealt with separately and with as much advice and counsel a girl can find among trusted authorities. We dare only offer the most general guidelines. If a father, after his

---

3   It is helpful when studying history to remember that all rulers are religious rulers because all governments are theocracies. Every government submits to a deity of some kind. Joseph knew Pharoah's deity was a rival deity. Joseph refused to worship false gods, but understood his duty to respect the authority structures of the nation, from the jailer to the pharaoh.

daughter's fervent appeals and prayers, still refuses to provide authority, leadership, and protection for his daughter and tells her she's on her own, it may be that he has effectively abdicated his authority over her without properly transferring it to a responsible party.

In this case, the general solution would be to locate an alternative protector. Until you're married, alternative authority figures would include your mother, a responsible brother, and/or a group of godly older men like the elders of a church, preferably those who would fit the qualifications for a bishop in 1 Timothy 3:2-9:

> "A bishop then must be blameless, the husband of one wife, vigilant, sober, of good behaviour, given to hospitality, apt to teach; Not given to wine, no striker, not greedy of filthy lucre; but patient, not a brawler, not covetous; One that ruleth well his own house, having his children in subjection with all gravity; (For if a man know not how to rule his own house, how shall he take care of the church of God?) Not a novice, lest being lifted up with pride he fall into the condemnation of the devil. Moreover he must have a good report of them which are without; lest he fall into reproach and the snare of the devil. Likewise must the deacons be grave, not doubletongued, not given to much wine, not greedy of filthy lucre; Holding the mystery of the faith in a pure conscience."

The reason we are focusing exclusively on fathers at this point is because this book just happens to be about fathers and daughters. Our mothers are very important, and their authority and guidance will be discussed in greater length in our section about the family in general. Even though we believe it is God's best for women to be under the authority of godly men, there will be cases where there simply are no responsible men available. The story of Ruth provides an important illustration of how a mother (or in this case, a mother-in-law) can lead and guide her daughter and even "provide security" for her by helping her locate a male protector (Boaz).

It is interesting to note that Ruth chose Naomi's protection rather than her father's. However, Ruth's case was different than that of a daughter's, as she was a widow with a need to take special responsibility for her own actions (see Numbers 30:9). However, most widows did return to their father's houses, as Orpah did. This is because authority is anything but a curse or bane—it is a great blessing, worth seeking diligently. When, upon the death of her husband, Ruth's legal status changed, she freely chose the guidance of God-fearing Naomi, instead of returning to her father's home, which was outside the covenant community.

CHAPTER SIX

DAUGHTERS, FATHERS, AND THEIR ENEMIES

WHO WOULD TURN YOU AGAINST YOUR FATHER

Do I really have enemies?

Yes. If you desire to live godly in Christ Jesus you will be persecuted.[1] And the more you embrace your calling to love and honor your father, the more your enemies will strike out at you in more fearful ways. At the moment, all fathers and daughters in general are under assault. Your father is being insulted, mocked, and guilt-manipulated by the media simply for being a man and a father. You are being pressured by the media and your peers and your entire society to dishonor and disregard your father. Why this vicious attack on fathers and daughters?

We need to understand that, since the beginning, Satan has been warring against God. From the beginning of history he has been using people—starting with Eve—to strike at God. Some people are more

---

1 See II Timothy 3:12.

useful to him than others, and some have been openly devoted to serving him. These are the most dangerous enemies of Christendom.

There is one enemy in particular who will come up several times in this book, primarily because his influence is so strongly felt more than a century after his death. His name is Karl Marx.

Who was Karl Marx?

Marx was a German philosopher who lived about the same time as Abraham Lincoln. He was a Satanist whose objective in life, in his own words, was "to dethrone God and destroy capitalism."[2]

He absolutely hated fatherhood and daughterhood. He hated patriarchy. He hated the concept of submission and honor to God-ordained authority. He hated everything about the father-daughter relationship that was nourished and modeled in the family. He believed the family stood in the way of his ambitions to replace Christianity with international socialism. His life's work was fueled by an extraordinary hatred of God's order.

Today Marx has millions of followers who help keep his hatred alive. Most of these followers are women who continue to help Marx with a kind of...daughterly loyalty. Isn't that ironic?

Why do I need to know about Marx?

You need to know about Marx because practically every person in the West today, including nearly all young women, including young Christian women, look at the world through Karl Marx's eyes. He has influenced modern thinking possibly more than any other person.

---

2   Karl Marx, cited in "Erasing Christianity" by Judson Cox, www.therealitycheck.org, April 1, 2005.

We can hardly help being influenced by Marxism. It appears in children's movies, Saturday morning cartoons, universities, seminaries and teacher's colleges, elementary schools, comic books, magazines, most movies, and the evening news. Watered down versions of Marxism are even taught from the pulpits of our local churches.[3] This isn't to say that pastors and all these other people are sinister revolutionaries. It is to point out that Marxism is widely influential. The entire Western culture has become so Marxist that all of us are relatively comfortable with a predominantly Marxist worldview.[4]

Many of these worldview issues were explained to us by our father, who was a Marxist before he became a Christian, and he understands the Marxist mindset very thoroughly.

How did Marx's ideas become so influential?

Marx became significant when his group of brilliant, devoted followers stumbled onto a formula for this cultural revolution that would sweep the globe.

In the early 1920s, a group of his followers launched a project that continues to weaken and bury the last remnants of Christianity. The Frankfurt School was organized in 1923 by dedicated Marxists who were determined to win a war they called "The Revolution." By this, they meant the non-violent overthrow of every nation in the name of communism. Russia was the first nation to fall, in 1917. It fell violently. The next two targeted nations were resistant, and this wasn't expected. When communist agents met to identify

---

3   See Appendix A for a short discussion about the Marxist worldview in modern churches.

4   A person's worldview is his religious mindset. A worldview is the theological lens through which one perceives the world. Our worldview is how we interpret and evaluate the things we see around us. Every person has a religious worldview.

the problem, they found they were in complete agreement. The problem was Christianity. They said the revolution would be stalled until Christianity was destroyed, not by guns, but by an alternative theology. They concluded that once a nation was socialized with this new theology, the revolution would proceed smoothly and without resistance. Christendom would be dead, and international communism would be the dominant religion of all nations.[5]

The Frankfurt School was set up as a think tank in Frankfurt, Germany to develop and teach this new theology as a clever "social science." They dressed it up as behavioral psychology and used ingenious methods of public relations to get the new ideas into every school, every movie studio, and every university in the West.

Their non-violent approach was simple. They identified each main element of biblical Christianity and then invented its opposite. They preached a strategy called "the great inversion," which was nothing more than the replacement of truth with error, then making error "politically correct."

Basically, their objective was to turn God's order on its head. Thus, if the Bible taught a family-based education model, they insisted on forced state schooling (with a curriculum of their own design). If the Bible taught male leadership, they insisted on forced cultural changes to place women over men in every area of society. If the Bible instituted marriage, they insisted on its removal. If the Bible placed high value on children, they insisted on developing a culture of widespread abortion and birth control practices. If the Bible

---

5   As Charles A. Reich summarized their strategy in *The Greening of America*: "There is a revolution coming. It will not be like revolutions in the past. It will originate with the individual and the culture, and it will change the political structure as its final act. It will not require violence to succeed, and it cannot be successfully resisted by violence. This is the revolution of the New Generation."

labeled evil as wrong, they defined it as right. Antonio Gramsci was a Frankfurt School colleague who explained this process in detail: "The civilized world has been saturated with Christianity for 2000 years,"[6] Gramsci wrote, reasoning that a culture rooted in Christian worldview and practices could only be captured from *within*.[7] Gramsci's recipe for total cultural domination was to "Marxise the inner man...to alter the Christian mind to turn it into its opposite in all its details so that it would become not merely a non-Christian mind but an anti-Christian mind."[8] He advocated a "slow march throughout the culture,"[9] a destroying of the civilization from within. "Everything must be done in the name of man's dignity and rights, and in the name of his autonomy and freedom from outside restraint. From the claims and constraints of Christianity above all," he wrote.[10]

This part of the revolution was deliberately non-violent. It was called *Cultural Marxism*,[11] because it saturated the culture by going straight to the minds of every man and woman. The goal of Marx's feminism was to Marxise the thinking of women, then men, then the entire culture. Notice how women were first on their list? Recall that Satan targeted a woman first, too. God's enemies have recognized that women are not only the weaker vessels, and

---

6   Antonio Gramsci, cited in "What is the Frankfurt School?" by Dr. Gerald L. Atkinson, CDR USN (Ret.), www.newtotalitarians.com, August 1, 1999.

7   Hence Gramsci's battle cry, "Capture the culture!"

8   Antonio Gramsci, cited in "Minds, Morals and Movies" by Dr. Peter Hammond, www.frontline.org.za, 2005.

9   Antonio Gramsci, cited in "A Statement of Bill Wood, Charlotte, North Carolina," waysandmeans.house.gov.

10 See Richard Grenier, *Capturing the Culture: Film, Art and Politics* (Ethics & Public Policy Center, 1991).

11 As opposed to "economic Marxism," which is the concept most people identify with the term "Marxism."

consequently more easily led, but they are incredibly influential over their husbands (think of Eve again) and children, *and they make excellent and loyal helpers.*

"Unless millions of women are with us," stated Lenin, "we cannot exercise the proletarian dictatorship, cannot construct on communist lines. We must find our way to them, we must study and try to find that way."[12] He insisted, "There can be no real mass movement without women."[13]

They found the way to the women's hearts and minds, all right. As Frankfurt School co-founder Georg Lukacs put it, "Such a worldwide overturning of values cannot take place without the annihilation of the old values and the creation of new ones by the revolutionaries."[14]

This destructive Frankfurt School worldview has been successfully transferred into Western culture. Even the Church has bought it and now combines it with a faint shadow of Christendom to create a superstitious, comfortable faith.[15] This new faith has feminized and Marxised even the minds of Christian women.

Many Christian women haven't been able to resist feminism. Some praise Betty Friedan, author of *The Feminine Mystique*, as a great liberator of modern women. How many Christian women know that Friedan was a Stalinist-Marxist activist, a professional propagandist working for the Communists? Author David Horowitz

12 *Lenin on the Women's Question; From My Memorandum Book*, by Clara Zetkin, first published in 1925 (www.marxist.com).

13 Ibid.

14 Georg Lukacs, cited in "Chapter II: The Historical Roots of 'Political Correctness,'" by Raymond V. Raehn, www.freecongress.org.

15 See Appendix A for a brief discussion about the Marxist worldview in modern churches.

points out that "…her interest in women's liberation was just a subtext of her real desire to create a Soviet America."[16]

Friedan embraced Karl Marx's overall plan for exploiting women. As Marx admitted in an 1868 letter, "Major social transformations are impossible without ferment among the women."[17] Friedan helped create ferment by following Lenin's example and making women unhappy with the joys and duties of womanhood.[18]

Perhaps Marx's most ingenious and successful move in tearing down Christendom was to inspire women to tear down their homes and families with their own two hands.[19]

Are you saying the feminist movement never had any good intentions? Wasn't it all about liberating women from oppression?

Feminists would like to have us think that Christianity and Christendom have trampled on women's rights and tried to extinguish their opportunities. As the official Declaration of

---

16 David Horowitz, "Betty Friedan's Secret Communist Past," Jan. 18, 1999.

17 Karl Marx, cited in "Karl Marx's Prescription for Women's Liberation" by Carey Roberts, mensnewsdaily.com, January 6, 2004.

18 In 1920 the Marxist Lenin described how "women grow worn out in petty, monotonous household work, their strength and time dissipated and wasted, their minds growing narrow and stale, their hearts beating slowly, their will weakened!" Every move necessary to the Marxist agenda was marketed as (again, in Lenin's words) "freedom for the woman from the old household drudgery and dependence on man, [which] enables her to exercise to the full her talents and her inclinations" (found in *Lenin on the Women's Question*).

19 "Every wise woman buildeth her house: but the foolish plucketh it down with her hands." (Proverbs 14:1)

Feminism openly announced, "All of history must be re-written in terms of oppression of women."[20]

The feminist movement would have us believe that justice, equality, and opportunity did not exist for women until the feminist movement created these things in the last few years.

The truth is quite the opposite. The most liberating force in all of history is Christianity. It has emancipated women the world over and elevated them to the place of honor God created them to occupy. Christianity offers women purpose, dignity, worth, and true power. As Christianity swept over the pagan world, women were liberated from slave-like or inhuman positions of gross inferiority. Every non-Christian society in the past has misunderstood and undervalued woman's worth, strength, and potential for influence. Every culture which shuns God's design for woman ends up degrading her, including the feminist invention which degrades man and makes him again a primitive exploiter of women.

In pagan cultures, women *have* been considered property, decorative objects, sexual objects, slaves, and/or the personification of evil. All of these things are wrong. But in preaching contempt for biblical womanhood, tearing down the institution of marriage, maligning the concept of godly submission, spitting on the office of motherhood, teaching women (and men) to despise the blessing of children, the feminist movement has only increased these problems in our generation.[21]

---

20 *The Declaration of Feminism*, November 1971 (cited in "Feminism and Society," a collection of quotes by Bill Wood, www.fathersforlife.org).

21 If you don't believe the feminists really advocated these things, take a look at their own words in Appendix B.

Women today are being used, exploited, and despised as much as ever. The difference is that the women who walked into this trap on their own feet are still calling it liberation. The stupidity of feminism is so self-perpetuating and blinding that most women who bought feminism when it was new and fresh in the 1960's—now depressed, guilt-driven, stressed-out, and heart-broken after years of being used and abandoned by men—are too loyal to wonder if they were cheated out of basic happiness by the feminism they swore by.

God created woman to be more than an oppressed victim of feminism. He had an important purpose and a high calling for her as the other half of the reflection of His image and glory. The feminists have taken us far away from this image of womanhood, the image found in the Old and New Testaments. It is the only view that ever accurately depicted where women can find true fulfillment and strength and achieve their fullest potential. It's also the only view that ever required women to be righteous and blameless in their hearts and to obey God's commands. This is why we believe the feminists hate biblical womanhood. Purity, holiness, and submission to God and His order are disgusting to them. Feminism is about "self" and cannot abide the principle of "God first, others second, ourselves last." The leaders of the feminist movement hate the things of light and love the things of darkness, and they hate the blessings God bestows on those who are faithful and obedient to Him.

Has feminism brought women any good things?

A lot of things people associate with the feminist movement have been good things, but this doesn't mean they were in fact the result of feminism. As Jennie Chancey points out in her article "You Don't Know Feminism":

Feminism has tried to plant territorial flags on "discoveries" it did not make. Being opposed to spouse abuse did not start with the feminists. Being in favor of fair inheritance and property ownership laws for women did not start with the feminists. Being opposed to rape and incest did not start with the feminists. The Bible was already there.[22]

If the word "feminist" meant "a defender of women" or "someone who believes women and men are of equal worth," then every Christian woman should be feminist. Unfortunately, feminism has not and cannot defend the God-ordained privileges and positions of women or promote equality and equity between the sexes. The happiness and rights of women never even entered into the agenda of the masterminds who dreamed up the feminist revolution. Marx wanted simply to use emotionally distraught women to subvert Christian society, then to exploit all who streamed from their homes into the factories.

Any movement driven by rebellion against God and His order can never bring anything good. A bad tree cannot produce good fruit. And no true good can, or ever has, come from feminism.

> *What is the most effective way I can help reverse the*
> *damage done by the Marxists and feminists?*

Sarah, after struggling with feminism for several years, asked herself this question. She shares what she learned.

My journey from feminism to faithfulness, by God's grace, is still continuing. Daily the Lord is refining me in areas where I still need work. I have found that the more I am delighting and meditating in His perfect Law (Psalm 1), the more I come to recognize and

---

22 Jennie Chancey, "You Don't Know Feminism," www.visionforum.org, January 23, 2003.

despise feminism for the sin that it is. Truly feminism is not a blessing, but a curse which must be warred against and destroyed. So how do we, as Christian women, defeat feminism?

We must recognize that feminism must be fought—and can only be successfully defeated—God's way. The way we wage war is by taking captive every thought to the obedience of the Lord Jesus Christ (II Corinthians 10:3-5). We must learn to recognize and reject the lies of feminism, including those that we ourselves unwittingly have adopted. We must never seek to conquer feminism by attempting to "Christianize" it. So-called "Christian feminism" is an oxymoron. Feminism in any form is rebellion and must be eradicated through *repentance*, not encouraged through syncretism. We cannot fight feminism with feminism. Nor should we promote any tactics that allocate to woman a different role than God has assigned her.[23] It is never permissible to disregard the Law of God for the sake of achieving a "greater good." We will not take back this culture for Christ by imitating our culture's rebellion to His Word.

The only way we will win the war against feminism is by obeying our Sovereign Commander. Our battlefield as women is being faithful to fulfill the calling Jesus Christ has given us. Our God-given mission is to help our fathers (or husbands) fulfill their God-given mission. They, as men, are to be the protectors, providers, prophets, preachers, leaders, statesmen, and warriors. Whether or not they are successful depends in large part upon us. Unless we are faithful to our biblical calling, our men cannot fully be faithful to theirs. How can we expect that men act like men as God designed them to be unless we are acting like women as God designed us to be? Let us therefore resolve to battle in our hearts and minds and lives anything that would divert us from this

---

23   I Corinthians 14:34-35; I Timothy 2:11-12; 5:14; Titus 2:3-5.

great and glorious task of womanhood. Feminism cannot prevail when women are content and obedient in the role God has given us, to be daughters, wives, mothers, helpmeets, and keepers at home. There is a deathblow struck against feminism every time a daughter/wife gives her heart to her father/husband and submits to him. There is a victory won for Christ's kingdom when a woman understands and embraces her God-given mission.

Rather than continuing in the deception of feminism as daughters of Eve, let us instead strive to be daughters of Sarah, who "obeyed Abraham, calling him lord" (I Peter 3:6). Rather than imitating Jezebel who dominated her husband and influenced him and the land for evil, let us instead make it our purpose to defer to, follow, strengthen, encourage, promote, support, and prosper our fathers (or husbands) for righteousness and the glory of God."

Unlike the feminists, we know God's design for women. This gives us the upper hand. Will we use it?

There is something that the feminists of the 20th century never fully realized. This is that women are hugely influential and *always have been*. Even during times when women were supposedly "shackled" to the house and kitchen, they were making their mark on the world by discovering true feminine freedom. Even when they were supposedly "enslaved to husbands," they were writing history. Even when they could do no more than rock cradles, they were ruling the world. And when they started staging power struggles with men, their influence became perverted—but it didn't wane.

We have a special kind of God-given influence, and we can either use it for His purposes or Satan's. We can use it to pull ourselves and our culture out of this big mess. We can use it to encourage our fathers and the other men around us to become men. We can do this by repenting from our natural inclinations toward feminism and becoming real women.

CHAPTER SEVEN

DAUGHTERS, FATHERS, AND VIRTUOUS WOMANHOOD

WHAT MAKES A DAUGHTER WORTHY OF BEING PROTECTED

What is a real woman?

Former U. S. Senate Chaplain Peter Marshall lamented back in the 1940s,

> Godly womanhood…the very phrase sounds strange in our ears. We never hear it now. We hear about every other type of women: beautiful women, smart women, sophisticated women, career women, talented women, divorced women. But so seldom do we hear of a godly woman—or of a godly man either, for that matter. We believe women come nearer to fulfilling their God-given function in the home than anywhere else. It is a much nobler thing to be a good wife, than to be Miss America. It is a greater achievement to establish a Christian home than it is to produce a second-rate novel filled with filth. It is a far, far better

thing in the realms of morals to be old-fashioned, than to be ultra-modern. The world has enough women who know how to be smart. It needs women who are willing to be simple. The world has enough women who know how to be brilliant. It needs some who will be brave. The world has enough women who are popular. It needs more who are pure. We need women, and men, too, who would rather be morally right than socially correct.[1]

A real woman is a woman who recognizes that she has been exquisitely and perfectly created by a loving God for a unique purpose. Out of genuine gratitude, awe, and a desire to please her Maker, a real woman joyfully embraces her femininity and submits every aspect of her identity—the attitudes and affections of her heart and mind, her appearance, her manners, her speech, her ambitions, and her beliefs—to God's original and unique design for her as a woman. A real woman understands that God designed femininity because masculinity was not enough in itself to represent God's image and glory. The differences between men and women glorify God, and downplaying these differences downplays God's glory. A real woman wants to bring glory to God by being a woman.

How can I be more worthy of my father's protection?

By simply being your father's daughter you are entitled to his protection. To be worthy of this protection, you must appreciate the reasons God has provided it for you, and then gratefully receive it from your dad.

Being truly worthy of protection starts with fearing the Lord. "Charm is deceitful and beauty is vain; but a woman who fears the Lord, she shall be praised" (Proverbs 31:30). A woman who fears

1   Peter Marshall, *Mr. Jones, Meet the Master*, cited in *Verses of Virtue*, compiled and edited by Beall Phillips (San Antonio, Texas: The Vision Forum, Inc., 2003) pp 8, 9.

God will strive to make every aspect of her character—specifically her heart—more like Christ's.

A woman worthy of being protected is in complete surrender to the Divine will and holds back no part of herself from God. She indulges in no pet preferences or habits that are not entirely pleasing to God. Think of Mary, the mother of our Lord, who made herself lowly, who had no ambition for anything but God's will, who said, "Behold the handmaid of the Lord; be it unto me according to thy word" (Luke 1:38).

The heroines of the Bible were praised for having such feminine qualities as graciousness, discretion, strength, dignity, kindness, purity, faith, generosity, diligence, courage, wisdom, and servants' hearts. We all need to work on cultivating these, as well as some of the more uncommon and neglected qualities. We have listed below some of the qualities that are the most challenging.

Self-denial

By self-denial, we mean something deeper than the usual meaning, "denying yourself things you want." Rather, we mean "denying that you have a 'self.' " 1 Corinthians 6:19, 20 tells us that we do not belong to ourselves, but have been bought with a price. Matthew 10:39 says, "He that findeth his life shall lose it: and he that loseth his life for my sake shall find it." We often hear people talking about "being true to yourself," "finding yourself," saying things like "That's just not 'me,' " "I need to follow my heart," or "I'm special because I'm me."

The natural "us" deserves to spend eternity in Hell. Being true to our natural selves and "following our hearts," which "are deceitful above all things and desperately wicked" (Jeremiah 17:9), condemns us to spiritual death. We have no "selves" that are worth being loyal to. Much of what makes up our natural personalities and the state of our hearts is dictated by our sin natures.

God does bless people, even in their sin, with gifts of natural abilities. Some people are naturally hard workers, some are generous, and so forth. One can be "true" only to the natural personality traits that are extolled in Scripture. So everything that makes us who we are—from things that seem like innocent personal preferences, to personality traits—must be examined and evaluated against Scripture.

Humility

> "Yea, all of you be subject one to another, and be clothed with humility: for God resisteth the proud, and giveth grace to the humble. Humble yourselves therefore under the mighty hand of God, that he may exalt you in due time." (1 Peter 5:5)

A woman with a humble heart doesn't seek her own glory and will not parade her greatness before others or try to "prove herself." Rather, she recognizes that she is nothing without God and seeks His glory alone.

A humble woman actively seeks to discover areas of her life she can change and repent from. Moving ever higher in godliness is her goal.

A gentle and quiet spirit

> "Whose adorning let it not be that outward adorning…but let it be the hidden man of the heart, in that which is not corruptible, even the ornament of a meek and quiet spirit, which is in the sight of God of great price." (1 Peter 3:3,4)

We hear about "free" spirits, fiery spirits, fiercely independent spirits, fighting spirits, proud spirits, revolutionary spirits, and just plain "spiritedness" paraded as the essential virtues for the ideal woman. Our culture views a woman with a gentle and quiet spirit as a pushover.

Psalm 37:11 promises, "But the meek shall inherit the earth; and shall delight themselves in the abundance of peace. The wicked plotteth against the just, and gnasheth upon him with his teeth. The Lord shall laugh at him: for he seeth that his day is coming."

God laughs at the militant feminists who mock the real woman for her meekness, promising that it will be the descendants of His meek servants who will inherit the earth. "The Lord lifteth up the meek: he casteth the wicked down to the ground" (Psalm 147:6).

A gentle and quiet spirit is not only imperishable; it is *precious* in the sight of God. It's also one of the hardest qualities to cultivate. Far from a sign of weakness, a gentle and quiet spirit is the sign of a woman who is strong in faith, mind, and character.

Dependence and non-self-sufficiency

These are unusual-sounding virtues these days. As strange as it may sound, to be able to "stand on your own" and not need anyone else, to be self-sufficient and independent, are *not* biblical virtues. In fact, they are unbiblical vices. Firstly, we must all have a dependence on God and lean entirely on him. Secondly, God did create us to be emotionally dependent on members of the body of Christ (the Church) and members of the families He put us in. The kingdom of God is depicted by relationships. It advances through relationships. Remember, it was not good for Adam to be alone. Thirdly, we are to be dependent on the guidance and leadership of the authorities God places over us. A rebellious, defiant personality is not cute. It's abominable to God.

"Self-confidence" and "self-esteem" are very popular terms right now. Our humanistic culture assures us that we are something special, something that we need to love, to indulge, to have confidence in, to be loyal to, to be easy on. These sentiments always follow hard on the heels of the idea that people are inherently good and have unlimited potential for progressive development. Humanists believe we can draw power from "ourselves" if we have faith in ourselves and believe in ourselves. But any ideas akin to "you can be anything you want to be" and "you can do anything you want if you believe in yourself" cut the sovereignty of God completely out of the picture.

God is our source of strength, and our confidence must be entirely in Him, because that is the only confidence that cannot be shaken. "It is God that girdeth me with strength, and maketh my way perfect" (Psalm 18:32). Trusting in our finite, fallible human abilities will leave us broken and destitute like the man in Psalm 52:5-9, whom God broke down forever, snatched up and uprooted, whom the righteous were to laugh at, saying: "Lo, this is the man that made not God his strength; but trusted in the abundance of his riches, and strengthened himself in his desire. But I am like a green olive tree in the house of God: I trust in the mercy of God for ever and ever. I will praise Thee for ever, because Thou hast done it: and I will wait on Thy name; for it is good before Thy saints."

How does a godly young woman act?

A godly daughter is her father's graceful pillar, fashioned for a palace (Psalm 144:12). In her daddy's palace, she is beautifying, supportive, and hospitable. When outside the walls of her daddy's palace, she is his ambassador, representative, and "arrow in the hand of a mighty warrior" (Psalm 127:4). Through her countenance, carriage, and demeanor, she leaves the world in no doubt that she is a girl submitted to her father's protection, the daughter of a king, a princess worthy of honor.

Amidst a generation of giddy, silly, loud, boisterous, undignified, clumsy teenaged girls, picture a girl who radiates dignity, regal serenity, respectfulness, grace, a gentle and quiet voice, poise, discretion, self-command, sincerity, peace, compassion, cheerfulness and humility. That girl would stand out as a woman of quality.

> "Let your light so shine before men, that they may see your good works, and glorify your Father which is in heaven." (Matthew 5:16)

I can see why learning to act with grace and gentleness is a good social thing, but is it an important moral issue?

There are three points we need to understand here.

Firstly, the thoughts in our hearts manifest themselves in the rest of our lives; as Jesus said, "A good tree does not produce bad fruit" (Matthew 7:18), and nor does a good woman produce bad behavior or attitudes in any outward way. *A woman's actions are a reflection of her heart and spirit, because our hearts dictate our behavior.* A rebellious, discontent spirit will be obvious in a girl's countenance, carriage, and speech. A boisterous, tomboyish, masculine spirit will reveal itself in the same way. What's inside of us will come out in many different ways, for all to see.[2]

Secondly, though God looks primarily on the inside, people can only see the outside. Is God's grace capable of turning a rebellious, defiant heart into a gentle and quiet heart? Do we show people the magnitude of God's grace by showing how our crude, unrefined behavior becomes gentle and quiet? Or do we give the world a reason to think that God is limited in His power because He was unable to

---

2   See Luke 6:45.

make our behavior (and so, of course, our hearts) conformed to His model for womanhood? We blaspheme God's grace by continuing to act like "ourselves" (sinful pagans). We glorify God's grace by overcoming stubborn pride and becoming gradually sanctified.

Thirdly, Christians are supposed to set an example to the world. That's what it means to be the salt of the earth. The apostle Peter wrote to the believers living in a generation much like our own: "But ye are a chosen generation, a royal priesthood, an holy nation, a peculiar people; that ye should shew forth the praises of Him who hath called you out of darkness into His marvellous light...Having your conversation honest among the Gentiles:[3] that, whereas they speak against you as evildoers, they may by your good works, which they shall behold, glorify God in the day of visitation" (1 Peter 2:9,12).

We are called to set an example both to believers and to unbelievers of what Christianity looks like, because we are the ambassadors of Christ. If the way we appear before others reflects badly on Him whom we represent, then we must repent and change.

> "Let no man despise thy youth; but be thou an example of the believers, in word, in conversation, in charity, in spirit, in faith, in purity." (1 Timothy 4:12)

How should a godly woman dress?

The theologian Henry Van Til accurately observed that culture is religion externalized. In the same way that a culture is a nation's religion revealed, clothing is an individual's religion revealed (and every person is religious). Clothes make a statement. They proclaim

---

3   Or "Keep your behavior excellent among the Gentiles..." This translation taken from the New American Standard Bible, ©1960, 1963, 1968,1971, 1972, 1973, 1975, 1977, 1995 by The Lockman Foundation. Used by permission.

to people who you are, what you believe, what you are worth, whom you belong to, what you admire, what you aspire to, what you are for, and whether you are protected or cheap.

Looking around us on the street, we can see girls of all shapes and sizes and social backgrounds and beliefs. Nearly all of them have one thing in common: they are hardly wearing any clothing. Like all clothing, the clothes that we don't see these girls wearing make a very obvious statement: *I am a shameless hussy…I am not worth much…I just want to get attention…I live for myself…I need to be noticed…I need to look like everyone else.*

We need our own messages to declare exactly the opposite—*I am loved, I am cherished, I am protected, I am a woman of virtue, I am submitted to God, I am part of a civilized society, I am worth more than rubies, there is a part of me that is not to be stared at by strangers because it belongs to my future husband.*

Unspoken statements like these can help us be salt and light in the earth.

But don't we have better opportunities for evangelism when we dress like the people we evangelize?

How is faith quickened in a person's heart? By the way we impress people? Or by other supernatural means? Of course, our clothing and manner can be advantageous to some extent in some situations, but only as long as we're not violating biblical standards for dress and conduct. However, here is an interesting insight we once overheard a girl share:

> I can remember several examples of people talking to me about Christianity before I was saved. I remember several girls in school who said they were Christian, but who behaved no differently to any of the other girls in the school. They would dress immodestly, go out with boys, use bad language and

many other bad things. In fact, the only way I knew they were Christians is because they would occasionally talk about attending church or activities with their church youth group. Now these girls were exactly like me, they dressed the same, they talked about the same things, and yet the fact that they were just like me wasn't a reason for me to listen to them talking about their religion; it was a reason for me *not* to listen, precisely because it seemed to me that they were no different. This religion they were talking about couldn't be a big deal if its followers seemed just like everybody else! Besides, why would I listen to 'advice' from people who seemed to act just like me— what could they possibly teach me?

What are biblical standards of dress for a protected woman?

A virtuous woman's dress must glorify God. Within this precept, there are three basic sub-principles to bear in mind when buying clothing. The first would have to be *modesty*, which begins with the heart. *Webster's 1828 Dictionary* says:

Modesty, as an act or series of acts, consists in humble, unobtrusive deportment, as opposed to extreme boldness, forwardness, arrogance, presumption, audacity or impudence. In females, modesty has the like character as in males; but the word is used also as synonymous with chastity, or purity of manners. In this sense, modesty results from purity of mind, or from the fear of disgrace and ignominy fortified by education and principle. Unaffected modesty is the sweetest charm of female excellence, the richest gem in the diadem of their honor.

As you might guess, the modesty—or lack thereof—in our hearts is manifested not only in our clothes but also in our behavior. It is possible for a girl to be dressed irreproachably but to be shamefully immodest in behavior—by flirting, being loud and boisterous, by attracting the wrong kind of attention to herself in the wrong way. As Proverbs 11:22 tells us, "As a jewel of gold in a swine's snout, so is a fair woman which is without discretion."

1 Timothy admonishes women to "adorn themselves in modest apparel, with shamefacedness and sobriety" (1 Timothy 2:9). So what does it mean to dress modestly? As regards clothing, modesty has two different meanings. The first and most obvious is the covering of oneself and not revealing things that the public has no right to see. The second is wearing unpretentious, quiet clothing that doesn't draw the wrong kind of attention to oneself.

As well as giving others the wrong impression, immodest clothing causes others to be distracted and tempts them to sin. It's wrong for us to dress in a way that tempts men to think of us in a way other than "as sisters, with all purity" (1 Timothy 5:2).

Matthew 5:28 warns, "But I say unto you, that whosoever looketh on a woman to lust after her hath committed adultery with her already in his heart." Adultery is a serious sin, and tempting men to commit a serious sin is seriously wrong. Yes, men are responsible for keeping their own thoughts pure. But when we do our brothers harm by tempting them to sin, we are sinning against them and against God.

> "We then that are strong ought to bear the infirmities of the weak, and not to please ourselves. Let every one of us please his neighbour for his good to edification. For even Christ pleased not himself; but, as it is written, The reproaches of them that reproached thee fell on me." (Romans 15:1-3)

Our bodies belong to our husbands—if we are not married, to our future husbands—and we need to see to it that we never reveal or show off what is for our husbands' eyes alone.

Our immodest clothing can also cause us to stumble ourselves.

Solomon was the wisest man in the world, Samson was the strongest man in the world, and David was the most righteous man in the world. But the one thing that was strong enough to defeat them all was the *femme fatale*, the fatal woman. We, as women, can wield a very dangerous kind of power, and that kind of power can be twisted to be very ungodly. Unfortunately, we may enjoy that feeling of power, and this is a dangerous feeling for us. If we enjoy the admiration and feeling of power we get from wearing a questionable garment, it is causing us to stumble, and we must repent of our vanity.

In every case, the chief thing to examine is your heart. We need to see to it that our adornment is not merely "that outward adorning of plaiting the hair, and of wearing of gold, or of putting on of apparel; But let it be the hidden man of the heart, in that which is not corruptible, even the ornament of a meek and quiet spirit, which is in the sight of God of great price" (1 Peter 3:3, 4).

When God judges Israel for her harlotry, He says:

> "Because the daughters of Zion are haughty, and walk with stretched forth necks and wanton eyes, walking and mincing as they go, and making a tinkling with their feet [caused by ostentatious ankle bracelets] therefore the Lord will smite with a scab the crown of the head of the daughters of Zion, and the Lord will discover their secret parts...And it shall come to pass, that instead of sweet smell there shall be stink; and instead of a girdle a rent; and instead of well set hair

baldness; and instead of a stomacher a girding of sackcloth; and burning instead of beauty." (Isaiah 3:16-24)

Jennie Chancey explains:

> It isn't the mantles, jewelry, fine linens, and veils that the Lord is judging here. It is the haughty, proud, and wicked heart of His people Israel. As Reverend Steve Schlissel explains, "It isn't the matter, it is the manner." We can dress in drab grays and browns, wear no makeup, and grease our hair back flat, but if we are haughty in heart and proud of our own "righteousness," we are as worthy of judgment as the "mincing" daughters of Zion.[4]

The next point of virtuous dress is *excellence*.

We are the ambassadors of the most High King. For His glory, we should dress in a way that is worthy of our high calling. Our appearances have to glorify God, though, and not ourselves.

When describing the ideal woman, Proverbs 31:22 says, "She maketh herself coverings of tapestry; her clothing is silk and purple." Note that the Proverbs 31 woman was dressed in fine clothing, not in rags. However, we must balance this with our duty to be good stewards of the financial assets God entrusts to us and not throw our or our fathers' money around extravagantly.

Finally, and possible the most controversial, is *femininity*. In the beginning, God created them male and female, and He called the distinction between the two "good." God specifically forbids the blurring of this distinction.

---

4 Jennie Chancey, *Modesty and the Christian Woman*, www.ladiesagainstfeminism.com, June 1, 2003 (quoting Rev. Steve Schlissel, Christian Student Worldview Conference talk, "The Covenant," July, 1999).

Deuteronomy 22:5 says, "The woman shall not wear that which pertaineth unto a man, neither shall a man put on a woman's garment: for all that do so are abomination unto the Lord thy God."

Jennie Chancey explains:

The word "abomination" is pretty unequivocal. It means "disgusting" and "wicked." In other words, God hates it, and we know from His Word that God "changeth not" (Malachi 3:6). Some approach the Deuteronomy passage by saying, "Yes, but in those days, both men and women wore robes, so you can't really say that men and women today have to dress differently. I can wear baggy trousers and a man's shirt and still look like a woman." But to assume that men's and women's clothing was interchangeable in "Bible times" would utterly negate the clear meaning of this verse. If there were no differences, there would be no need to even discuss cross-dressing. However, there were distinctions between men's and women's attire among the Israelites. The Hebrew word *kaeliy* (used here as "that which pertaineth to a man") often refers to armor in other scriptural passages (see BlueLetterBible. org). During the time the Israelites entered the Promised Land, the pagans dwelling there used cross-dressing in their temple ceremonies. Specifically, women often donned men's military armor in the worship of the goddess Astarte (Venus). Matthew Henry notes, "[I]n the worship of Venus, women appeared in armour, and men in women's clothes; this, as other such superstitious usages, is here said to be *an abomination to the Lord*" (emphasis in the original). There were and are distinctions in dress that do more than reveal our different genders; they also reveal our God-ordained roles. The woman who wears a man's clothing is, in essence, declaring herself to be a man and able to do whatever a man does (enlist as a soldier, defend cities from attackers, and take an arrow like a man). The man who wears a woman's clothing declares that he has shunned his maleness as God defines it and prefers not to protect, fight, defend, or even fully provide for those under his care. Pagan societies repudiated God-given male-female differences and roles, as reflected in their idolatrous practices. So we must take care to see that our clothing is a correct portrayal of who we are—whether male or female. As women, our clothing should tell the truth of our position in God's economy. We are the "weaker vessel," softer and gentler than the man and in submission rather than in leadership. When we dress for the day, does our clothing declare that we are feminine and precious—people to be protected and cared for? Or does it proclaim that we can earn our own way in the world and slay our own dragons? The woman clomping around in "tank pants" and combat boots doesn't bespeak maidenly virtues or a need to be treasured and cared for. In fact, she invites others to treat her as "one of the guys," slapping her on the back, slamming doors in her face and leaving her to fend for herself in a dark parking lot. But the woman of gentle, discreet femininity invites honor and distinction. Men hush their rough talk when she enters the room. Men think twice before letting a door close in her face. No one would dream of slapping her on the back or sharing a coarse jest with her. The clothing she chooses to wear partially explains the preferential treatment she receives, but it goes deeper than what is on the outside. Her feminine beauty grows from within—from her obedience to God's commands for womanly behavior. As our culture continues to toss aside male-female distinctions in favor of "gender neutrality," we must strive even more to be womanly and make modesty look as wonderful as it really is.[5]

---

5   Ibid.

Genevieve tells of her journey in learning to dress like a protected woman:

I was raised to dress modestly. To me, being modest meant wearing clothing which was not skimpy, tight, or revealing. But somehow, along the way, in seeking to become modest, I became masculine.

I always was something of a tomboy growing up. I preferred trousers to skirts, mainly because I didn't like any of my skirts, but also because feminine attire would have been unpractical for a young girl who liked to romp with her younger brothers, climb trees and dig holes with them in the garden! As I grew up and matured, and as the fashions changed, it became harder and harder to find clothing which I considered to be modest. The clothing in the women's sections all seemed too flimsy and impractical, and they seemed to be made for women much smaller than my height of 5'11". And so I turned to the men's section to find garments which were loose, baggy, and 'modest' enough for me to feel comfortable wearing.

Then one day, I looked down at myself and thought, "I look just like a man." It was true. From my shoes to my sweater, my clothing had all come from the men's section. This is when I realized that in seeking to be modest I'd become masculine. I was truly horrified. I'd been seeking to please God with my modesty, but realized that I wasn't pleasing Him by being masculine. In fact, I realized that my masculine appearance sent the message that I was rejecting God's gifts of womanhood and femininity to me. It struck me that that was what I was missing: femininity. I needed to be feminine just as much as I needed to be modest. This would be pleasing to God.

The area of femininity became a major subject of study for me. I read books, talked to peers, sat under the teaching of older women, and attempted to learn all I could about being feminine. One book I read described femininity as being the opposite of masculinity. This helped me a lot. I connected this concept with the ideas that I was learning that colours and colour combinations can be feminine or masculine, that various fabrics can be feminine or masculine, that patterns on fabric can be feminine or masculine, that cuts and styles and forms of tailoring can be feminine or masculine. My wardrobe went through a reformation, and indeed continues to reform as I learn more about femininity.

To ensure that I keep learning and growing and don't start to cruise, I've put into place a number of initiatives. Firstly, I review my wardrobe every six months or so either by myself or with the help of a family member or friend. Immodest/unfeminine clothing simply has a way of making its way into my wardrobe. Secondly, I've started a folder on femininity. Articles, pictures of feminine looking women or pieces of clothing, fabric cuttings, color combinations, and other findings relating to femininity all go into my folder.

The Lord is good. Not only has He opened my eyes about the importance of femininity, but He has shown me how important a witness I have as a Christian girl to this pagan world in the way that I dress. May my wardrobe continue to reform in ways that please the Lord. I praise the name of the Lord.

Where should I get guidelines for modest, excellent, feminine dress?

This is where our protectors come in. In the same way that they are responsible to keep you from making a foolish vow or commitment, they are to protect your character and reputation, and to protect you from making a mistake by revealing yourself. If your father (or mother) is concerned about the way you dress, *you are blessed!* You have a parent who loves you enough to want to protect you. We need to *ask* our fathers to set standards and make guidelines for us, instead of resisting them or pushing their limits. Because our fathers are men, they know what other men would find a stumbling block. They also know how they want their ambassadors to represent them.

Expect a dramatic change, not only in your life but in the lives of those around you, when you start following biblical principles for modest, excellent, feminine dress. In her article entitled "Men's Wear Lost, Feminine Wear Regained," Bethany Vaughn tells how she conducted a one-week-long experiment she called "The Feminine Dress Challenge," committing to wear nothing but feminine dresses for one week and keeping a journal of the results throughout. She reported:

> I immediately noticed that I felt more feminine. I felt like a woman! I felt lovely and wonderfully beautiful, delicate and charming, dainty and glowing. I know you may think I took a dive into sheer craziness, but something really happened to the way I perceived myself. Hole-y jeans and a tee-shirt cannot even compare. There is some truth to the saying, "clothes make the man."
>
> The next thing I noticed was that I became keenly aware of my movements and physical actions. Climbing over the seat in the van or running up the stairs or even sitting were oftentimes done in a very unfeminine way. When I have a dress on, I am careful to sit like a lady. I walked and carried myself differently.
>
> Another thing I noticed was positive public reaction. I experienced numerous acts of chivalry and respect when I went out in public. When we were out and about, my daughter and I, more times than not, had doors opened for us by men. One man tipped his hat to us and said, "Good Day, Ma'am." We had young men at the grocery store answer with, "Yes, Ma'am" and

"No, Ma'am" and help lift heavy loads. These were not rare acts, but the respect and chivalrous actions noticeably increased, and I believe that our attention to feminine dress was what spurred these comments and actions from strangers.[6]

Femininity has a strange effect on the outside world. To our lost culture, it is foreign, but it is fascinating. It inspires awe and respect. It can even inspire today's feminized men to be manly, protective, and chivalrous. Never underestimate the power of godly femininity.

---

6   Bethany Vaughn, "Men's Wear Lost, Feminine Dress Regained," www.ladiesagainstfeminism.com, October 28, 2003.

CHAPTER EIGHT

DAUGHTERS, FATHERS, AND FEMININE STRENGTH

WHY PROTECTION GIVES US POWER

Is it possible to be feminine and delicate, protected and sheltered, and also be a strong, dynamic warrior for Christ?

First, we need to properly define some words: strength, and femininity.

The world has given us a warped idea of strength, a view confined to physical strength, vocal volume, assertiveness, toughness, size, commanding leadership, and other masculine traits. It excludes any of the more subtle definitions extolled in Scripture, which we will talk more about in a minute.

The word "femininity" is also fraught with derogatory misinterpretations. It is a common misconception that femininity is all about being fluffy, pink, prissy, flirtatious, bimbo-like, or trivial. These are descriptions that the world brings to mind when the word "feminine" pops up, but nowhere in Scripture are such things mentioned as being signs of godly womanhood.

Rebekah hated these false ideas of femininity. She tells us:

> My concept of femininity had been warped and twisted by
> the feminist culture that I grew up in, though at the time
> I was not aware of it. I thought that being feminine meant
> that a woman was so dainty and delicate that it rendered her
> incapable, or that she was so weak and dependent that she was
> powerless to provide anything for herself. It seemed to me that
> the constraints of femininity would produce a woman who
> was incompetent and of little use; someone so "good" that she
> would be good for nothing. Because I was repulsed by (this
> distorted view of) femininity, I embraced the antithesis, not
> realizing that there was a biblical truth, which was solid and
> balanced between these two extremes.

Being feminine and being warriors for Christ are not contradictions. God wouldn't require all Christians to be warriors and dominion takers and then demand that women become useless parasites and good-for-nothings. God wants us to serve Him. He will not make it impossible for us. A proper understanding of both requirements shows us that the one (femininity) can lead to the other (powerful purpose). **Rebekah** came to realize:

> God's perfect ways are not exclusive, but inclusive, of strength.
> Strength is manifested in ways such as being obedient even when
> it is difficult, and standing firm and decided in one's convictions.

Do girls who have "tomboy-ish" inclinations have to change?

Rebekah was a "born tomboy." She says:

I found my life as a girl to be rather dull and unexciting while growing up. It seemed to me that a boy's life was more desirable than a girl's. To solve this erroneously-perceived problem, I made it my mission in life to be a tomboy. I set about undertaking the task of fulfilling my goal by accepting every opportunity I had to prove my strength and refusing to show any sign of weakness or cowardice (both of which I loathed). I never allowed myself to cry because crying was for sissies. Even though I am the middle sister of three sisters, I was more like the brother my sisters never had. I have always been physically stronger than my sisters—a fact that I took great pride in. In order to avoid compromising my "tough" persona, I shunned all things that I deemed "girlie" or "weak"—what I thought was feminine.

And so I became a tomboy and a romp, and for a while I quite enjoyed it. Sin often seems sweet at first, but is bitter in the end (Proverbs 20:17; 16:25). In fact, I not only delighted in being boyish and different from those "feminine" girls whose chatter often bored and irritated me, I also liked to do things for the shock value and to see how far I could push the limit. Since I had always been a person more of action than of words, communicating physically rather than verbally, I found that I could more easily relate to boys because of that similarity. My attraction to boyish things and the adventure and excitement that came with them fueled my aversion toward femininity as I saw it. My quest to become "one of the guys" led me to yield to my sinful nature and develop a competitive and independent spirit, causing me to lose one of the sweetest traits of girlhood—that of gentle trustfulness. As I began to indulge my independence (which was rebellion against God's order and not submitting to my parents), I was proud of the fact that I needed no protection or sheltering (so I mistakenly thought)—I was "tough" and could make it on my own. At first I was quite pleased with myself and whom I was becoming, but the longer I drank from the well of feminism, the sicker I grew. Instead of gaining contentment, there was a sea of discontentment welling up within me. Instead of the serenity and gratification that I was seeking, it brought greater dissatisfaction and frustration than I had felt before. After realizing that, no matter how hard I tried, I could never be a boy, I then began to resent that I had been created a girl. I questioned God as to why I had (what I thought was) the unfair misfortune and oppression of being a girl.

The Lord answered my question, though not right away. Years later, as He took control of my heart, Christ began to turn it toward Himself, placing within it new desires—desires that would honor and please Him. He drew me away from the poison water I had been consuming and led me to the fountain of life (Proverbs 14:27). Through a variety of ways, God began to expose the fallaciousness of my thinking and thus my way of living. The Holy Spirit used His Word, faithful biblical preaching and teaching, books I read, and young women I met who were examples of godly femininity to open my eyes to the fact that I had been in sin. My rebellious behavior was a reflection of my rebellious and sinful heart; because my heart was deceitfully wicked (Jeremiah 17:9), my understanding of my role and femininity was perverted (see Proverbs 4:23). I could now see these godly influences in my life demonstrating that young women should be gentle in speech, voice, and manner, full of love for home—that there was no shame in that, for it was God's perfect will and plan for women. As the Lord continues to teach me to delight in and be thankful for being a young woman, I am discovering the contentment I desired but missed out on while pursuing the lie of feminism in regards to femininity. Thankfully, the Lord revealed to me that I was indeed not a strong young woman but a foolish young woman, simple and knowing nothing. I was beginning to understand that a woman's true strength lies in her femininity, not in her physical being or in stubborn willfulness, and that true femininity is anything but weak. I am not saying that being feminine will make one strong, but that strength is developed through, manifested in, and drawn from being obedient to fulfill God's calling as a woman.

In what ways can women be strong without being masculine?

Rebekah continues:

The Lord has shown me that, as a woman, I can be just as strong as a man, but that strength is evinced in a different way in a woman's life than in a man's life. The agency of a man's strength is not better, but it is different than the agency of a woman's strength. Both men and women are called to be soldiers for Christ, but we are commanded to be so in different realms. Man is fitted, qualified, and created for taking dominion in the storms of public life; we as women are ordained by God to occupy and keep the domain of home. As women, we are not to rival man by seeking to be a replica or copy of him, nor are we to compete with him, but we should seek instead to complement him and be his counterpart as God created us to be (Genesis 2:18). By exhibiting such virtues as meekness, gentleness, kindness, forbearance, obedience, reverence, modesty, and purity in a responsive, submissive manner, we bring a balance and completeness to man's assertive qualities as an initiator, warrior, provider, leader, and protector (see 1 Peter 3). These and other such godly traits are the God-ordained elements of a girl's influence in her father's life and someday in the life of her husband.

A truly strong woman is not masculine or mannish, but is firm in decision, character, beliefs, and action; she has all the softness that does not imply weakness in the wrong way; she is possessive of a firmness that is not harsh or domineering or exclusive of delicacy. She has the ability to provide for herself, but in restraint does not. Instead she channels that ability by supporting and building up her father or husband, enabling him to fulfill his God-ordained role. The strong woman is loving toward family, helpful whenever she can be; she is competent, capable, and intelligent, yet dependent on, trustful of, and submissive to the Lord and her father or husband. I had never before understood the harmony that existed between being strong and being feminine. Yet a feminine woman is a strong woman, because her strength comes from embracing and fulfilling the role that God has given to women.

For the greater part of my life, I had no idea of the importance of our God-ordained mission as women. What responsibilities are attached to our work! What strength is required for and found in the pursuit of biblical femininity—more than I ever had while pursuing feminist ideals and indulging my flesh. Performing the role that the Lord has given us as women is never degrading, boring, unimportant, unexciting, or shameful, but quite the opposite—it is a wonderful and fulfilling privilege and blessing. The Scripture teaches that there are consequences to our actions: both negative for disobedience and positive for obedience (Deuteronomy 28; 29; 30:15-20). Our faithfulness as daughters and wives to welcome our responsibilities and do our duty will better enable our fathers and husbands to more fully and easily carry our their God-ordained mission in life.

It should be every girl's aim to possess in her character all the capacity of womanhood and to not only do the work the Lord has called us to as women, but to embrace and delight in that work. In order for this to be possible, our hearts must be right with the Lord and must be kept right. Our motivation and desire must be to please the Lord and bring glory to Him. I cannot stress to you enough the importance of a yielded and submissive heart—first to our heavenly Father, and second to your earthly father or husband. The kind of life you will have—in fact your very life—depends on the condition of your heart. Remember the warning of Deuteronomy 11:16: "Take heed to yourselves, that your heart be not deceived and ye turn aside..."

Be, oh, so careful to guard your heart and keep it stayed on Christ, for He will most certainly make you strong to do His will—your duty: exemplifying biblical strength in femininity. For we are not strong in and of ourselves, but we are weak and we must depend on Christ. Let me, the former tomboy, encourage you to do as I am able to do by the grace of God: treasure, embrace, take pleasure in, and delight in being a woman and in being feminine, for this was God's perfect will when He created you. Train, or re-train as I have had to do, your mind to think and work according to the guidelines that our Father God has given to us as women in His Word; ask the Holy Spirit to renew your heart and mind after Jesus Christ and to stamp His Word in your heart and mind.

May we always glory in the true greatness and real dignity of the sphere that God has ordained for us as women to fill. Let us labor to qualify ourselves to accomplish our mission with distinguished success, by God's grace. As we set the biblical ideal before ourselves of strong, beautiful girlhood and womanhood, let us bend all of our energies toward it and use the strength afforded us from our gracious heavenly Father to attain this. May the Lord grant that we would be strong enough in our biblical femininity and brave enough to always be loyal to our calling of biblical womanhood, for His glory.

What would a society be like where the women were truly strong?

There have been a few societies filled with, and consequently, usually built by, such women, but the one which instantly springs to the authors' minds is early America.[1]

Though modern history books have twisted the truth about our foremothers, we can learn a lot from the fascinating first-hand accounts from this time. We can discover much about the mothers of our country from reading their journals and letters and memoirs. Nannie T. Alderson writes in her autobiography, *A Bride Goes West*, the story of how, in the 1880s, she left her wealthy, upper-class West Virginia family in her early twenties to go with her husband

---

1   When the first brave wives came with their husbands to the shores of Plymouth in 1620, they brought character and the customs of Christendom with them. Unfortunately, most modern history books give inaccurate depictions of women from this time, and often focus entirely on the "feminists before their time" who did little or nothing to build up their society, and often had little cultural significance. Often they pick and choose various brilliant and impressive women in history, such as Abigail Adams, and present them as feminists. In many cases, including Abigail's, the women they have tried to recruit to their cause were in fact submissive wives, devoted mothers, and joyful keepers-at-home. Most truly strong women from this era do not feature in the feminist rewriting of history. "All of history must be re-written in terms of oppression of women." ("The Declaration of Feminism," November 1971.)

to live in a one-room cabin on the barren, uncivilized cattle lands of Montana, with the threat of Indians massacring and scalping never far away, no other women to talk to, and none of the luxuries she was brought up with. After getting word, the day after she gave birth to her firstborn, that Indians had burned their cabin down, she admits, "I saw that I was beginning to feel sorry for myself—the lowest state to which a woman's mind can fall. And I made up my mind to stop it. Many times in the years that followed I forgot this worthy resolve, but I always came back to it sooner or later. I still think it the most important lesson that any wife can learn, whether she lives in a house of cottonwood logs or in a palace."[2]

Mrs. Alderson's strength of character was typical of the women of her time, which was not so long ago, in the late 1800s.

Alexis de Tocqueville was a young French nobleman who came to America in the early 1830s to study, analyze, and report on the state of this new nation. His observations of America and the American people became the well-known study *Democracy in America*. He was struck by the young American women he encountered, and their courage, and he commented on their feminine strength of character:

> The same strength of purpose which the young wives of America display, in bending themselves at once and without repining to the austere duties of their new condition [marriage] is no less manifest in all the great trials of their lives. In no country in the world are private fortunes more precarious than in the United States. It is not uncommon for the same man, in the course of his life, to rise and sink again through all the grades which lead from opulence to poverty. American women support these vicissitudes with calm

2   Nannie T. Alderson and Helena Huntingdon Smith, *A Bride Goes West* (University of Nebraska Press, 1942), p. 128.

and unquenchable energy: it would seem that their desires contract as easily as they expand with their fortunes.

I have often met, even on the verge of wilderness, with young women who, after being brought up amidst all the comforts of the large towns of New England, had passed, almost without any intermediate stage, from the wealthy abode of their parents to a comfortless hovel in a forest. Fever, solitude, and a tedious life had not broken the springs of their courage…I do not doubt that these young American women had amassed, in the education of their early years, that inward strength which they displayed under these circumstances.

…Hence it is, that the women of America, who often exhibit a masculine strength of understanding and a manly energy, generally preserve great delicacy of personal appearance, and always retain the manners of women, although they sometimes show that they have the hearts and minds of men.[3]

These are the women that the feminists of today refer to as poor, oppressed victims of a chauvinist society, imprisoned in long skirts, chained to the family hearth, and prevented from realizing their full potential. These are the women true historians refer to as the mothers of our nation, the heroines who built our society. They were courageous without being authoritative. They were sympathetic, compassionate and considerate of the feelings of others without being driven by their emotions or obsessed with their feelings. They enjoyed being feminine and beautiful without being slaves to fashion or their appearance. They were firm of resolve without being feministically stubborn; strong in faith, mind, and character without

3   Alexis de Tocqueville, *Democracy In America* (New York: Penguin Books USA, Inc., 1956), pp. 237, 244.

being independent; and self-disciplined without being self-centered. Most of all, they were proud to be women. They had no need to feel guilt or confusion over their role and had no wish to act like men.

Should we be just trying to go back to how things were 200 years ago?

There were many wonderful, biblical aspects of American society 200 years ago, due to that society's strong Christian heritage, and there are many lessons to be learned from studying those who came before us. There were also mistakes made during those times that we can learn from. We should not aspire to merely duplicate a previous era, but rather to build on its good points and learn from its bad ones. We should identify the legacy in all its richness, then build on it.

We, in a sense, are also pioneers. We should not try to cling to a bygone era—rather, we should try to build something new, something greater and more biblical than has ever been seen in any past society. And we must never underestimate the power women have to influence whole societies in this way. But in order to have this kind of influence, we must be women. Not men. This is where we find the mysterious feminine power that God gives us.

Alexis de Tocqueville again:

> [I]f I were asked, now that I am drawing to the close of this work in which I have spoken of so many important things done by the Americans, to what the singular prosperity and growing strength of that people are mainly to be attributed, I should reply, to the superiority of their women.[4]

---

4 Ibid., p. 246

CHAPTER NINE

FATHERS, DAUGHTERS, AND THE RIGHT CAREER AT THE RIGHT TIME

THE HIGHEST AND NOBLEST VOCATION OF ALL

All my life I've wanted to have a career.
Is this a godly ambition?

Because our culture has departed so far from biblical patterns of life and thought, we must examine every tradition of men. Right now, let's examine the concept of young women chasing exciting and impressive careers in the name of personal fulfillment, security, interest, ability, adventure, or personal affluence.

Don't I have a duty to stand on my own two feet and
support myself with a career outside the home?

Biblically, the duty to provide is given to the man. As we read in Genesis 3, because of Adam's sin, God cursed the ground so that it would be hard for Adam to provide for his family. The curse God gave Eve was completely different:

"Unto the woman He said, I will greatly multiply thy sorrow and thy conception; in sorrow thou shalt bring forth children; and thy desire shall be to thy husband, and he shall rule over thee." (Genesis 3:16)

Nowhere in Scripture does it even hint that a woman has a duty to provide for herself. Even in a worst-case scenario, our Heavenly Father has arranged for masculine protection for needy women.

Here is an interesting perspective. Throughout history, men have had to bear only the curse God gave directly to them. They work hard to provide for and protect their families. They don't bear children. In our society, women are freely embracing a double curse—the curse of the man (difficulty in providing) in addition to the curse of the woman (pain in childbirth).

What about women who are abandoned, divorced, or widowed? We must remember that God is not silent on this issue. Scripture goes into detail about how women without fathers or husbands are to be provided for. Both Old and New Testaments are full of exhortations to protect and provide for the widows and fatherless. The immediate responsibility rests with family. "If any provide not for his own, and specially for those of his own house, he hath denied the faith, and is worse than an infidel" (1 Timothy 5:8).

"But if any widow have children or nephews, let them learn first to shew piety at home, and to requite their parents: for that is good and acceptable before God" (1 Timothy 5:4). Widows without relatives to provide for them are to be cared for by the church. "Pure religion and undefiled before God and the Father is this, to visit the fatherless and widows in their affliction, and to keep himself unspotted from the world" (James 1:27).

R.J. Rushdoony explains, "The word *visit* in Greek is a form of *episkopeo*, and it means to visit with help, to care for, to exercise oversight."[1]

Some argue that Ruth was a biblical example of a widow who got a job to support herself and her mother-in-law. Closer reading of the book of Ruth reveals a woman living off the charity of a benevolent man who understood God's order. She did have to go out, into the fields, to collect the food he instructed his young men to leave for her. Boaz assumed responsibility for her safety and support, extending his protection and cautioning her to stay on his estate with the other young women.[2]

Some women (abandoned, divorced, or widowed) have no family able or willing to support them. If this happens, churches should step in and carefully provide both spiritual and financial protection. Churches have a duty, however, to qualify the help they give. It can only go to those who have proven themselves obedient to God's standards for family-centered living.

Though men are supposed to be the providers, and fathers and husbands must support their daughters and wives, this does not exempt any women from their duty to *work*. There is a distinction between the work women are supposed to do in fulfilling the duties God has given them and being a wage slave to strange men in the "workforce."

---

1 Rushdoony, *Law and Society: Volume II of the Institutes of Biblical Law* (California: Ross House Books, 1986), p. 133

2 The book of Ruth is a fascinating portrayal of God's design involving young women, protection, provision, and authority. The happy ending? The faithful, virtuous young woman is blessed with a husband and children. Though she was a Gentile, she was welcomed into the covenant community. God blessed her obedience supernaturally and placed her in the line of Christ.

What is the ultimate occupation I should be preparing for and aspiring to?

We have already mentioned that God created woman for a special purpose and that she is most productive when she devotes herself to fulfilling this role. When He created woman, He gave her an occupation. This lifework is her sphere of dominion and seat of authority, whereby she is to gain praise and honor and achieve influence.

First, woman was created to be her husband's helper.

Second, woman is called to be the mistress of a functional home.

The apostle Paul rarely gave instruction specifically to young women, but one of the instances where he did so is in Titus 2:4, 5: "…that they may·encourage the young women to love their husbands, to love their children, to be sensible, pure, **workers at home**, kind, being subject to their own husbands, that the word of God may not be blasphemed."

Jennie Chancey explains: "Going to the Greek, the word for 'worker at home' used here is *oikouros*, which literally means 'guard or watcher of the house.' Thayer's *Lexicon* renders the meaning 'keeping at home and taking care of household affairs.'"[3]

William Einwechter writes: "In Paul's charge to the younger women, he exhorts them to 'marry, bear children, guide the house…' (1 Timothy 5:12). The verb 'guide' (*oikodespotein*) is an expressive term meaning to *rule* the household, to *manage* family affairs. It indicates that the sphere of a woman's authority is the home…

3   Jennie Chancey, "Jennie Chancey Responds to Titus 2 Cynics," www.visionforum.org, December 10, 2003.

Furthermore, 'guide' is a present infinitive indicating that managing the home is the wife's constant occupation, her full-time job."[4]

Women were designed by God to be the happiest, most fulfilled, most productive, most appreciated, and most honored as homemakers. No other career can come close to the importance of homemaking. Most other careers actually undermine God's order by cheating women out of their first and best calling and taking civilization in the wrong direction. This is because homemakers are so central to guiding and shaping civil society. When women leave that domain to pretend to be men, it's not just silly, it's detrimental to a woman's life and her culture.

Third, woman is called to be a trainer of children.

What could be more important than raising up the future generation of warriors for Christ? By bringing up our children in the nurture and admonition of the Lord, we are raising armies for Christ! In 1905, when President Theodore Roosevelt addressed the nation on the importance of motherhood, he revealed a mature understanding of the biblical position:

> No piled-up wealth, no splendor of material growth, no brilliance of artistic development, will permanently avail any people unless its home life is healthy...unless the average woman is a good wife, a good mother, able and willing to perform the first and greatest duty of womanhood, able and willing to bear, and to bring up as they should be brought up, healthy children, sound in body, mind, and character, and numerous enough so that the race shall increase and not decrease. There are certain old truths which will be true as long as this world endures, and which no amount of

4   Rev. William Einwechter, "Exegetical Defense of the Woman as Keeper at Home," www.visionforum.org, February 9, 2004.

progress can alter. One of these is the truth that the primary duty of the husband is to be the home-maker, the breadwinner for his wife and children, and that the primary duty of the woman is to be the helpmate, the housewife, and mother…Into the woman's keeping is committed the destiny of the generations to come after us…The woman's task is not easy—no task worth doing is easy—but in doing it, and when she has done it, there shall come to her the highest and holiest joy known to mankind; and having done it, she shall have the reward prophesied in Scripture; for her husband and her children, yes, and all people who realize that her work lies at the foundation of all national happiness and greatness, shall rise up and call her blessed.[5]

There is nothing confining or restraining about this "career" God has called us to.

Notes William H. Felix, a Southern Baptist minister who lived from 1838-1912, in his essay "The Work and Sphere of True Womanhood":

Woman's work is foundation work for society, for the state, for the kingdom of Heaven. In the homes of America are born the children of America; and from them goes forth American life. Who has the hand upon these springs of life? Woman. These children of American homes go out with the stamp of these homes upon them, and only as these homes are what they ought to be will these children be what they ought to be….Woman may think her sphere and work are limited and contracted, but in this she was never found in a graver mistake. In the home she is imprinting herself upon the man; in him she builds up society, in him she builds up the state, in him she legislates, in

---

5   Theodore Roosevelt, "On American Motherhood," a speech given in Washington on March 13, 1905, before the National Congress of Mothers (cited in Jennie Chancey's "When Momma Wears Combat Boots").

him she executes, in him she rules. She makes man what he is, so far as human power can operate. Yes, if she never does anything else but "nurse babies," she can do no grander work. May God impress upon our women the high, heavenly, holy duty of rearing the children of our country, and making our homes places of joy and comfort. Alas! for the state! if our women are to leave the work of our homes and run hither and thither in search of larger rights and larger powers.[6]

Where did the "outside the home" careerism concept come from?

You've probably been told all your life that careerism is the most acceptable option for women. We've all been told this. How did it become so acceptable?

Careerism for women became "correct" simply because the alternative has become "incorrect." Women of this century are surrounded by savage ridicule of the choice to stay at home, help their husbands and train their children.

The first ridiculers of homemaking were not ordinary women who had found a better, more fulfilling path. The ridiculers were the same Marxists we introduced in Chapter Six, who knew there would be no cultural transformation if mothers continued to strengthen Christian civilization from their strong positions of influence in the home. They didn't want wives helping their husbands. They didn't want mothers training their children. They didn't want mothers

---

6   From the essay by W. H. Felix entitled: "The Work and Sphere of True Womanhood" in J. W. Porter, ed., *Feminism: Woman and Her Work* (reprint ed., Bloomfield, New Mexico: The Historic Baptist, 1995), pp. 129-130.

teaching their children anything. The ridiculers were primarily revolutionaries with political agendas.

Because Western nations have listened to these ridiculers, women are now operating on new customs and traditions that are revolutionary. The revolutionaries have succeeded. The family has been revolutionized. Men and women think differently than they ever have in many thousands of years. How did this happen?

Forcing women into employment was one of the primary tactics of the cultural Marxists. One of the oldest tricks in the socialist book is the widespread exploitation of women for their labor in the deliberate effort to destabilize the home. As we have seen, Marx was no friend of women, and neither was his colleague Frederick Engels. Engels wrote, "The first condition of the liberation of the wife is to bring the whole female sex back into public industry, and this in turn demands the abolition of the monogamous family as the economic unit of society."[7]

This also would fulfill one of their other goals: the eventual end of private labor and private property.

In *From the Old Family to the New,* revolutionary communist leader Leon Trotsky explains how the socialists planned to end private domestic labor: "We need more socialist economic reforms. Only under such conditions can we free the family from the functions and cares that now oppress and disintegrate it. Washing must be done by a public laundry, catering by a public restaurant, sewing by a public workshop. Children must be educated by good public teachers who have a real vocation for the work."[8]

---

7   Frederick Engels, *The Origins of the Family, Private Property and the State,* (New York: International Publishers, 1942).

8   Trotsky, *From the Old Family to the New,* www.marxists.org.

In other words, mothers, at all costs, must be kept from working in their natural sphere, the home. Why? Because devoted, full-time mothers inevitably realize too much. Many instinctively know that the family and socialism do not mix. Mothers, realizing their true potential for influence in their original role—wives co-ruling a self-contained, miniature kingdom called the family, with its own hierarchy of authority, its own property, its own economic provision, its own governance—wives helping their husbands take dominion of the earth without an approved government agenda—women like these stand in direct opposition to socialism. Their standing firm in their roles as wives, homemakers, and trainers of children is what prevents socialism from taking hold.

For this is the third, and possibly most important, reason for the Marxists to strive above all to persuade women to leave the home in search of more "important" work: to prevent them from training their children.

> Marcuse said that women should be the cultural proletariat who transformed Western society. They would serve as the catalyst for the new Marxist Revolution. If women could be persuaded to leave their traditional roles as the *transmitters of culture*, then the traditional culture could not be transmitted to the next generation…What better way to influence the generations than by subverting the traditional roles of women? The Marxists rightfully reasoned that the undermining of women could deal a deadly blow to the culture.[9]

In the name of freedom for women, the Marxists killed three important birds with one stone, simply by luring women into

---

9   William Borst, Ph. D. American History, "A Nation of Frogs," *The Mindszenty Report Vol. XLV-No. 1* (January 2003, emphasis added).

outside employment.[10] They forced women into industry, they made family life the business of the State, and they took control of the children so they could secure the loyalty of the next generation.

Looking at society as a whole, the movement that took women out of the home and put them in the marketplace was damaging for women and Western culture. Many parties have cashed in, but none more than the State. Families are the big losers.

According to Scripture, is chasing a career outside the home a sin?

Because only God can dictate what sin is, and because sin is a very serious thing, we must be very cautious about what we label as sin. Career*ism* may not technically be a sin in theological terms, but doing one's best to get out from under God's order for families and society may be a sinful action done with sinful motives. It may not be "want of conformity to the *law* of God,"[11] but it does appear to be want of conformity to His design for civil society.

Let's look at the Titus 2 command again. As we pointed out before, the original Greek for "workers at home" is *oikouros*, which literally means "guard or watcher of the house." Jennie Chancey points out, "A woman cannot both 'keep at home' (or 'guard the house') and 'keep' in a separate workplace...A simple glance at the domain which the wife is commanded to oversee and rule—yes, rule—should demonstrate beyond a doubt that it is not possible

---

10 Actually, they also killed a few other minor birds, such as instilling despair, guilt, and depression in women, driving them to psychologists, "the agents of social change."

11 From the definition of sin according to the Westminster Standards.

to be an effective, capable keeper at home while pursuing another (outside) occupation."[12]

This does not mean that women should be kept prisoners in their homes. It means that women should be the *guards, protectors, and keepers of their homes.* God did not create the home to be a "house" or a cage for women, or a place to keep the women because they weren't allowed to be anywhere else. But devoting herself to any other sphere would be a waste of her time and her life and would keep her from realizing her full potential. The home is the best workplace for her abilities. The home is the place where she can be the most productive. The home is where she can give the most glory to God, because she is embracing His wonderful design for women. The work she will do as keeper-at-home, when understood biblically, is work only a woman can do, and it is the most worthy work she can aspire to. And though her work does not take place in the gates, it is praised in the gates, as Proverbs 31:31 tells us: "Give her the fruit of her hands, and her works will praise her in the gates."

Isn't there a biblical kind of careerism? What about the Proverbs 31 woman?

The heroines in the Bible were very hard-working and productive, and some had the time to augment their families' wealth through their business acumen. The Proverbs 31 woman, for example, recognized that although "the God-ordained and proper sphere of dominion for a wife is the household and that which is connected with the home...her domestic calling, as a representative of and

---

12 Jennie Chancey, "Jennie Chancey Responds to Titus 2 Cynics," www.visionforum.org, December 10, 2003.

helper to her husband, may well involve activity in the marketplace and larger community (Gen. 2:18ff.; Prov. 31:10-31; Tit. 2:4-5)."[13]

It would be wrong to call the Proverbs 31 woman and any of the other great women of the Bible "career women." They did not "work alongside men as their functional equals in public spheres of dominion (industry, commerce, civil government, the military, etc.)."[14] They did not make themselves the vocational helpers of men other than their husbands. They did not devote their lives to selfish ambition and the pursuit of personal glory. They did not make their husbands and children and homes second priority after the office and the co-workers and the paycheck. They were not wage slaves. They understood God's design for women's highest and noblest vocation of all.

What about women who are childless or whose children are grown and gone?

Women, regardless of whether or not they are busy full-time taking care of children, are too precious to the body of Christ to be squandered in worldly pursuits. Older women are instructed to teach the younger women. In his first letter to Timothy, Paul describes a woman worthy of honor as one with a reputation for "good works," a woman who has lodged strangers, washed the feet of the saints and relieved the afflicted (1 Timothy 5:9, 10). We see that the Proverbs 31 woman stretched out her hands to the poor and needy. Throughout Scripture, women are praised for laboring in building up the body of Christ through deeds of benevolence and generosity. There is a

---

13 The Tenets of Biblical Patriarchy, drafted by Phil Lancaster of *Patriarch* magazine, www.visionforum.org.

14 Ibid.

desperate need for women doing these things in our churches! If we are too busy earning that second income to reach out to others, it shows that we have followed the world's path of skewed priorities and are not worthy of honor. It is precisely those women who have no children to keep them busy who are available to fulfill these great needs.

The idea of women going out into the sphere of public industry to compete with men for jobs in pursuit of "their true potential," public recognition, prestige, self-fulfillment, and, of course, that pay-check,[15] was pushed by God-hating Marxists who wanted to keep woman out of her natural element, tear apart the family, and destroy Christianity. If we really want to put an end to this, we should recognize that accepting and pursuing this mode of life perpetuates the feminist agenda and extends the curse on our society and economy even further. Christian women should be taking an active stand against this.

We should not be asking ourselves, "How unbiblical is it for a woman to get a career?" or "In what circumstances would it be permissible?" These questions amount to "How close can I get to the fire without being burned?" or "How far away can I get from God's perfect will without crossing the line into technicalities of sinning?" Isn't this kind of "testing the limits" the course of passive rebellion in itself?

Rather, we should be asking, "How can I run further and further from the fire into a realm of greater godliness? What decisions can I make with my life right now that will encourage God's blessings on our society instead of curses? How can we retake this culture for Christ?"

---

15 Working for a paycheck is often referred to as wage slavery, because wage earners tend to build lifestyles around their jobs that restrict them from freedom and obedience to God.

What if I've been given gifts that, if properly developed, will lead me outside the biblical role for women?

Some people interpret the parable of the talents to mean that Christians have an obligation to pursue their interests, passions, and abilities, whatever these might be. It should be noted first that the Bible never encourages us to follow our passions or pursue our dreams. And though it speaks of using our *spiritual* gifts, it doesn't permit us to use any gift or ability for purposes that are contrary to God's order or God's timing.

But insofar as our aptitudes and gifts can be used for the glory of God, we should use them. Church and families thrive on the diversities of gifts women can develop. Gifts in music, academics, medicine, and many other areas can be channeled into womanly, God-honoring realms, and used to enrich and edify fellow believers.

However, we can't structure our lives around our gifts, but rather around our calling as women, as helpers in the Dominion Mandate (though this calling may well involve these gifts). We have to be willing to set them aside if duty calls.

"For whosoever will save his life shall lose it; but whosoever shall lose his life for My sake and the gospel's, the same shall save it" (Mark 8:35). Losing our lives for His sake may involve giving up our own interests and abilities. Our father, a very gifted artist, had to lay aside his love of painting in order to focus on his church and family duties. Our mother forfeited a life as a professional musician in order to devote herself to her husband and children. God has often provided them with avenues to use these abilities *within the lives they have chosen*, but they had to be willing to forsake these to follow Him (Matthew 19:29).

But seek ye first the kingdom of God, and his righteousness; and all these things shall be added unto you. (Matthew 6:33)

We believe that most gifts God gives to women can be developed and used, in some way, for His glory. But we can't let them lead us into fields that are off limits to us. Just because a woman might be brilliantly talented in business affairs doesn't mean she should be the CEO of a giant corporation. But she may use this ability to be an outstanding helpmeet to her husband. Regardless of interests or talents, there are some roles that women aren't meant to assume.

Can I serve God as a woman pastor?

We wish it could be said that any girl with a Bible will know the answer to this question, because the answer is so painfully clear. The Bible is sufficient to provide the answer. But because women "Bible teachers" and women pastors have been playing fast and loose with the texts, it is important for us to say, "You need your Bible to answer this question, and you also need a willing heart to obey what you read in the Bible."

All our lives we girls will be tempted with the sin of seizing authority from men, just as they will be tempted to run away from responsibility. We must not twist Scripture in order to justify our sinful ambitions. And men must not surrender their duties to women just because women have clever arguments about the "cultural contexts" of scriptural commands. If we want to start getting choosy and selective about what parts of Scripture we will believe and obey on the flimsy grounds of "cultural relevancy," we might as well throw out the whole book of 1 Corinthians, because it was clearly not written to us, but to the Corinthians! This is obviously nonsense. "All Scripture is given by inspiration of God, and is profitable for doctrine, for reproof, for correction, for instruction in righteousness: that the man of God may be perfect, thoroughly furnished unto all good works" (2 Timothy 3:16).

Look up the verses—such as 1 Corinthians 14:34, 35: "Let your women keep silence in the churches: for it is not permitted unto them to speak; but they are commanded to be under obedience, as also saith the law. And if they will learn any thing, let them ask their husbands at home: for it is a shame for women to speak in the church," or 1 Timothy 2:11-15: "Let the woman learn in silence with all subjection. But I suffer not a woman to teach, nor to usurp authority over the man, but to be in silence. For Adam was first formed, then Eve. And Adam was not deceived, but the woman being deceived was in the transgression. Notwithstanding she shall be saved in childbearing, if they continue in faith and charity and holiness with sobriety."

There are women who argue that when Paul wrote to the women to keep silent in the churches, he was specifically directing this at a group of unruly women in the church at Corinth. However, the reason Paul stated was not "because certain women in your specific congregation are too noisy," but ...for Adam was first formed, then Eve." It is God's command to all women, based on His created order and founded in His moral law. If God does not permit us to speak in the churches, we should be content to discover the wisdom of that command by obeying willingly. The women who obey the commands about woman pastors and woman teachers know exactly what God means and why He was so clear about the issue.

Should women ever get into politics?

There seem to be four biblical principles to consider here:

The headship of the man

We have already explained that the man was made first and is the head of the woman (Genesis 2:7, 1 Timothy 2:13). In 1 Corinthians

11:3 we see that the biblical chain of command is God–Christ–Man–Woman. As William Einwechter points out:

The Bible explicitly states that the man has headship over the woman, and that this headship is not based on cultural factors, or even the fall; rather, it is based on the created order established by God Himself.

Now it is also plain in the Bible that God has ordained that the order of the headship of man must be maintained in each governing institution set up by God. There are three primary institutions established by the Lord for the ordering of human affairs. These are the Family, the Church, and the State. Each of these institutions has authority to govern within its appointed sphere. We could say, then, that there are three "governments" in the world: family government, church government, and state government. In each of these governments, God has commanded that men bear rule. The man has headship in the family (Ephesians 5:22-24), the church (1 Timothy 2:11-14; 1 Corinthians 14:34-35), and also by implication and command, in the state as well (1 Corinthians 11:3; Exodus 18:21; see point 2 below).[16]

The qualifications for a civil official

God clearly states in many places in Scripture the necessary qualifications for anyone who would bear rule in a civil sphere. In *every one*, the basic requirement is that he be a *man* (see Deuteronomy 1:13, Deuteronomy 17:14-20, 2 Samuel 23:3; Nehemiah 7:2; Exodus 18:21).

---

16 William Einwechter, "Should Christians Support a Woman for the Office of Civil Magistrate?" www.visionforum.org, July 8, 2004.

The position of the ideal virtuous woman

Though the Proverb 31 woman's work was praised in the gates, it
did not take place in the gates, but in the home. It was the woman's
husband who took his place in the gates (Proverbs 31:23), and the
implication is that his success and influence was largely due to his
wife's being faithful to her calling rather than trying to usurp his.
And what were the gates? According to Rev. Einwechter, "The 'gates'
in Old Testament times referred to the place where the leaders of the
city (i.e., 'the elders of the land') would gather to discuss community
affairs, administer civil law, and judge in criminal and civil cases. The
'gates,' therefore, is a reference to the 'city hall,' the 'capital building,'
the 'courthouse' or, in short, to the seat of civil government."[17] The
virtuous woman did not take a visible role in this sphere.

Women rulers as a sign of judgment

When the nation Israel was being judged for her unfaithfulness to
God's laws and design, the prophet Isaiah lamented her condition,
saying, "As for my people, children are their oppressors, and women
rule over them…(Isaiah 3:12).

Rather than a sign of "progress" for a nation to have women
rulers, it is a sign of God's judgment and displeasure with that
nation! Women holding seats of authority, whether it be in business,
church, family, law, or politics, is one of the distinguishing marks of
a society under God's curse.

Rev. Einwechter again: "It is weakness and a sin [on the part
of the men who allowed it] because it is an abdication of their
responsibility to be the leaders God has called them to be…it is a

---

17 Ibid.

sign of confusion and judgment. It is a sign that men have utterly failed to exercise the leadership required of them."[18]

But since our society is under God's curse,
aren't there things that a godly woman
magistrate could do to make things better?

If a woman wants to do her society a favor, the last thing she should do is extend God's curse even further by perpetuating the feminist tactics that helped invoke His curse on our society in the first place. However good a woman's intentions may be, the ends never justify the means. As William H. Felix put it: "Give woman the ballot, put her upon the platform, make her the equal of man in every respect, and let her enter the arena of political strife and religious reformation under the idea that her power must be utilized, and you *thwart* the end by the wrong use of the means."[19]

A godly woman might seem more qualified to serve the office of civil magistrate than any man around, and, in fact, she might be more qualified. She might be able to do more immediate outward good, but in the end it will be to the ultimate detriment of her society. It has been God's practice to bless entire nations because of an individual's godliness and obedience (one example is Joseph in Egypt). The best thing a woman can do for her country, regardless of its situation, is to pursue God's perfect design for her life and her role as a woman, so that her righteousness will entreat God to revoke His judgment on her country and instead shower blessings on it.

---

18 Ibid.

19 From the essay by W. H. Felix entitled: "The Work and Sphere of True Womanhood" in J. W. Porter, ed., *Feminism: Woman and Her Work* (reprint ed., Bloomfield, New Mexico: The Historic Baptist, 1995), pp. 98-99 (emphasis added).

But what about Deborah? Wasn't she a judge?

People who want to make a biblical case for women taking leadership in the civil realm point to Deborah in the book of Judges. "We should be judges, like Deborah!" is a rallying point. Before jumping to any conclusions, we should first seek to understand what exactly Deborah was doing.

The scene is Israel, at a time when the "children of Israel again did evil in the sight of the Lord" (Judges 4:1). Deborah describes the scene in Chapter 5, verses 6 and 7: "The highways were deserted, and the travelers walked along the byways. Village life ceased, it ceased in Israel…" Commentators note that, "Israel's failed leadership had resulted in chaos and foreign domination. It was not like the days in which God had been the warrior at the front of Israel (vv. 4-5). The roads were abandoned because they were not safe for travel on account of the foreign oppressors and robbers."[20] Israel was under severe judgment from God, and the context of Judges 5:2 suggests that the reason was that the leaders were not leading.

Verse 7 continues: "…until I, Deborah, arose, arose a mother in Israel." Chapter 4, vv. 4-5 tells us, "Now Deborah, a prophetess, the wife of Lapidoth, was judging Israel at that time. And she would sit under the palm tree of Deborah between Ramah and Bethel in the mountains of Ephraim. And the children of Israel came up to her for judgment." Rev. William Einwechter explains:

> Deborah's role in Israel was that of a "prophetess," but not that of a civil ruler or military leader. The text does not support the idea that she was a civil magistrate. She "judged" Israel (Judg. 4:4) only in the sense that she was sought out by the people for

---

20 New Geneva Study Bible (Nashville: Thomas Nelson Publishers, 1995), p. 339.

advice and judgment in the settlement of disputes because of her wisdom from God. Apparently the priests and Levites were so corrupt that the people had to seek wisdom and judgment from this godly woman.

...the judges during this period were more military leaders or "avenging deliverers" than they were civil magistrates (cf. Judges 2:16-19). Because of this fact, we must ask ourselves if we can even consider Deborah to be a "judge" in the same sense as the other judges in the book. The account of Deborah is unique in that she did not lead Israel into battle herself (as did the other judges in the book), but, rather, the Lord choose Barak to be the military commander.[21]

Verses 6-8 say, "Then she sent and called for Barak...and said to him, 'Has not the Lord God of Israel commanded, "Go and deploy troops at Mount Tabor; take with you ten thousand men...and against you I will deploy Sisera...and I will deliver him into your hand"?'And Barak said to her, 'If you will go with me, then I will go; but if you will not go with me, I will not go!' "

As a result of Barak's cowardice in effectively hiding behind Deborah and asking her to do what he had been assigned to do, Deborah announced, "I will surely go with you; nevertheless, there will be no glory for you in the journey you are taking, for the Lord will sell Sisera into the hand of a woman" (Judges 4:9).

Deborah's society was being judged in much the same way as ours, but the level of judgment seems to have been more severe. In this very unfortunate time, when it appears that there was not even one man who would take the responsibility of leadership, God

21 William Einwechter, "Should Christians Support a Woman for the Office of Civil Magistrate?" www.visionforum.org, July 8, 2004.

did raise up a woman to encourage and support the men, and also to shame them for their cowardice. It's important to note that not all the women in Israel were called to lead the way Deborah was, and even she tried to pass the leadership to Barak when God so instructed. The role of a "Deborah" is not one we should be hoping for, but one we should be trying at all costs to prevent. If our society ever sinks to the level where *one* Deborah is necessary, it will be a sign that God is phenomenally displeased with our culture and is inflicting a colossal curse on it. Deborah was glorified and blessed by God as a "deliverer" of Israel, and, in essence, what she did was to bring men back into leadership.

A one-time Deborah wanna-be, **Sarah,** explains her journey "from feminism to faithfulness":

> As a young girl, I was told (and therefore believed) that my mission was to "be something" when I grew up. Thus, I thought that the purpose of my education was to train for a career, and the purpose of my family was to raise me to be independent. From public school to Christian schools to home schooling to the local Christian college, my general goal of earning a degree and getting a job remained the same, though the specifics and motive altered when I became a Christian. Rather than being motivated merely to fulfill "society's expectations," I was also convinced that I had a responsibility to take an active place in the gates of the land and retake them for Christ. Even though I planned on getting married someday and home schooling my own children, I thought that the best investment of the gifts and abilities God had given me was to pursue a career in the field of law. And looking at the wicked state of our culture, my reasoning (seconded by encouraging family and friends) was: We need righteous lawyers and judges; I should do that, like Deborah in the Bible.

Not too long after coming to this conclusion, my family attended Vision Forum's Faith and Freedom Tour in July of 1999 (I was twenty-one years old). It was a life-changing experience for us—especially for me. Through the faithful and courageous teaching of Mr. Doug Phillips, I was challenged to rethink my positions on a woman's place and mission, including questioning my adamant support for women winning the vote and serving as lawyers and judges. That summer I diligently sought to know the truth. Could I really have been wrong all this time? Did the Word of God speak definitively on this subject? I found that, indeed, it did, as I searched the Scriptures and read John Knox's polemical treatise *The First Blast of the Trumpet Against the Monstrous Regiment of Women*, and the prophetic writings of Robert Lewis Dabney. I soon came to realize just how wrong I had been in my reasoning. By His grace, God convicted me to see that the very culture that I was trying to change was actually the influence behind my thinking. At first, I denied it. How could I, who considered myself to have taken a strong stand against "radical" feminism, be, in reality, a feminist?! And yet, I was—in my thinking. Even though I wasn't seeking to have a career for career's sake or to glorify independent behavior—I was truly wanting to have an influence of righteousness on our world before I married and had children—God showed me that though my intentions may not have been wrong, my standard (the means I was using) was not in obedience to His Law. And while claiming to be serving Him, I was really dishonoring Him.

Through passages such as I Corinthians 11 and I Timothy 2, I learned that a woman is always to be under authority—whether her father's or her husband's—and be learning from him, not apart from him. It is not my place or responsibility to conquer the public arena or take an active role in the gates of the land,

no matter how equipped I thought I was to do so. It is my job
to support my father as he does that. At first I was disappointed
to learn that the sphere that God had ordained for women
(that of the home and family) did not include being lawyers
or judges or taking dominion in the political arena. But as I
studied His Word, God graciously began to convict me to see
that the problem was not with His design, but with my heart. I
wasn't content to submit to His will because I was rebellious and
because I had adopted the lies of feminism.

Gradually I began to see how much my thinking had been
influenced by feminism. I had been duped into believing
feminism's lie that says: "When you graduate from high school,
you either have to go to work full-time or go to college."
I believed the lie of feminism that "you are only making a
difference or being productive with your life if you are out 'doing
something.'" I believed feminism's lie that says: "Women should
do everything that men do—women can do anything they want
to do." And I believed feminism's lie that "a woman's fulfillment
is not in the home but outside of it."

By God's grace, I repented of my feministic beliefs and
independent spirit. I surrendered to Him my will and my fears
of being ridiculed by the world for not pursuing a career, and
I turned my heart towards home and my role as a daughter
and sister. I now take great delight in serving the Lord and my
parents and advancing their vision—making my father's home
and work and ministry as productive as possible. It is such a
blessing to be under my father's roof—under his authority,
protection, and leadership. No longer do I seek to leave it in
search of a more "significant" position. It is such a joy to be
part of a family that is a team—a unit—that works together to
further God's kingdom. I am so thankful for the Lord's mercy in

turning my heart and allowing me to experience the wonderful privilege of being a daughter in my father's house as He designed it to be.

And my message to all you daughters is this: Don't miss it! Don't miss out on the blessings of obedience by investing your time and energies serving your own pursuits. Don't make the same mistakes that I did! Don't be deceived by the lies of feminism that lead you to look for your mission outside the context of the home and family. Don't believe those who would tell you that being a daughter and a sister is not enough. There is no greater work that you could do—there is no better work that you could do—because it is the work that God created you for.

The mission of true womanhood is beautiful, wonderful, exciting, glorious. It is the most important work we could ever do. Let us then equip ourselves for the task and be faithful to fulfill it. Let us be wary of "good" causes which would entice us away from our true duty. Our obedience or disobedience to the high calling Jesus Christ has given us as women will affect future generations and the future of nations, either for good or evil. May the Lord make us faithful, and by His grace, we will change the world for the glory of God.

CHAPTER TEN

FATHERS, DAUGHTERS, AND HIGHEST EDUCATION

THE TRAINING OF A PROTECTED WOMAN

How important is it for women to be highly educated?

Christian women have a duty to be highly, highly educated. They should take this duty very seriously. They should be just as serious about their *standards* of education. Christian women have a duty to protect themselves from defiling ideas and trivial pursuits that may falsely be called "education." Fathers of unmarried daughters should help daughters guard this duty.

The right education can make a Christian woman a powerful asset to a father's estate and an even more powerful co-ruler of her husband's estate after she marries. The wrong education can pollute her mind, corrupt her heart, and make her useless as a tool for God's glory. The wrong education can lead a young woman away from the blessings God may otherwise have bestowed on her.

What kind of education are you saying is important?

We are referring to the kind of education that makes us useful to God, in contrast to the schooling that makes a pupil useful to the State. In the mid-1800s, loving father William B. Sprague explained the essence of the "right" education to his daughter.

> I would have you, then, in the first place, bear in mind that the great object of your education is to enable you to bring into exercise the powers which God has given you in such a manner as shall contribute most to His glory. For all the noble faculties with which you are gifted, you are indebted to the same Being who gave you your existence: on Him also you are dependent for their preservation; and it is a first dictate of reason that they should be employed in His service. ...The object of education then is twofold: to develop the faculties and to direct them; to bring out the energies of the soul, and to bring them to operate to the glory of the Creator. In other words, it is to render you useful to the extent of your ability.[1]

An education can be defined as the training and shaping of the heart, soul, mind, and strength. An education consists not only in the learning of facts and skills, but also in the developing of affections and worldview. Our worldview is how we see and judge our culture and the world around us. Anything which affects our worldview and affections—in fact, anything which influences our hearts, souls, minds, or strength—is educational, whether for good or for evil. And this means that *all education is inescapably religious.*

Godly education is purpose-driven. Because our purpose as young Christian women should be to glorify God and obey Him,

1 Sprague, William Buell, 1795-1876, *Letters on Practical Subjects, to a Daughter,* 11th American ed., New York, n.d.

our educations need to be our tools in this task. As the great scholar R.J. Rushdoony points out, "…the purpose of Christian education is not academic: it is religious and practical."[2] Therefore, the kind of education we need to pursue *first* is the training and shaping that will equip us to do His work comprehensively.

The line is drawn between the two competing types of educational priorities at the very beginning of the Bible. As Tom Eldredge points out in *Safely Home*, "The first conflict in recorded history was a battle over education."[3] He explains that Adam and Eve were given a choice between knowing God and walking with Him, gradually discovering more and more of His truth and wisdom; or a shortcut to instant knowledge—to eat the fruit and know everything, good *and* evil. These two education philosophies—the empty, shallow knowledge centered around man, and the wisdom of God, which comes only through knowing and fearing God—are still at war today. According to Eldredge: "[The humanist philosophy] emphasizes the autonomous reason of man and his eternal quest for personal philosophy, on the one hand, and social utility as defined by the State, on the other. [The Christian philosophy] emphasizes obedience before God, a key component of which is the development of wisdom and godly relationships."[4]

We live in an age where even Christians don't question the importance of pursuing trivia, nonsense, political correctness,

---

2   R.J. Rushdoony, The Philosophy of the Christian Curriculum (California: Ross House Books, 1985), p. 25.

3   Tom Eldredge, *Safely Home*, (San Antonio: The Vision Forum, Inc., 2003) p. 3.

4   Ibid. p. 5. Eldredge says: "Only when men fear the One True God can they have knowledge, wisdom, or understanding. Every thought must be taken captive to the obedience of Christ, and the autonomous mind of man must be called what it is—a fallen, sinful, and imperfect tool which must be renewed by God before it can truly function properly. Logic and rhetoric find value insofar as they are derived from biblical presuppositions and used to advance holy causes."

and credentials, and view these as the educational priorities. In a culture devoted to the pursuit of wealth, pleasure, comfort, and entertainment, shallow, man-centered education is now higher education. Academic "qualifications" have become a goal that has nothing to do with learning or wisdom.

It's interesting to note that the specific humanist philosophies that dictate education and lifestyle today flowered in Ancient Greece and Rome. In a nutshell, the Greco-Romans worshiped man. They placed great faith in man and worked hard at keeping that faith strong. From a practical perspective, they glorified the body and the mind and devoted their lives to the disciplining and perfection of these, seeking to elevate them to a divine level.

From an historic perspective, every society that becomes infatuated with the Greco-Roman curriculum and worldview and puts such an emphasis on human reason and physical development suffers moral decline. The Renaissance and the Enlightenment were steps backward, not forward. Without biblical wisdom, a nation cannot stand.

Is college where young women should go to get the right kind of higher education?

In 1850, every college in America was a Christian institution of higher learning. Most schools attempted to direct students into useful knowledge and virtuous stewardship of intellectual gifts and abilities. This is no longer true. By the early 1900s, even the semblance of academic rigor was dying, and now colleges have become intimidating reformatories of anti-Christian, politically-correct accreditation.

For young women, college campuses have become dangerous places of ongoing anxiety, wasted years, mental defilement, and moral derangement.[5] The wisdom and discernment they bring with them to the campus are not strengthened, but taken from them. Today's college experience can lead young women away from real knowledge and blessing and into estrangement from both their heavenly Father and earthly fathers. New York State Teacher of the Year John Taylor Gatto notes in *The Underground History of American Education,* that American universities, which once served the individual and the family, began following a German tradition of forcing universities to serve industry and the political State in the 1920s.

Observed H. L. Mencken in 1928, "The great majority of American colleges are so incompetent and vicious that, in any really civilized country, they would be closed by the police…In the typical American state they are staffed by quacks and hag-ridden by fanatics. Everywhere they tend to become, not centers of enlightenment, but simply reservoirs of idiocy. Not one professional pedagogue out of twenty is a man of any genuine intelligence. The profession mainly attracts, not young men of quick minds and force of character, but flabby, feeble fellows who yearn for easy jobs…Their programmes of study sound like the fantastic inventions of comedians gone insane."[6]

In order to survive by attracting students, colleges falsely represent themselves as the abiding centers of academic freedom and higher education, according to the American tradition. It's time to admit that they are none of these things.

---

5   Moral derangement was one of the specific goals of the politically-correct curriculum advocated for government schools, particularly universities, by the Frankfurt School faculty. The condition opens the student's mind to alternative theologies and philosophies, it was reasoned.

6   From H.L. Mencken, "The War Upon Intelligence," *Baltimore Evening Sun,* December 31, 1928.

Then what does the college curriculum teach?

We stated previously that all education is religious. This means that all centers of education are, by definition, centers and teachers of religious values. Which religion is being taught in universities? In a word, Statism.[7] To be more specific, Cultural Marxism. Modern universities serve the State and teach their students to serve the State.

The college curriculum would do you more harm than good—unless it is your ambition to be comfortable in the world's system, to attain the world's standards of personal peace and affluence. If this kind of syncretism is a young woman's chief ambition, college is the most beneficial place to spend from four to eight years. The modern college experience can help one succeed in a certain kind of artificial life that is independent of the Christian institutions of family, church, and limited biblical government. Success in this artificial life requires pessimism and contempt for Western culture. Today's college experience is designed to provide the worldly student the "sensitivity" to maintain a lifelong critical attitude toward all things Western, including faith, family, and freedom. The world is ready to reward people with this worldview and this conditioned sensitivity.

Why are college degrees considered so important?

The "advanced" degree will always be important to desperate colleges that survive by maintaining a monopoly. They sell degrees to people who think university credentials are important—mostly to parents who

---

7   Statism is the rival religion that puts the government in the place of God. The Messianic State assumes God's authority in the preserving and governing of all His creatures and all their actions. Known in America as the Welfare State or the Nanny State. Its main characteristics are compulsory government schooling, high taxes, an entrenched bureaucracy, police-state powers, and an ever-growing body of laws and regulations.

want to buy a college degree for children who have little direction in life. To receive a degree, a graduate is supposed to demonstrate his agreement with the curriculum, part of which is a university sales-pitch: "Your college degree is proof of your intelligence, of your worth to society, and of our special privileges to award the degree to those who believe what we tell them." People who spend $40,000-$140,000 for these degrees tend to perpetuate the idea that degrees are important.

A college degree *is* important if one wants to impress a bureaucratic hiring agency, or if one wants to pretend some sort of academic or intellectual superiority over others who may not have a degree. But as proof of academic achievement, the modern college degree is a deception.

I know that, as a young woman, I shouldn't be aspiring to become a career woman or wage slave, but isn't it true that holders of degrees perform better and make more money than those who don't have a degree?

Graduates who work in government or university bureaucracies do command higher salaries than those without advanced degrees, but usually only at the entry levels. In the real world—the business world—it is no longer true that college grads make the big dollars.[8]

---

8   With the possible exception of the engineering vocations, college graduates are not higher earners. Historian Gary North has documented studies across the 20th century that tracked the performance of adults who attended college and their professional counterparts who did not, or who learned by correspondence courses. The college graduates are not the top achievers. According to North, "Recent studies have revealed that students who have been educated in an off-campus learning setting produce higher performance rates than conventional classroom-based education does." North also cites articles published in *Business 2.0*, *National Post*, the *Chicago Sun-Times*, and the *Chronicle of Higher Education* by Stanford Business School professor Jeffrey Pfeffer, who concluded that even "earning" an MBA does not guarantee a successful career or a higher salary. Summarizes North,

However, even if graduates did have higher earning potential, is material success a reason to invest several years in a corrupt institution, exposing oneself to defiling ideas and experiences, and dishonestly representing oneself as a scholar in a setting that does not permit honest scholarship?

Where does real success come from? Where does material success come from? It comes from the hand of God as a personal blessing of obedience. The lessons of Scripture are clear. Cowardly syncretism with the world's system brings chastisement, not blessing. Yoking oneself to the world's system does not invite the fatherly blessings of God. God commands: "Be ye not unequally yoked together with unbelievers: for what fellowship hath righteousness with unrighteousness? and what communion hath light with darkness? And what concord hath Christ with Belial? or what part hath he that believeth with an infidel? And what agreement hath the temple of God with idols? for ye are the temple of the living God; as God hath said, I will dwell in them, and walk in them; and I will be their God, and they shall be my people. Wherefore come out from among them, and be ye separate, saith the Lord, and touch not the unclean thing; and I will receive you. And will be a Father unto you, and ye shall be my sons and daughters, saith the Lord Almighty" (2 Corinthians 6:14-18).

Surely not all colleges are so anti-Christian that they need to be shunned. What about the engineering schools, the Christian colleges, or the military academies?

The pressure is being increased on every accredited university to conform to established patterns of cultural Marxism as the foundation

---

"The training or education component of business education is only loosely coupled to the world of managing organizations."

of all orientation, sensitivity, and curricular studies. These schools, even formerly Christian colleges, retain professors who practice what is known on campus as repressive tolerance. There is no free exchange of intellectual ideas permitted. The defense of Christendom cannot be permitted by any professor who wants tenure. This is policy.

According to the *Wall Street Journal*, even the Massachusetts Institute of Technology is tied to such a policy and a political agenda "that regulates not only students' behavior but their attitudes and consciences."[9]

Even the United States Naval Academy has now abandoned former standards of ethics, propriety, and academic honesty. This is a frightening development when one considers the pagan ideas our future military leaders are now required to embrace in order to rise to the top of their classes.

We were born in the shadow of the Capitol building in Washington, D.C., where our father was working as a political consultant at the time. One of his favorite weekend trips was to take us to the Naval Academy campus in Annapolis, where we could stroll the expansive grounds and feel the sea breezes. On the beautiful lawns, historic battle monuments taught us about decisive events of courage and fortitude that secured our nation's freedoms. But later he stopped taking us there, because the atmosphere was changing. Sounds of childish conduct and the strains of lewd rap music drifted from the dormitories. Campus standards of sobriety were falling. We remember our father's growing concern, even in the early 1990s, about the slipping standards of discipline among the cadets and faculty.

---

9   Alan Charles Kors and Harvey A. Silverglate, "Colleges Aim to Control Thinking, but Not Drinking," October 15, 1998, *The Wall Street Journal*, Page A22, Dow Jones & Company, Inc.

As just one example at the Academy, a *mandatory,* anti-morality "ethics" curriculum now requires students to embrace the teachings of euthanasia advocate Peter Singer.[10] Furthermore, Navy chaplains are forbidden to continue their historic role assisting future United States naval officers in moral development, gentlemanly conduct, and ethical decision making.

This is the essence of the current collegiate danger. Colleges are no longer places of academic exploration and free expression, but of enforced, rigorous religious indoctrination.

Even the Christian colleges?

The Nehemiah Institute has found that the Christian worldview of some Christian college graduates is weaker upon graduation than it was on entering the college.[11] All American colleges were once

---

10 Dr. Gerald L. Atkinson, "Cultural Marxism at the Naval Academy," www.thenewtotalitarians.com, July 4, 2001. The author cites a copy of an e-mail memo, dated 3/22/01, from an Executive Department Navy lieutenant to all instructors who teach the NE-203 [Ethics and Moral Reasoning for the Naval Leader course] during the Spring of 2001. This memo informed the instructors that Peter Singer's *Egoism, Altruism, and Sociobiology* text has been placed on the mandatory reading list for this New Age 'ethics' course. Singer is the neo-Marxist "ethicist" who teaches moral relativism by recommending bestiality and infanticide as necessary milestones on the road to the moral and ethical liberation of the West.

11 Since 1988, the Nehemiah Institute has given the PEERS test to thousands of teen-agers and adults in order to determine their worldview. The PEERS test determines an individual's worldview in five key areas: politics, economics, education, religion, and social issues. Results from each category are classified into one of four major worldview philosophies: Christian Theism, Moderate Christian, Secular Humanism, and Socialism. From 1988-2000, average scores of Christian school students dropped by 30.3 percent. Contact the Nehemiah Institute to obtain declining scores of students at specific Christian colleges, www.nehemiahinstitute.com.

Christian. The same theologies and ideas that corrupted the older colleges are corrupting the colleges currently labeled "Christian."

But the "college experience" is supposed to be something so special. Lots of people say I can't go through life without it. Why is this?

Many people have never thought of an alternative for the bright, gifted girl. Some think that an environment of debauchery is a necessary initiation for real life. Well, occasional brushes with danger do tend to strengthen character, but long-term immersion in an environment of false religious ideas can destroy good character and does corrupt morality.[12]

The bulk of the *classroom* experience is learning to bend one's thinking toward the Marxist worldview with everyone else, so that life in a Marxist society can be comfortable. The *campus* experience is hedonistic revelry. The *networking* experience is, largely,

---

12 "Be not deceived: evil communications corrupt good manners" (1 Corinthians 15:33).

Enter not into the path of the wicked, and go not in the way of evil men. Avoid it, pass not by it, turn from it, and pass away. (Proverbs 4:14,15)

And have no fellowship with the unfruitful works of darkness, but rather reprove them. For it is a shame even to speak of those things which are done of them in secret. (Ephesians 5:11, 12)

I have not sat with vain persons, neither will I go in with dissemblers. I have hated the congregation of evil doers; and will not sit with the wicked. I will wash mine hands in innocency: so will I compass Thine altar, O Lord. (Psalm 26:4-6)

Blessed is the man that walketh not in the counsel of the ungodly, nor standeth in the way of sinners, nor sitteth in the seat of the scornful. But his delight is in the law of the Lord; and in His law doth he meditate day and night. (Psalm 1:1, 2)

yoking oneself with others who are also attempting to justify the investment of four years in a dishonest environment that has so little to do with the real world.

Most university students would agree that much of the college experience is about learning to "fit in." This is really a very good way to describe it. That's exactly what they're supposed to get out of the college experience. They're supposed to learn to respond as a mass. This is how statists achieve national uniformity in thought, word, and deed, which is exactly what they need to maintain cultural dominance. Learning to "find my place in the world" translates in the practical language of life as "finding my little slot in the big State machine."

Yes, there is a lot of hype about the "college experience." It may be adventurous, but it is so cruelly depleting. One commentator said the college degree proves nothing to an employer except that the graduate has learned to tolerate four years of boredom. If boredom was the only danger, and wasted years the only risk of the college experience, we would not make such a big deal about "the experience." However, we believe it ranks as the most foolish spiritual investment a girl can make in the flower of her youth.

Can't mature Christians survive the dangers of college and come out with experience and credentials that might be useful in God's service?

Many young Christian college graduates have asserted that, yes, they have survived the college experience with their faith and morals still strong. A mature young Christian friend of ours has recently graduated from a strongly anti-Christian college which she knew would try to indoctrinate her. She feels like she has won, because she exited with a degree *and* what she thinks is an intact soul. What she doesn't know is that the college is laughing at her, because it knows it is the real winner. It doesn't mind her keeping her personal hobby religion, because now it knows it won't interfere with a statist agenda. The university took tens of thousands of her dollars, and in exchange for her generous contribution, it has given her fear. It has intimidated her so that she will always give the "right" answer instead of the Christian answer, regardless of what she really believes. It has proof of her allegiance and her agreement with its religion on paper in her handwriting. It has made her tolerant of and even comfortable with anti-Christianity and has made her terrified of ever being "intolerant" of the anti-Christian worldview. This will render her powerless as a possible troublemaker. And in our friend's false feeling of triumph, she's not even aware of these things.

Listen to the Christian-college experience of **Jennie**.

I can remember my first day of college so clearly. Although I had gone away to school under protest, I did feel a keen anticipation about sitting under learned lecturers and studying my favorite topics (literature, writing, and history). The very air seemed electric with possibility as I marched down the cobblestone walkway to my first class. Even the smell of the new books in my arms was magically thrilling.

Having been homeschooled for seven years, I was well prepared for college academics. In fact, I'd won a full scholarship to college (my parents' own *alma mater*). Six months earlier, I had begged my parents to let me stay at home, but the scholarship had made their decision firm, so I finally decided to make the best of things and dive into college life with all my energy. In spite of terrible homesickness, college life did have its charms. I was truly in control of my life in a way I never had been before.

Though I often sought my parents' counsel over the phone, the final decisions rested upon my shoulders. I could pick the classes I wanted to take, set my own daily schedule, get involved in extracurricular activities, and go out with new friends (at all hours!) My parents had given me excellent study habits, and I found it very easy to keep up with the pace of my major (English, with a concentration on writing).

But something started to bother me only a few weeks into my time at college. When my Western Civ. professor declared that history was really a series of "uncoordinated" and "random" events, alarms went off in my head. I believed that God sovereignly orchestrated all of the affairs of men—that history was really "His story." But I quickly quieted my fears, believing the professor would shortly explain himself and get us onto the right track. Well, as his worldview continued to unfold, I could only sit in utter disbelief. My Christian professor made it quite clear that he was a theistic evolutionist and did not hold to the belief that the Bible is infallible. I called home right away. My father assured me that he'd sat under that same professor when he had gone to college, and he urged me to ask questions and make it a point to disagree with the professor in my term papers ("He'll admire you for it," Dad said). I also found two other like-minded students in the class, and we purposed to pray together and constantly raise questions in class.

When one of my literature professors began to reveal her feminist beliefs and advocate "women's studies" (including "love poetry" written by lesbians), I wondered if I was really in a Christian school. The New Testament professor under whom I sat for several semesters used every one of his lectures to advance his pet belief that all the male-female roles in Scripture were solely 'cultural' and did not apply to Christians today. He inserted feministic jabs at the reliability of Paul's writings at every opportunity. I'd known before that there were people who rejected the plain teachings of God's Word, but I did not expect to encounter them in a small, 'conservative' Christian college. I purposed to keep my eyes open and my brain in gear as I sat in class and engaged my professors. But I didn't factor in the ability of the constant immersion in opposing worldviews to wear down my resistance.

In almost every course I studied over the next four years, a subtle but definite shift began to take place in my outlook and way of thinking. As the seeds of doubt (in God, in my family, in the Church) began to take root in my mind, I felt my heart hardening. No longer did I possess an unqualified joy in God's creation or even in His work in my life. After all, if "science" had "proved" the Bible wrong and outdated, Truth stood on a very shaky foundation. Could even logic be reliable in a world where Truth Himself could be called into question? Perhaps all of those injunctions of St. Paul's really were "cultural" and irrelevant in our times. Perhaps my New Testament professor was right when he said that, if Jesus had come to earth in our day, He would have chosen a woman to be one of His disciples! Three years before, I might have questioned that notion and fought it with all my being—but month after month, my foundations had been eroded to the point that I didn't even know how to argue any more. I just gave up and put the answers on the tests that would give me the coveted "A."

Now, lest you think I was a "sheltered" child before college, let me make it clear that my parents had not hidden me from the world's philosophies. In fact, they had worked hard to instill in me a thoroughgoing biblical worldview, teaching me to think, debate ideas, and stand firm on the Truth. Yet four years after entering college, I walked out a bitter, cynical "Christian feminist," turning my back upon all the things my parents had given me, and determined never to marry. What had happened in four short years to undermine my parents' hard work and my own precious beliefs?

As I mentioned at the start, when my parents sent me away to college, it was over my protests. I had no desire to leave my home and family to pursue a degree. I hoped to become a writer like my father, and I believed he could give me the best possible instruction as I helped him with his own writing, research, and editing (he was a renowned aviation historian and wrote 59 books and over 2,000 articles in his lifetime). But my parents truly believed I could not develop my skills unless I went to college and studied under other professors. They were not worried about me changing my beliefs or losing my desire to marry and have children, because they had brought me up to embrace a biblical worldview from birth. I went to college totally committed to the Lord's design for marriage and family and focused upon developing my gifts to use later to bless and help my future husband and to train my own children.

However, when I returned home four years later, I was not the optimistic 19-year-old my parents had sent away. Four years of liberal teaching (heavily influenced by "Christian" Marxism and the "social gospel") had slowly worn away my resistance and left me confused and doubtful. But the liberal teaching really wasn't the crux of my change. I also graduated from college bitter towards my parents and certain the Proverbs 31 model was just not for me. I had lived in a false "real world" for four years—a world that divorced me from my family, alienated me from the Church, and (after seeing serial dating in practice) convinced me that men live only for paychecks and trophy wives and are not to be trusted. Even at a fairly strict Christian school, girls sought birth control from the school nurse, went off-campus to drink at parties, got pregnant, or just got involved in unhealthy dating relationships with young men. Unprotected and "independent," all of us were vulnerable. Thankfully, I came out of college even more strongly committed to purity before marriage, but many of my friends left with deep regrets. It certainly left me cynical about men—not to mention secretly bitter towards my father, because he had not been able to protect me long-distance.

It is amazing how far removed we are from our own history when it comes to the education of women. The notion that an unprotected young woman should leave her home and family to "gain independence in the real world" is less than 140 years old. For that matter, so is the notion that a college degree is equal to a thorough education! We've become so shackled to that symbolic piece of paper that even we homeschoolers feel we haven't "arrived" or "proved ourselves" until we have a degree on our wall. While there are certainly occupations that require long years of institutional study (perhaps medicine or law), a college degree does not validate one as a thinking person.

I can honestly say that I have learned far more in the past nine years of marriage to my husband than I ever learned in four years of college. In fact, I spent three of my four years on campus "spinning my wheels," because most of the courses I had to take for my major were essentially repeats of what I had already studied at home—with a dash of egalitarianism[13] thrown in for good measure. I graduated with the highest honors (*summa cum laude* with honors in independent study), and I really do not feel I earned those laurels. I am no genius, yet college wasn't a challenge academically after all my years at home with my very involved parents. When I was homeschooled, my parents

---

13 Egalitarianism is the idea that all men must be equally needy of strict government provision and supervision.

divided the teaching duties according to their own personal strengths. Mom taught us math, science, and "home ec." My father taught government, history, economics, and writing. In addition to "class time," I spent four happy years helping Dad with his research and learning to edit under his tutelage. What a blessed time that was for me, especially since my father died at a young age (49). If I hadn't enjoyed those years of close fellowship and study with him, I think his death would have been all the more tragic, as I mourned the years I missed. I still wish I'd had four more years with him, but the Lord works all things for our good, and I can rest in that. I am thankful for the years of learning I did enjoy with him, because he laid the foundation for everything I have subsequently studied as an adult.

But all academic considerations aside, college put me into a kind of "Twilight Zone" for four years, disconnecting me almost completely from the real world of home, family, little children, grandparents, and even deep church involvement. For four years, I lived in an environment totally unlike the real world I'd be reentering when I graduated. It was a world where my own preferences ruled: I could get up late, stay up all hours, eat whatever I wanted whenever I wanted, go out with friends any time, take the classes I chose, and, most importantly, slowly disconnect myself from my own family back home. Their concerns were no longer mine. They were no longer closely involved with the decisions I had to make on a day-to-day basis, and I didn't feel obligated to concern myself with what they did, either. My younger sister and I grew so far apart that it took six years for us to heal our relationship. Mind you, this didn't happen overnight, but it happened all the same as the weeks and months rolled on and I got into the practice of being on my own.

Shortly before he died, my father confessed to me that he felt he had made the wrong decision all those years before when he forced me to go away to college. He asked me to forgive him, then prayed with me, thanking the Lord that He had "restored the years…the locust had eaten" (Joel 2:25). God is faithful! He can preserve us and protect us in spite of wrong choices. His grace is truly amazing! I am thankful for the good things He did bring out of my time in college—in particular two excellent English professors who worked closely with me to develop my writing skills—but I wouldn't wish those years on another young woman. I've heard many speakers advocate the whole "college experience" as a must-have for young people. While I do believe men are called to go out into the world and establish themselves in the profession the Lord has called them to, I am willing to say openly that I do not believe there is a reason to send a young woman away to get an education.

How can parents be so zealous about wanting to send their daughters off to get a detrimental "education?"

Many parents are willing to pay lots of money for their children's "higher" educations to ensure that their children can enjoy the worldly rewards that come with embracing an anti-Christian worldview.

This is probably because the Christian life is not an easy life. Many professing Christian parents want their children to avoid the troubles experienced by God's people. If they would admit it, what they really want for their children are the passing pleasures of Egypt. In a recent poll,[14] Barna Research found patterns of deliberate syncretism in Christian families, led by parents. Said founder George Barna, "We found that the qualities born-again parents say an

14 "Parents Describe How They Raise Their Children," February 28, 2005, The Barna Group, Ventura, Calilfornia, www.barna.com.

effective parent must possess…[are] indistinguishable from…parents who are not born-again."

"Only three out of ten born-again parents included the salvation of their child in the list of critical parental emphases," he noted. By far the top-rated outcome was "getting a good education," presumably the kind that would ensure that Christian children are indistinguishable from the world's children.

Many fathers freely admit that it is not necessarily an "education" they desire for their daughters, but the approval of the State—for the State to officially pronounce that the girl has bought whatever academic ideals she needs in order to be comfortable and accepted in a statist economy. Other fathers admit they want their daughters to meet a husband who will take the daughter off their hands. Other fathers say they want their daughters to build an address-book file of fellow students to make business networking easier in the real world. Other fathers take the crass position that any protection they once provided for their daughter is about to end and the girl is out there on her own.

However, the reason most parents give for sending their daughters off to college is that they believe their daughters won't be successful in life without the college degree. We so wish families could break out of this way of thinking. We know parents who worry bitterly about college, wanting their children to go there and wanting to be able to pay for it, yet not being able to afford it since the parents are still paying off *their* student loans because the degrees they earned did not help them find employment that was good enough to get out of debt.

There is something wrong with this picture, isn't there? If "higher" education is supposed to make one smarter, then why can't impoverished graduates see the folly of this whole racket? Because college teaches them to see only what the State would have them see. The poor parents learned the wrong lesson and don't realize just how thoroughly they were lied to. Even in middle age they tend to treat college as a kind of religious sacrament. Instead of covering daughters with the protection they need at a critical time of life, daughters are often covered with guilt if they even contemplate an alternative to the college experience. Let's try to find and prove the wiser alternatives.

We know families who skipped the "college experience" whose lives are filled every day with joy and excitement—even professional fulfillment. Family businesses can be not only fun but successful. We know daughters who work with their fathers and fathers who work with their daughters. We know fathers-in-law who work with their sons-in-law. We know of bank accounts that are in the black instead of in the red. These are stories of happiness because the families broke out of the enslaving mentality that "success is impossible without a college degree."

So what are a girl's alternatives? How can we become thoroughly well-educated in the right ways without going to college?

First, we can go to our fathers to appeal for a better alternative. We are happy to report that many fathers respond favorably when daughters can outline a truly superior alternative that includes:

a) Remaining at home to help the father's business, as preparation for marriage;

b) Pursuing true academic learning by correspondence or self-study; or

c) Applying oneself to advanced homemaking studies in preparation for real life.

We know fathers who were once dead-set on sending their girls to college, who changed their minds when they saw the wisdom in this better alternative. When the goal of the young woman is not laziness or self-centeredness, but the thorough training of her mind in preparation for a fruitful life, a father's heart can melt and be turned toward his daughter, sometimes for the first time. When fathers see the way daughters give them their hearts for protection, they can embrace a more responsible relationship with their daughters. When fathers see how much their daughters truly want to help them and honor them, they seriously rethink the folly of sending their girls into compromising environments.

A good education does not have to be expensive and is easily within the reach of any girl who can read and get access to good books. John Taylor Gatto observes:

> Close reading of tough-minded writing is still the best, cheapest, and quickest method known for learning to think for yourself…Reading, and rigorous discussion of that reading in a way that obliges you to formulate a position and support it against objections, is an operational definition of education in its most fundamental civilized sense…Reading, analysis and discussion is the way we develop reliable judgment, the principal way we come to penetrate covert movements behind the facade of public appearances.[15]

So there are ways to obtain academic credentials without living on the college campus?

Yes. But a student and a father should know exactly why these are useful before they are pursued. They may be completely unnecessary

---

15 John Taylor Gatto, *The Underground History of American Education*, (Oxford Village Press, 2001), p. 56.

for future success. If they represent a specialist foundation for further studies, that foundation can be obtained in many cases by correspondence and new internet opportunities for distance learning.

> *Are there ever any circumstances that might make college attendance, on campus, a legitimate option for young women?*

The Bible never says college is off limits to girls, and we are trying very hard in this book to advance only those ideas that can be defended exegetically.[16] We are attempting to raise a simple question that is too rarely asked by our generation:

> *"If a young woman was determined to think and act biblically, how would she live?"*

She would rediscover God's design for virtuous womanhood for every stage of her life and try to conform her service to God to that plan. Central to that plan is a virtuous heart, a pure mind, the right education, a strong father-daughter relationship, a wisely contracted marriage, and wise, God-fearing descendants.

Too many fathers and daughters build their lives around the wrong questions:

> *"How can I be popular and successful in the world's eyes?"*

> *"How can I make the most money and conform my priorities to a money-making lifestyle?"*

> *"How can I avoid the stigma of being too 'Christian' or too 'legalistic?'"*

---

16 Exegesis is the drawing of truth directly from Scripture in the right interpretation.

"How can I conform myself to the world's way of doing business, doing education, doing family, doing fun stuff, doing marriage, doing children, doing retirement, doing everything?"

The wrong questions lead us in wrong directions. When we start asking the right questions and begin to be transformed by the renewing of our minds,[17] the things of the world no longer enslave us but begin to present themselves to us as tools we might appropriate for our mission in life. Money can enslave one or equip one. Books can enslave one or equip one. A course in bio-chemistry might enslave and harm a student or equip one. Most students attend college asking the wrong questions and find themselves quickly enslaved to the predominant worldview.

Unless the current university setting is made more honest, it will continue to be a deceptively dangerous place to spend the best years of one's life.

But what about becoming a teacher in the non-Christian government schools? It seems that would be such a wonderful "ministry" job, especially if I have children later and want to teach them at home. Shouldn't I go to teachers' college, especially while all my friends are there?

A few personal observations: it is our opinion, after observing the damage done to Christian daughters in education colleges, that *of all the fraudulent courses in the modern college, the education major is the most dangerously deceptive of all.*

The Frankfurt School faculty (mentioned in Chapter Six) knew that teachers were some of the most powerful and influential people on earth, for they trained and discipled the next generation.

---

17 See Romans 12:2.

As Lenin put it, "Through the schools we will transform the old world…the final victory will belong to the schools…the final sketch plan of the socialist society will belong to the schools."[18] So the Frankfurt School targeted and took control of the teachers' colleges in order to control what was being taught to the children.[19] In fact, if we were asked to what primary cause we attribute the astounding transformation of Western society, we would reply, to the Marxist infiltration of the teachers' colleges, universities, and schools. Today the education colleges are hotbeds of religious Marxism, and young teachers are forced to go through possibly the most rigorous courses of indoctrination available in any universities.

In order to get accreditation and employment, they are required to absorb Frankfurt School doctrines.[20] Not just a few doctrines, but most of them.[21] They come away pessimistic, with the conviction that Christianity is outdated, dangerous, and inadequate and must not interfere in the developmental process of individual children.

18 Vladimir Lenin, quoted in Deerwood Studios' *Certain Failure*, television documentary series, 1995.

19 Gatto records: "In 1928, a well-regarded volume called *A Sociological Philosophy of Education* claimed, 'It is the business of teachers to run not merely schools but the world.' A year later, the famous creator of education psychology, Edward Thondike of Columbia Teachers College, announced, 'Academic subjects are of little value.'" John Taylor Gatto, *The Underground History of American Education*, p. 39.

20 John Taylor Gatto, says in *The Underground History of American Education*, (Oxford Village Press, 2001), p. 135: "Where the whole tendency of education is to create obedience," [Orestes] Brownson said, "all teachers must be pliant tools of government."

21 In 1970, the then-president of the NEA, George Fischer, told NEA representatives during an assembly, "A good deal of work has been done to begin to bring about uniform certification controlled by the unified profession in each state …With these new laws, we will finally realize our 113-year-old dream of controlling who enters, who stays and who leaves the profession. Once this is done, we can also control the teacher training institutions." (Brannon Howse, "Is NEA a 'Terrorist Organization?'" WorldNetDaily, February 27, 2004.)

Young teachers also come to believe in a sacred duty they owe the State to facilitate the State's every wish, conditioning young minds to comply with new ideas, which will constantly and continually be superior to old ideas because of their "secular" nature.

Our friends who have been through these courses lose their discernment with every compromise they are required to make in education college. They are expected to make many compromises in order to get passing grades.[22] The courses target those students who know how to think and marginalize them, punishing them for traditional thought.[23] After two or three years in this environment, conditioned responses seem to govern our friends' worldviews. They embrace the Frankfurt School worldview.[24] They can no longer see the religious nature of secular thought. It seems so nice and modern and pragmatic and scientific and "neutral." This is the primary problem for every incoming freshman at any major

---

22 One of our friends informed us that none of her papers reflect her own convictions, but must be conformed to what the teacher's college expects to be the uniform conviction of every student. Any deviation means a failing grade.

23 One popular device for embarrassing Christians includes the "Delphi Technique," in which a class facilitator focuses intense ridicule and humiliation on a nonconforming student until the student complies with class consensus. Teachers are taught this technique to ensure conformity among their own students and even within community groups of parents, if necessary.

24 This worldview was summarized well by New York State Teacher of the Year John Taylor Gatto: "Hundreds of millions of perpetual children require paid attention from millions of adult custodians...Utopian schooling isn't ever about learning in the traditional sense; it's about the transformation of human nature." The purpose of schooling, according to Frankfurt School doctrine, is to prevent children from becoming responsible, thinking adults so that an arbitrary State can manipulate the masses at any time according to any policy. See John Taylor Gatto, *The Underground History of American Education*, (Oxford Village Press, 2001), pp. xxxi., 16.

university for any course of study, but it is especially concentrated in the "education" major.[25]

As for serving the State in a State classroom, a Christian teacher can simply *not* be a Christian teacher there, because biblical presuppositions are off limits both in the mind and in the classroom. Every Christian teacher is required to teach the rival religious presuppositions of the State curriculum.[26] Non-compliance means dismissal, and you should know this before you invest one day or one dollar in an education college education. Once fired from the State system, you will find that the better independent schools do not hire teachers who have education credentials from State schools, because the training has nothing (this is not an exaggeration)—nothing—to do with teaching academic content to eager students. Education majors learn how to facilitate a non-academic State curriculum, how to function bureaucratically, how to ride herd on a large number of peer-dependent, disrespectful students, and how to be faithful members of the teachers' union until retirement.

---

25 Gatto describes the purposes of the training techniques used on both teachers and students, saying, "…all were built around the premise that isolation from first-hand information, and fragmentation of the abstract information presented by teachers, would result in obedient and subordinate graduates, properly respectful of arbitrary orders. "Lesser" men would be unable to interfere with policy makers because, while they could still complain, they could not manage sustained or comprehensive thought. Well-schooled children cannot think critically, cannot argue effectively." See John Taylor Gatto, "The Public School Nightmare: Why Fix a System Designed to Destroy Individual Thought?"

26 Here's a separate issue Christians should seriously think about. By teaching in government schools, Christians continue to endorse an institution that is not biblical. Neither in the Bible nor the Constitution is the government allowed to be involved in education. This unlawful situation will not be remedied if Christian parents and teachers continue to endorse the system by their participation.

As to your qualifications to teach your own children one day, you must realize that you will be eminently more qualified to do this than any other teacher, because you will be the children's mother. Besides, home education is not about schooling, it is about education. It is about helping your children learn to think, about "treating them seriously when they are little, giving them responsibilities, talking to them candidly, providing privacy and solitude for them, and making them readers and thinkers of significant thoughts from the beginning."[27] Home education tends to follow the Smithsonian Institution's recipe for genius and leadership: "Children should spend a great deal of time with loving, educationally minded parents; children should be allowed a lot of free exploration; and children should have little to no association with peers outside of family and relatives."[28]

What are some important subjects for young Christian women to study?

Jennie continues:

> Becoming a woman of God is certainly more than just learning to cook, sew, and take care of babies—although those things are extremely important! A man needs a "helper suitable for him." He needs someone who can share his concerns, talk about them intelligently, and help him come up with solutions. He needs a co-regent who will rule their home wisely and well. When God gave the Dominion Mandate, He gave it to both Adam and Eve. He didn't make Eve subhuman or tell her to be

---

27 Gatto's recipe for true education, from his essay "The Public School Nightmare."

28 Jessie Wise and Susan Wise Bauer, *The Well-Trained Mind* (New York: WW Norton & Co., 1999), p. 589.

strictly ornamental. No one who advocates biblical standards for educating daughters believes this. Woman was made for man because man was not complete without her—together male and female constitute the image of God.

I am not at all implying that women should be uneducated, ignorant, and unwise—or that they should suppress the natural gifts the Lord has given them. The women hailed in the Bible as examples for us were exceedingly wise, clever, intelligent, capable, and quick-witted. They were not shackled to the home, brainless and without ambition. But their ambitions were God-oriented and God-directed.

I can say without hesitation that sending a daughter away—divorcing her from her family obligations and relationships for four years—is not a recipe for success either educationally or spiritually.

It is unfortunate that the topic of college for Christian young women has become a touchy one in recent years. Bringing it up even among close Christian friends can often cause misunderstandings or hurt feelings. Those of us who do not advocate sending daughters away to college are often viewed as judgmental or pietistic. Some people mistakenly believe that we really don't think girls should be educated at all. This is simply not the case. I believe God calls all of us—male or female—to develop our brains, to learn to think and speak cogently, and to be prepared to educate the next generation thoroughly. But I can tell you unequivocally that my college experience did not prepare me for the life I now live as a Christian wife and mother.

As Christians, we need to be willing to talk issues like this over in a gracious manner, looking to Scripture first for our precepts, examples, and direct commands. While good Christians can and do disagree about certain issues, we should not divide the Body over them but seek to grow ever closer to our Head, Christ. As we prayerfully consider the education of our daughters, I hope that we will commit to dig into God's Word and seek His paths. When St. Paul says that he "command[s] that the younger women marry, bear children, [and] guide the house" (I Tim. 5:14), we need to say "amen" without coming up with a list of qualifiers. When he writes that the older women be "teachers of good things; that they may teach the young women to be sober, to love their husbands, to love their children, to be discreet, chaste, keepers at home, good, obedient to their own husbands, that the word of God be not blasphemed" (Titus 2:3b-5), we need to understand that these things are not antithetical to academics. The woman at home is a ruler (literally the "despot of the house" in the Greek). I believe the best environment to prepare her for her future queendom is the godly home—a home where parents and children make learning lifelong and do not train the next generation to believe that wisdom is tied to a piece of paper.

"But where can wisdom be found? And where is the place of understanding? Man does not know its value, Nor is it found in the land of the living. The deep says, 'It is not in me;' And the sea says, 'It is not with me.' It cannot be purchased for gold, Nor can silver be weighed for its price. It cannot be valued in the gold of Ophir, In precious onyx or sapphire. Neither gold nor crystal can equal it, Nor can it be exchanged for jewelry of fine gold. No mention shall be made of coral or quartz, For the price of wisdom is above rubies. The topaz of Ethiopia cannot equal it, Nor can it be valued in pure gold. From where then does wisdom come? And where is the place of understanding? ...God understands its way, And He knows its place...And to man He said, 'Behold, the fear of the Lord, that is wisdom, And to depart from evil is understanding.'" (Job 28:12-20, 23, 28)

We believe girls should develop their talents and pursue their interests insofar as these can be used for the glory of God. Setting our interests aside, there are a few preliminary subjects that all aspiring helpmeets and mothers should study.

Our father always taught us that in order to be responsible cultural leaders, young ladies must possess:

a) A consistently biblical worldview, which comes from studying God's Word (theology), the revealing of God's plan for mankind (history), and an understanding of our times; and

b) The tools to develop messages and pass those messages on to others, especially the mastery of the English language, both spoken and written. These could be called the tools for discipleship.

Our father believes that learning to write well is necessary, not only because it is an effective and efficient way of communicating ideas, but because it develops the mind's ability to think, form convictions, and teach. Our father emphasizes how the pursuit of these things will require a lifetime of diligent academic study.

He also points out to us the ongoing discipline we need to apply in academic fashion to those practical skills we will need in our future vocations as Proverbs 31 women. We must study hard how to be virtuous and accomplished. We have so much to learn about effectively running a home estate, dealing with children, demonstrating hospitality, discipling younger women, ministering to other families. We started young, but we're just coming into an age where we can embrace these lessons thoroughly.

Proverbs 31:12 says of the ideal woman, "She will do him [her husband] good and not evil all the days of her life."

We have always found it interesting that this verse doesn't say, "She will do him good and not evil as soon as she is married to him," but rather that she will do him good and not evil *all* the days of her life. This means that we young women should be actively doing our future husbands good *right now*, even if we don't know who they are or when we will marry them. One of the ways we can do our future husbands good right now is by preparing to bring many assets into the marriage. The greatest assets we can give our husbands are our own skills and excellent character. We should be training to be the best helpmeets we can possibly be.

A wife should be "a helper suitable for him," a co-regent and co-laborer to him in the Dominion Mandate. Proverbs 31:11 says, "The heart of her husband trusts in her, and he will have no lack of gain." A husband should be able to entrust his wealth to his wife and trust her to extend the borders of his estate. Therefore, it might be wise for us to invest some of our time in studying to acquire business acumen, accounting skills, and political knowledge.

It's also prudent for us to learn the craft of home-making. In another letter written by William Sprague to his daughter back in the 19th century, this wise father says:

> It is important that you should cultivate a taste for the management of domestic concerns as early as possible. As no part of your education is more practical than this, it were unsafe to neglect it even for a short period, as the consequence of such neglect would probably be, that you would form other habits uncongenial with domestic employments, and which perhaps might give you an aversion to them which you would never overcome…I beg you to bear in mind, that the knowledge of which I am speaking is to be acquired only in a single way, and that is by actual experience.

You may study the science of domestic economy as carefully as you will, and you may receive lessons from experienced and skilful managers, and after all, you will be little wiser till you come down to the actual reality of participating in the every-day concerns of a family. When you actually put your hand to the work, you will begin to learn; but unless you put your hand to it frequently, and learn to think it no dishonour to engage in anything appertaining to the economy of a family, you can never expect to become an accomplished housekeeper.[29]

A girl who assumes she does not need extensive training to be a homemaker is a girl who would fit the feminists' caricature of a housewife.[30]

The sheer mechanics of housekeeping, when performed properly, are like a high art form. As Cheryl Mendelson states it:

[W]hat a traditional woman did that made her home warm and alive was not dusting and laundry...Her real secret was that she identified herself with her home, [and]...it is illuminating to think about what happened when things went right. Then her affection was in the soft sofa cushions, clean linens, and good meals; her memory in well-stocked storeroom cabinets and the pantry; her intelligence in the

---

29 Sprague, William Buell, 1795-1876, *Letters on Practical Subjects, to a Daughter*, 11th American ed., New York, n.d.

30 "[Housewives] are mindless and thing-hungry...not people. [Housework] is peculiarly suited to the capacities of feeble-minded girls. [It] arrests their development at an infantile level, short of personal identity with an inevitably weak core of self. ...[Housewives] are in as much danger as the millions who walked to their own death in the concentration camps. [The] conditions which destroyed the human identity of so many prisoners were not the torture and brutality, but conditions similar to those which destroy the identity of the American housewife." Betty Friedan, *The Feminine Mystique*, 1963.

order and healthfulness of her home; her good humor in
its light and air. She lived her life not only through her
own body, but through the house as an extension of her
body; part of her relation to those she loved was embodied
in the physical medium of the home she made. My own
experience convinces me that there is still no other way to
make a good home than to have attitudes toward home and
domesticity modeled on those of that traditional woman.
...Advertisements and television programs offer degraded
images of household work and workers. Discussions of the
subject in magazines and newspapers follow a standard
formula. ...It is scarcely surprising, then, that so many people
imagine housekeeping to be boring, frustrating, repetitive,
unintelligent drudgery. I cannot agree. (In fact, having kept
house, practiced law, taught, and done many other sorts
of work, low- and high-paid, I can assure you that it is
actually lawyers who are most familiar with the experience of
unintelligent drudgery.)[31]

G.K. Chesterton likened wifely duties to those of a monarch,
a powerful merchant, and a teacher of theology, manners, and
morals—all performed simultaneously. "I can understand how this
might exhaust the mind, but I cannot imagine how it could narrow
it," wrote Chesterton. "How can it be a large career to tell other
people's children about [arithmetic], and a small career to tell one's
own children about the universe? How can it be broad to be the
same thing to everyone, and narrow to be everything to someone?
No; a woman's function is laborious because it is gigantic, not
because it is minute. I will pity Mrs. Jones for the hugeness of her
task; I will never pity her for its smallness."

---

31 Cheryl Mendelson, *Home Comforts: The Art and Science of Keeping House*, pp. 9-10.

In addition to basic housekeeping and cookery skills, it is also advantageous for us to know something about nutrition, health, medicine, and first aid. There is more to home-making than housecleaning chores. The Proverbs 31 woman did more than clean a house—she ruled a home.

To rule, guide and keep a home is to create an entire culture, filled with godly or ungodly aesthetics. Because of the importance attached to this, we should know the difference between the elements of culture which honor God, or dishonor Him.

There are so many other things it would be helpful to study, we can't really include a list. We've only tried to spotlight a few of the most important, and often most neglected, disciplines of home life.

But what if I can't get married? What if I can't have children? What if my husband dies and I have to support myself? What if my father refuses to protect and provide for me? Surely I don't have time to train myself for marriage. Isn't it wiser to train myself for a worst-case scenario?

We live in a cynical society that anticipates decline, decay, and defeat. In God's order, for the Christian woman, there is no circumstance where a widow or abandoned woman is forced to support herself. The reason this question is often asked is because fathers and churches and other responsible parties are not being responsible.

The role of the Proverbs 31 wife and mother is not a role that can be "slipped into" easily. In fact, to do it really well takes a lifetime of training. What are our priorities? Learning to "survive" can teach girls attitudes of independence, hardness, authoritativeness, and cynicism. Can this be wise or godly if it damages our ability to become Proverbs 31 women?

We should be bending all of our energies toward making God's ideal a reality in our lives, pursuing the best-case scenario with all our might. Settling for the status quo will not help pull our society up out of the mire, but choosing the better course can.

CHAPTER ELEVEN

DAUGHTERS, FATHERS, AND THE FAMILY MISSION

HOW YOU FIT INTO YOUR FAMILY AND HOW YOUR FAMILY FITS INTO GOD'S PLAN

How important to God is the family?

Many people believe that we have blown the importance of the family unit way out of proportion. However, it is impossible to over-emphasize the biblical importance[1] of a unit that is based on God's nature itself. The family is an intrinsic part of God's nature, because it is based on God's own being. He is Father and Son. Christ and His Church are the foundation for marriage. Believers are referred to as brothers and sisters in Christ. The greatest celebration of history will take place as the Eternal Groom is finally united with His bride.

The entire Bible—in fact, the very elements of Christianity—are written in terms of family relationships. This is an interesting insight into how important the family is to God.

---

1 The importance which the Bible prescribes it. For the family to usurp the powers of the other institutions would be wrong.

God makes it very clear through Scripture that He is displeased with people who don't place enough importance on their families. We read in 1 Timothy 5:8 that "But if any provide not for his own, and specially for those of his own house, he hath denied the faith, and is worse than an infidel."

Esau is an interesting example of someone who misunderstood the importance of the covenantal family. The firstborn's right was to be the heir to the family's estate, but it also included inheriting the responsibility of caring for the aged parents and unmarried daughters. The firstborn was blessed with becoming the next leader of the entire clan. The act of selling his birthright was an open rejection of his family's heritage, and showed that he even despised it (Genesis 25:34b). It demonstrates that he had no regard for the covenant blessing bestowed on him as firstborn (a position which was important to God) and despised his place in the line of covenant promises. And for this, the Bible calls him a "profane person" (Hebrews 12:16). The anti-blessing he received found fulfillment through his descendants, who were to live away from the "fatness of the earth...and the dew of heaven" (Genesis 27:39). One of them was Herod the Great. Esau's line was cursed because he had despised his family heritage.

Another example of a man who brushed off family importance was Eli. Eli was a godly man who devoted his life to serving God in the temple, making his family second priority. According to modern thought, God should have been pleased with this. But in fact, because Eli placed his ministry priorities above his duty to train his sons in the way they should go (Proverbs 22:6) and to restrain them when they consequently did evil (1 Samuel 3:13), God sent upon him a curse "at which both the ears of every one that heareth it shall tingle" (1 Samuel 3:11). "...and there shall not be an old man in thine house for ever…and all the increase of thine house shall die in the flower of their age" (1 Samuel 2:32,33).

This curse of dying young is a striking contrast to the promise given to those who honor their parents: "…that you may live long on the earth."

God set up society to be made up of family dynasties rather than individuals. And usually His blessings, curses, and promises were given to entire families, to carry on for generations within those families.

> "And I will establish my covenant between me and thee and thy seed after thee in their generations for an everlasting covenant, to be a God unto thee, and to thy seed after thee." (Genesis 17:7)

> "…for I the Lord thy God am a jealous God, visiting the iniquity of the fathers upon the children unto the third and fourth generation of them that hate me, and shewing mercy unto thousands of them that love me and keep my commandments." (Deuteronomy 5:9,10)

In the New Testament we see even more examples of God's grace bestowed on entire families, as in the case of the Philippian jailer ("And after he brought them out, he said, "Sirs, what must I do to be saved?" And they said, "Believe in the Lord Jesus, and you shall be saved, you and your house." Acts 16:30,31) or the case of Cornelius ("And [Peter] shall speak words to you by which you will be saved, you and all your household." Acts 11:14) or the case of Lydia ("And when she was baptized, and her household…" Acts 16:15).

What did God intend the family to do?

When God created man, He provided order for society and a structure for the administration of his kingdom. He created three separate institutions: the Family, the Church, and the State (the civil government). The Church was instituted to be God's ministry of mercy and reconciliation. The State was to be God's ministry of justice. The family was for the bearing, nurturing, and bringing up the future generations in the admonition of the Lord. The family is the heart of society; the condition of the family will determine the condition of civilization.

What's more, the family is God's primary tool of dominion. He gave the Dominion Mandate to a *family* and not a ministry organization, and the method it was to pursue was to fill the earth and subdue it. The bearing and training of godly children is the most effective long-term strategy of discipling all the nations and taking dominion. "Train up a child in the way he should go, and when he is old he will not depart from it" (Proverbs 22:6). Whoever trains the children controls the future. A chain is only as strong as its weakest link, and a society will only ever be as strong as the families in it.

Does the state of the family actually have much cultural significance?

Doug Phillips, president of The Vision Forum, Inc., has pointed out that "Every generation has its defining challenge. Ours is the systematic annihilation of the biblical family."[2]

Many Christians focus on fighting obvious crises such as prostitution, abortion, civil unions, broken marriages, and child abuse. They might be more fruitful if they recognized that these are only the outgrowth of a more serious problem—that the West has forgotten what marriage, children, and the family in general are all about.

---

2   Doug Phillips, "The Biblical Family Now and Forever," A Line in the Sand: *The Vision Forum Family Catalog*, 2005, p 1.

The ironic thing is that God's enemies seem to have understood how important strong, functional families are to Christianity better than God's own people do.

As Gerardus Van der Leeuw stated, "Religion, thus, is seen as a projection of the family, and the family must therefore be destroyed in order that religion may also be destroyed."[3]

"Marx was on to something more profound than he knew when he observed that the family contained within itself in embryo all the antagonisms that later develop on a wider scale within the society and the state," wrote Shulamith Firestone, a disciple of Betty Friedan, in her 1970 tract *The Dialectic of Sex*. "[U]nless revolution uproots the basic organization, the biological family...the tapeworm of exploitation will never be annihilated."[4]

R.C. Sproul, Jr. laments in *Bound For Glory* the way families have been reduced to mere groups of individuals living under one roof. Innocent-seeming norms such as separate workplaces, separate hanging-out places, day-care, rest-homes, age-segregated classrooms, and even relationships have actually been fragmenting the family by slotting each member into a different group and sending it in its own direction, alienated from the rest of the family.

> But it gets worse...we have much the same problem in the Church. ...Mom goes off to her Women in the church...circle. Dad heads off to his Promise Keepers meeting. Princess is at her youth group meeting, while Junior is watching videos of vegetables in children's church. ...We seem to think that if we

---

3 Gerardus Van der Leeuw, *Religion in Essence & Manifestation, A Study in Phenomenology*. (quoted in *Institutes of Biblical Law, Volume One*, by R.J. Rushdoony).

4 Cited in William Norman Grigg's article "Gramsci: A Method to the Madness," www.grecoreport.com.

can keep all this separateness together under one roof we are doing okay. But the truth is, we are failing miserably, even when we think we are succeeding. We're allowing our families to be torn apart because we are allowing our families to be molded by the wisdom of the world.[5]

Perhaps the greatest triumph of the cultural Marxists was to enlist the help of Christians in undermining the family's importance as the first and basic institution of society, with the Church leading the way in programming family relationships out of existence. Christian parents are content to stand back and watch passively (sometimes approvingly) as their families are broken into pieces. They don't realize that new practices like age-segregated classrooms and age-segregated church services were devised to split up the family by fostering peer-dependence instead of family-dependence, promoting disloyalty to family ties, traditions, and religion.

"We have a lot of churches these days that instead of reaching the unchurched are unchurching the churched," notes Dr. Michael Horton. "What do I mean by that? Modernity has already virtually torn apart the generational fabric and rootedness that comes with long-term commitments. According to some of the statistics I've seen, the average candidate for a seeker church is not an unbeliever but a lapsed churchgoer or a churchgoer who has been so uprooted and transplanted in his or her life that belonging to a seeker church—with its more transient feel—is more desirable. A spiritual tourism, if you will."[6]

---

5   R.C. Sproul, Jr., *Bound for Glory: God's Promise for Your Family* (Wheaton, Illinois: Crossway Books, 2003), pp. 25, 26.

6   Michael Horton , *Seekers or Tourists?: Or the Difference Between Pilgrimage and Vacation*, Alliance of Confessing Evangelicals, 2002.

Why do God's enemies want to split up families?

Because as strong, cohesive units, families pose a huge threat to God's enemies. Take a family where each member is pursuing his own schedule, his own life, his own friends, his own ministry. Though today it wouldn't be seen as *dysfunctional*, it is not functioning the way the family was created to function. A *real* family is "a self-sufficient, fully functioning, economically viable agent for the dominion of God."[7]

A family is more than the sum of its parts. A "fully functioning" family thinks like a team. Each member has different abilities, but all share a vision and work toward the same goal. That is why the famous Von Trapp family's motto was *Cor Unum*: One heart.[8] Proverbs 29:18 says, "Where there is no vision, the people perish," and where there is no united family vision, the family perishes. The weak and dysfunctional families are the families without a united goal and purpose. Though the members may be diligent in pursuing their own separate ministries, there will always be a limit to how much fruit these can bear, because *families are most productive when the members are united in vision and work together to execute a common mission.*

We have had many opportunities to observe and compare all kinds of families from all over the world living in many different circumstances. The ones that have a dynamic, united life purpose, who see life as a battleground instead of a playground, where the members are each other's best friends, all involved, and all building each other up and discipling one another, are the most incredibly fun, exciting, adventurous, and productive units. Most of all, they

---

7   Doug Phillips, audio recording, "What's a Girl to Do?"

8   The Von Trapp family of *Sound of Music* fame was a real family who fled for their lives with few possessions and was forced to work together to survive away from their homeland. Because of their practical unity they not only survived, but prospered.

bear the most fruit and have the most influence, if only because families like this never go unnoticed.

Isn't there a time in a girl's life when she should be "on her own," independent of her family?

It's a given in our society that before marriage, a young woman should have a few years to "test her wings," free, independent, and single. "Singleness" these days means more than being unmarried. It's more than a state. It's a stage—the stage when you slowly become disconnected from your family, when you learn to think and act as an independent agent, when you become uninvolved in your family's concerns (and reluctant to let them be involved in yours). Friends begin to take the place of family, and making and hanging out with friends becomes the most important priority.

This kind of singleness does not feature in God's plan for society. In fact, because of all the destructive ideas associated with the word "singleness,"[9] we never refer to ourselves as single. We're unmarried, but we're not "single." God put us in a family.

If God was so kind as to let you grow up in a family, then you are not single. You have been put into an important unit for an important purpose. To pursue singleness (singleness meaning, being outside a family) is to reject this gift. This is how God views single people: "He setteth the solitary into families" (Psalm 68:6a). Being solitary is something that God, being all-knowing and loving, and

---

9   For the sake of discussion, when we use the word "singleness" in this chapter, we are referring to this specific stage of familial isolation, rather than to our unmarried years, which are a gift from God like any other time of our lives. Our teen years are unique in ways we need to rediscover. We also dislike the term "teenager" because the teenage culture invented itself in selfishness, waywardness, and independence.

merciful, delivers His children *out* of. So He blesses His daughters by making singleness a non-issue for them. He puts them into families.

Many girls respond to this with, "But you don't know *my* family!" No, we don't, but God does. Some people say, "You choose your friends, but your family you're stuck with." We prefer to say, "You choose your friends, but God chooses your family." Before the foundations of the earth, God was putting together all the members of your family, and He chose each one for a purpose, as He does everything. If you look at the family in terms of a group of souls whom God chose from all the other souls, to put together to share a life, it gives you a whole new perspective into what a wonderful miracle a family is.

CHAPTER TWELVE

DAUGHTERS AND A FATHER'S ROOF

WHERE YOU CAN BE PROTECTED AND PRODUCTIVE

If I'm supposed to be an active part of my family, then does that mean I should live at home until I'm married?

In historic biblical circumstances, a girl lived at home under her father's roof until she was married.

But that was then and this is now, right?

What women have now is neither progress nor improvement. Western women are much worse off than they have been for a long time. Our plans and desires should not be based on what we want or what the culture says we need. We should seek God's best. We should seek and welcome God's protection. We should also seek and welcome our father's protection until we have our husband's protection. It may not be unlawful to live in an environment that doesn't offer protection, but is it profitable?[1]

It is a father's responsibility to provide for his daughter, lead her, and protect her body, soul, mind, and emotions. If a daughter is wise enough to understand her need to be *fully* under the authority and protection of her father, it's logical that she would seek those *all the way*, instead of giving them a token nod ("Sure, I only see my father every few months, but if he tells me to do something, I obey.")

Throughout the whole Bible we see examples of young women who lived at home under their fathers' protection until they were given in marriage. One example of a daughter who left home to seek friends outside the covenant community is Dinah, who is interestingly called "the daughter of Leah" instead of the daughter of Jacob. Look her up in Genesis 34 and see what a mess she made for herself, her family, and the entire neighboring kingdom.

Fiona talks about one of the greatest dangers and temptations facing the unprotected young women of today:

> When a young lady is out from under the protection of her father—this can be a physical and a spiritual thing—the world looks so attractive. All the things she never noticed before seem to be everywhere and readily available. The boys, clothes, music, easily-acquired finances, cars, jewelry…I think the worst is probably the boys who are there waiting for a nice, pure, lonely young lady in need of attention and caring. The rest is history. I have seen this happen to so many people I know. It is painful and leaves emotional scars.

---

1 See I Corinthians 6:12.

When I ask myself why I left home when I was 17, the answer is simple. I rebelled against my father, did not respect his authority, and quite simply wanted to live life the way I wanted. No, it was not well with me. From the moment I left home, life was fraught with difficulties. I had car accidents, I lost my wallet, I couldn't keep a part-time job for longer than six months, I got myself almost immediately in financial bondage. I was truly in a state of "spiritual blindness," walking up and down the streets of "Vanity Fair," not registering anything or anyone.

The weight of biblical passages seems to strongly indicate that the home is the woman's domain. Why should this be true only for married women? Proverbs 7:11 describes one of the wiles of the harlot: "She is boisterous and rebellious, her feet do not remain at home." This description could match many of the Christian girls we know. They would be outraged and insulted to be likened to harlots, but they are unwittingly acting like them. The godly woman loves to be in her home.

Sarah says:

It is such a blessing for me to be under my father's roof—under his authority, protection, and leadership. No longer do I seek to leave it in search of a more "significant" position. It is such a joy to know that I am part of a family that is a team—a unit—that works together to further God's kingdom for the glory of God. We are no longer a household of individuals with our own ministries and activities independent of one another— for then the family cannot function as God designed it. I am amazed at the difference in our lives due to the work God has done in our hearts.

Can a girl really accomplish as much living at home as outside it?

We know the idea of moving back home sounds absolutely insane to most girls at first. They just can't reconcile the idea of living at home with doing important things for God. This is because few people understand what the home is really all about anymore. If you think we are advocating you move home to lie around on the sofa, watch movies, and read teen magazines, think again. The Proverbs 31 woman did not eat the bread of idleness, and neither can we. The biblical home is not a center of leisure and entertainment, as most modern homes are, where the TV has replaced the family hearth as the center of the home.

The biblical home is not just a place to chill out and be entertained—it is a *center for industry.* A real home is set up so that the members *work* together in it.

I don't want my parents to have to support me. If I live at home, how can I keep from being a drain on my family?

Biblically, it is a father's duty to provide for his daughters. However, a girl should be worth her keep, one way or another, at the very least. There is no reason why a girl should be a drain. On the contrary, the presence of a diligent, cheerful, industrious daughter in the family is so beneficial that, even if she isn't contributing to the family income, her family will be in a much better financial state with her than without her. It may be that a daughter can be better at helping her family save money than at earning it. These days, due to taxes on everything you earn and everything you buy, a penny saved is *much* more than a penny earned. Because all families' circumstances are different, we can't tell you all the ways you may be able to help your family. But a girl who has her family's best interests at heart, who works toward the family vision with all her might, and through her faithfulness and enthusiasm is a good example to the others, would be such a blessing to her family that they would be much better off financially with her at home than having her live anywhere else.

Is there a time and a place for me to earn some money of my own by working on projects of my own?

Probably. While serving our families is the top priority, many young women have additional time on their hands. What did the Proverbs 31 woman do with her "spare" time?

"She seeketh wool, and flax, and worketh willingly with her hands." (Proverbs 31:13)

"She considereth a field, and buyeth it: with the fruit of her hands she planteth a vineyard." (Proverbs 31:16)

"She perceiveth that her merchandise [is] good: her candle goeth not out by night." (Proverbs 31:18)

"She layeth her hands to the spindle, and her hands hold the distaff." (Proverbs 31:19)

"She maketh fine linen, and selleth [it]; and delivereth girdles to the merchant." (Proverbs 31:24)

This woman is amazing. Not only does she see that every aspect of her household is kept ship-shape, but then she has time to engage in "cottage industry." We doubt this woman involved herself in business dealings for the fun of it, or because it made her feel more "fulfilled," or even because she personally needed the money for herself. Her whole life was about serving her family to the best of her abilities. Her additional hard work and diligence was presumably to increase the family's holdings, extend its productivity, and bring as many assets into it as she could.

While we young women are yet unmarried, we often have some spare moments. We should invest these in learning more skills and putting them to use. If we help our families as much as possible and still have more time, it could be a wonderful thing for us to be able to acquire assets to bring into our future families, as the Proverbs 31 woman did for her family.

What kinds of money-earning projects could I get involved in?

Crystal says:

> There are some basic principles which must be followed in order for any young woman to be earning money in a God-honoring manner.
>
> There is danger in a woman working for a man who is not her husband or father. The rates of workplace marital infidelity are high. There is protection in being under the right authority. We cannot be under the protection of our fathers or husbands if we are off serving another man 40 hours a week. I have held a number of different jobs in different situations during my life, but one thing has been the same about all of the jobs: I have either been working for a Christian woman, for myself, or for my authority. I could never, under any circumstance, feel safe and protected doing otherwise.
>
> There are a multitude of jobs a young woman can do from her home or in others' homes that will allow her to still be under her father's authority. Whatever her gifts or skills, there is always a creative way to use those talents without being out from under authority.

My parents always raised me with a vision to be a godly wife and mother. I did not aspire to be anything else as a young child, nor as a young adult. They taught me that true success does not come from being well-known or making a lot of money. True success is achieved through honoring God by serving others. They always encouraged me to minister to others without expectation of personal reward. My siblings and I were first required to prove ourselves faithful servants in our own home before we ministered to those outside of our home.

When I was 12, my parents allowed me to begin helping a large family from church. As time moved on, the Lord began opening up other doors. I started teaching violin to a few students and gradually found myself with 17 students. A local Christian homeschooling mother (whose children were grown) opened a lovely Victorian tea room. With my parents' blessing, I began working there one day a week. Other opportunities arose in the following months and years: I helped edit a book for Christian young women, published a newsletter encouraging young women in godliness, and assisted a few families who owned home businesses at their booths at homeschool conferences, among other things. I can honestly say that I sought none of these jobs or ministries. In each instance, someone approached my parents or approached me about them, or the Lord just laid them in my lap.

As I look back, I see how the Lord used everything I was learning through those jobs and ministries to help me to better fulfill God's calling in my life today. The things I learned through helping families, serving at the tea room, and teaching helped me to be much better equipped and prepared to be a wife and mother. The opportunities I had to help with small businesses and the people I met through my ministries to young women have been an invaluable resource to me in starting and running our home business.

The vision for our business, Covenant Wedding Source, was first born in 2002 when my husband and I were planning our own wedding. After just a few months of trying to find modest gowns and God-honoring ideas, we quickly became aware there was a real lack of conservative Christian wedding websites available. The Lord began to put in our hearts the desire to fill this void. Over the next several months, we began praying and thinking about what God would have us do. In the beginning of 2004, we felt the Lord leading us to launch our own website to provide a God-honoring alternative to the secular wedding industry. In April of 2004, our dream became a reality, and Covenant Wedding Source began.

For the first eight months, we operated a full-fledged wedding business offering custom made gowns, veils, invitations, and more. Things were going extremely well and God was blessing our endeavors more than we could have ever hoped for. But, as time went on, I gradually lost my focus on what my most important priorities were and I began putting Covenant Wedding Source above my husband and home.

A few months after I began losing my focus, our first precious daughter was born. Her birth meant my time was much more limited and I was struggling even more with my priorities. I kept thinking if I just tried a little harder or managed my time a bit better, I could keep up with everything. But alas, my husband and daughter were getting short-changed, and I knew in my heart this was not God's will. I kept stubbornly plodding along, hoping somehow things would get better. Instead of getting better, things got worse. Our sales, which had been phenomenal, now almost dissipated. The weddings I was helping to coordinate became major fiascoes with just about everything possible going wrong and the end results costing me a lot of money.

We had never had this problem in the past! I couldn't figure out what was wrong until I finally realized maybe God was trying to tell me something. As I started examining my heart and I realized Covenant Wedding Source had become "my" business, no longer "our" business. I was seeking to fulfill "my" vision of what I thought God wanted me to do, instead of seeking to expand my husband's vision and ministry. In the process, I was creating more stress for my husband rather than being the helpmeet for him God has designed me to be.

After a lot of struggle and tears, God enabled me to confess my wrong priorities to my husband and seek his forgiveness and the Lord's forgiveness. The Lord has given me a peace about this. Even though I love coordinating all the details for weddings gowns and other things, I know that someone else can do this and my place is to focus on my relationship with the Lord, with my husband, with my daughter, and caring for our household. I know that this is what God wants for me and so I am excited to press forward and follow Him.

God has been so faithful to bless this obedience. Shortly after coming to this realization, the Lord worked out the details so that Covenant Wedding Source can continue, just with a lot less involvement from me. By restructuring the company, we have been able to still provide this resource to brides, without it encroaching upon the needs of my husband and daughter.

I share this so that maybe others can learn from my mistakes. No matter what you are doing, even if it seems so right, constantly seek God's direction through your authorities. A home business can be a great thing, but if it begins to hinder your ability to be what God would have you to be, drop it or pray about a creative alternative. *It is not worth it to make a little extra money here on earth and lose eternal rewards.*

There's no end to the list of good home businesses appropriate for either married or unmarried women. In their spare time, friends of ours have earned money from dressmaking, catering, childcare, wedding organizing, pet-sitting, tutoring, teaching music and art, giving classes in literature, writing, etiquette or cooking, doing graphic design, website design, and free-lance journalism. Others have helped their siblings start or expand independent businesses (one of which was recently sold for $40 million). Others, who have poured their spare time and creativity into their fathers' businesses, have contributed commercially valuable ideas.

Friends of ours in rural situations have done market gardening, plant propagating, livestock rearing, horse and dog breeding, and raising chickens to sell eggs, among other things.

Here's an important point to remember: Find out from your father what the overall goal is. Even during the Great Depression, when literal survival was in the forefront of many daddies' minds, families found much happiness simply living together and living simply, together. Many have recalled, "We were happy, and we didn't even know we were poor."

What is the goal for your family's existence? How many fathers have taken time to think deeply about this? You can help your father by being different from the average teen girl who is never content and pressures her father to give her a more worldly life. What would it do for your father if he knew he had a daughter who wanted to give and not take? A daughter who wasn't mammon-hungry? A daughter who was not unreasonable and demanding?

The goal of most Western families is affluence. They want "more"—more of what everyone else has. This goal becomes a lifestyle often driven not by the plans of the father but by the demands of wives and children. This mammon-centered lifestyle is what drives average families into debt, distraction, disharmony, dysfunction, and such fragmentation that they don't know each other.

The reason this kind of family life is not happy? It's not *stuff* that makes people truly happy. What if we discovered that family relationships make us happy? What if we reorganized everything around a father's wishes to have more time together? What might happen?

Before Laura Ingalls Wilder wrote her *Little House* books, she wrote a regular column for a rural Missouri paper, mostly about homemaking and farm life. In one column she registered her concern for families who overburden their lives with expansion—hundreds of acres, more animals, more work, less time together. She then proceeded to explain how easy it is for a family to make a good living on a small farm of five acres, leaving enough time for a freer, happier, healthier life.

Her main point had nothing to do with farming or even living in the country. She was trying to get her readers to focus on priorities of family and community and how happiness is found in relationships.

Mrs. Wilder also pointed out the benefits of living closely to other neighbors who also have smaller holdings, so that all can enjoy "pleasant social gatherings in the evenings," thanks to being in such close proximity.[2] She was suggesting that we will never discover the real meaning of family life if we're absorbed with goals of affluence.

In 1632, William Bradford made an interesting comment in his journal. The strong Puritans of Plymouth became weak when they

2   Stephen W. Hines, *Little House in the Ozarks* (Nashville: Thomas Nelson, 1991), p. 30.

began accumulating more land and then more land and then more land around the original community that made up their remarkable biblical commonwealth. There is nothing wrong with land acquisition. There is something wrong about putting it ahead of other duties. The Puritans began losing the relationships they enjoyed, because their new pursuits made assembling together so difficult.[3] It was the beginning of the end of the happy Plymouth colony and the biblical characteristics that went with it. Bradford predicted God's displeasure at this loss of "comfort and fellowship." Why? Because relationships matter.

Does your father know this? Most Western men do not. We cannot begin to describe the influence a daughter can have on her entire family when she embraces this idea and then begins relating to every member of her family in loving, appreciative ways. Do you realize that modeling this kind of love in your homes may be the most revolutionary action taking place in the Christian world? You will be bringing to life something that has been dead for too long. Seeing this kind of behavior for the first time can be a revelation to fathers and can revolutionize your family.

What kind of lifestyle is most appropriate for people living in the kingdom Christ rules? What kind of lifestyle would your father want if he really gave it careful consideration? Did you know there may be many similarities between the two? Chances are your father's dreams will be impossible, unless he has the help and support of his family. If that support started with you, what might God do for your family? What riches might you discover in the relationships you have all around you? Could you make the impossible probable by your godly influence in the home?

---

3   Quoted by Peter Marshall and David Manuel, *The Light and the Glory* (Grand Rapids: Fleming H. Revell, 1977), p. 216.

CHAPTER THIRTEEN

DAUGHTERS, FATHERS, AND FAMILY DYNAMICS

A DAUGHTER'S INFLUENCE IN THE HOME

Most girls can only dream about having the kind of family you just described. What can we do if our families are just average?

Our culture has taught us to be cynical and without hope. Christian circles have picked up on this pessimistic attitude. Most girls who recognize that we live in a corrupt generation have been given a vision for no more than "survival." They believe it's impossible to have anything better than second best. Thus, the excuse many girls use for not pursuing the ideal and following a biblical pattern is that "our society just isn't set up to take God's ideal—it's too far gone. Our families just couldn't apply these things, because they're in too bad a state, and these ideas are too radical. We are just trying to survive."

We must have a better battle plan than this if we want to do anything to lift our society up out of the mire. The lines of action we've shown you—such as living at home, putting ourselves under the protection and authority of our fathers, preparing for marriage—

are drastic. But if we want to do anything to start reversing society's downward spiral, we will have to do something drastic. The very fact that society is not set up for this is why we must take our stand, now.

The real question is: Can we daughters repair the damage done to our fathers, our mothers, and our siblings, by introducing a biblical vision? Do we have the power to pick up the broken pieces of our families and our society? Will our influence make any difference?

We can do all things through Christ who strengthens us (Philippians 4:13). We can have a huge effect on our fathers and families. In fact, we are probably already having much more influence over them than we realize; both good influence and bad. A daughter can't save her family, and it may not be God's will for her family to reverse its direction and become an agent for His dominion, but she can and should be a good influence on them and pray for God's blessing. Already, much of your family's direction depends on you.

"…that our daughters may be as corner stones, polished after the similitude of a palace." (Psalm 144:12)

The role of a "corner stone" or "corner pillar" is very important. *Webster's 1828 Dictionary* defines a pillar as: "2. A supporter; that which sustains or upholds; that on which some superstructure rests." Think of your father, your parents, your family, as being this superstructure. It rests, in a large part, on you, whether you know it or not. A building is only as strong as that which supports it. A daughter can make or break her family.

There is lots of hope for daughters with less than perfect families. To doubt that reformation of our families is possible is to doubt that God is sovereign and in control, that His plan is perfect, and that He blesses people who obey Him.

The story of Rahab in Joshua 2 and 6 shows an example of a daughter who was able to save her entire household through her faith. She said to the Israelite spies, "…for the Lord your God, He is God in heaven above and on earth beneath. Now therefore, please swear to me by the Lord, since I have dealt kindly with you, that you also will deal kindly with my father's household, and give me a pledge of truth, and spare my father and my mother and my brothers and my sisters, with all who belong to them, and deliver our lives from death" (Joshua 2:11b-13). The spies kept their promise, and because of this one daughter's belief, the entire family was protected.

Joseph is another example. "It came about that from the time he [Potiphar] made him [Joseph] overseer in his house and over all that he owned, the Lord blessed the Egyptian's house on account of Joseph; thus the Lord's blessing was upon all that he owned, in the house and in the field" (Genesis 39:5).

The principle we see in these examples is that God blesses entire households just because of the faith and obedience of one member. One faithful daughter can have a sanctifying influence and invite God's blessings on her whole family.

How can I strengthen and support my parents?

Our parents have a huge responsibility before God to represent Him to us and our siblings, and they are accountable to Him for the way they lead. They have to provide for us, protect us, teach us, set standards for us, keep order in the home—and they are accountable to God for the ways they do these things. In our generation, because of the war against parental authority, it's especially hard to be a parent. So if we want our parents to do a good job and lead the family in a good direction, we need to work especially hard at treating them the way

God wants us to. Doing our duties as daughters makes it easier for them to do their duties as parents. This may require a drastic change of heart for many daughters, as it did for a girl we know.

Susan was an average 15-year-old Christian-on-her-own-terms, who figured she was being honoring to her parents because she was no worse than any of her friends. However, she was aware that there were a few things in her life that made her parents uncomfortable—offensive music, questionable clothing, and undesirable friendships she pursued over her cell-phone.

Somewhere along the line, God convicted her that she was sinning against Him, His order, and the parents He had given her. She repented. She then went to her father, giving him the cell-phone and objectionable CDs and clothing, asking for his forgiveness and for his prayers that she would have the strength to submit to him and seek his will for her. It wasn't easy for her at first, because what her parents wanted for her was rarely what she wanted, but when she started looking for their guidance instead of resisting it, they started paying more attention to the guidance they were giving her. Because they were no longer at war with their daughter, it became easier to see how to give constructive input to a girl who was listening. As a result, they started cutting back the restrictions and letting her use judgment that was grounded in an understanding of God's will. Susan was able to do this, because she had given her parents her heart.

Being able to fulfill our duties as daughters will require nothing less than this kind of radical change of heart and priorities. To give our parents our hearts means to consider their wishes as more important than our own—to sacrifice our own selfish desires to our parents.

Our friend **Amber** told us how God used a simple moral test to show her just how drastically she needed to change her priorities. She was thrust into the dilemma of having to choose between keeping her own schedule, or structuring her time around her father's.

> [A]t this point my frustration was beginning to rise, my entire schedule was now off, I was now nearly 45 minutes late for a lunch date, and the snow was coming down even harder. My mind was twirling with a million thoughts, "Didn't my father realize he was messing up my schedule?" "Doesn't he care about considering other people's time?" This conversation with myself continued, until all at once a deep sinking feeling hit me. Whose priorities, wants, desires, and plans were coming first in my life? The answer was quite obvious—MINE!

How is one to prepare for being a suitable helpmeet, if one's entire life up until marriage has been filled with a me-first mentality? It is nearly impossible to learn selflessness if we have not learned to practice it prior to marriage. For each of us, God allows various forms of trials and tribulations to form us into His image, causing us to learn to be selfless rather than selfish. As Peter the apostle once penned, "…that the trial of your faith being much more precious than gold that perisheth, though it be tried with fire…" (I Peter 1:7). It is often the "unimportant" little things that God brings into our lives—for instance, dropping off paperwork—that truly show our sense of honor, humility, and, ultimately, a servant's spirit. It is amazing how often God brings so many little things into my life to show me my own self-centeredness. But it has been the day-in and day-out little "trials and tribulations" that God has put me through, which have spoken so loudly to a culture so foreign to the concept of serving.

For many years, I struggled with what I would fill my single years with, and what I would do with my life if I were to never marry. It wasn't until my father and I wrestled through this issue together that I truly understood what my calling was. Almost two years ago, my father asked me to completely take over the bookkeeping side of his business. I must admit the thought of bookkeeping wasn't on my top ten list of interesting things to learn as a single young woman; it was more in the nightmare category! I knew this was an opportunity to serve my father, but at that point I did not realize the impact it would have on my life. After some study and a few minor problems on the computer end of things, I began to learn the art of bookkeeping, although I must admit it was a bit overwhelming at times. As time progressed and I was initiated into the field of bookkeeping, I began to learn that it was not the activity that brought enjoyment and contentment; it was in the fact that I was pleasing my father. The job merely became an outward manifestation of a deeper desire to serve my father. Such freedom came for me in the realization that contentment was not in the state I was in but in the fact that this act of service brought joy to my father. The opportunities God has brought for me through serving my father have been incredible, and the relationship we have built is irreplaceable.

I can see the panic-stricken faces reading this article, worrying that God is going to assign them some type of dreadful task. Please do not worry. In the process of working with my father, I have begun to see how uniquely my talents fit my father's needs. These gifts and talents are not only meant for my benefit, but to encourage and support those whose authority I am under. Though my "occupations" in life will continually be changing, God's principles never deviate, remaining the same throughout all of history. I am absolutely confident in the fact that, had I chosen to follow the world's philosophy of womanhood, I would still be wrestling today with the issue of life purpose. Though I have much yet to learn, my father and I are working together, and I thank him for his patience with me. For each one of us the story is very unique, but my point is, are we willing? Above all, we must learn to make our time secondary to that of our family—which is a constant battle for me and an area I will be attempting to conquer for years to come. Truly, what a blessing it will be to our future husbands that we have learned what it means to make our own wants, desires, and goals secondary to the goals of the ones we are serving.

I can't count the number of job offers I have received over the years due to the fact that I am serving my father. The loyalty, determination, and honor I have learned in the process of serving is what is so appealing in our culture, which is literally dying for women with servants' spirits. Many of the skills I have gained in the process have definitely not been in what I would consider to be in my field of expertise, but it is amazing how, when we change our attitude, we often accomplish far more than we ever imagined. Often in the Bible, God used those least qualified to accomplish His greatest work. It is men like Noah, Moses, Joseph, Gideon, and David who are hailed as men of faith and humility and who are noted as the heroes of the faith in Hebrews 11. They stood against the tide, were considered "weird" or not "normal," and, I'm sure, were asked, "Why can't you just get with the program and do what everyone else is doing?" But it was their willingness to choose God's ways over man's humanistic philosophies that made them men of faith and conviction.

Though it is still difficult to remain faithful to God's calling for true godly womanhood in a society which despises and disallows any sense of femininity, we must stand firm as the faithful saints of old once did, unflinching in the face of adversity. I challenge you to remain faithful, whether married or unmarried, to the call of servanthood.

Why is pleasing our parents so important to God?

Romans 13:1, 2 instructs, "Let every person be in subjection to the governing authorities. For there is no authority except from God, and those which exist are established by God. Therefore he who resists authority has opposed the ordinance of God; and they who have opposed will receive condemnation upon themselves."

God ordains authority to establish and maintain order in society. God has ordained authorities in churches, in the government, and in the home. These authorities actually have the responsibility to *represent God* and His laws and standards to those under them. When we try to resist this authority, we are resisting God. When we mock this authority, we mock God.

What are the consequences of not honoring our parents? How serious is this to God?

This warning in Deuteronomy 27:16 comes directly after, "Cursed is he who makes an idol": (Note: this is in the same font size and form as a blockquote, but should not be part of the blockquote),

> "Cursed be he that setteth light by his father or mother." (KJV)

> "Cursed is he who dishonors his father or mother." (NASB)

> "Cursed is the one who treats his father or his mother with contempt." (NKJV)

Setting light by your father or mother means mocking or making fun of them. It may seem innocent enough, but God places it on par with idol-making. To make fun of our parents invites the curse of God, and invokes His judgments on the rest of our lives. In short, if you belittle your parents, you are asking God to make your life miserable.

"The eye that mocks a father, that scorns obedience to a mother, will be pecked out by the ravens of the valley, will be eaten by the vultures." (Proverbs 30:17)

People like to set this verse aside, because they think it sounds too bizarre to be taken seriously. We don't believe this verse is talking about literal ravens and vultures, but it is certainly talking about a form of predator or scavenger. When a daughter rejects the instruction of her parents, she suddenly becomes prey for the predators of our generation—bad influences. Her parents' guidance is a shield from these bad influences as long as she takes it to heart, but once she rejects it, she becomes vulnerable prey to these predators. They come and peck her eyes out. By that we mean that they take away her spiritual eyesight. Suddenly she is blind and can't tell the difference between wisdom and folly. She'll wander around thinking she can see, but she'll keep stumbling and falling down, bringing trial after trial and judgment after judgment into her life.

There is an interesting connection between honoring parents and being able to see clearly. Proverbs 6:20-23 tells us that the instruction of our parents, which means even the restrictions they place on us, are a guide, a lamp and a light; and their discipline—their punishments for us when we disobey—are the way to life.

"If a man curses his father or mother, his lamp will be snuffed out in pitch darkness." (Proverbs 20:20)

When we reject their opinions, their restrictions, and their punishments, that lamp, that blessing that God gives us to guide us, is snuffed out, leaving us blind and unable to see that we are stumbling around, making a mess of our lives.

When she was young, our mother had a Christian friend who disregarded her father's instruction in making a very important decision, and it ruined that girl's life. For the past 25 years, she has had nothing but curses and judgments coming down upon her life. But in the same way that dishonoring our parents brings us a life of curses, honoring our parents brings us a life of blessings.

> "My son, if you accept my words and store up my commands within you…then you will understand the fear of the Lord and find the knowledge of God." (Proverbs 2:1, 5)

One of the most blessed families in the Bible was the family of Jonadab the Rechabite, in Jeremiah 35.

God commanded the prophet Jeremiah to go to the Rechabites, and offer them wine to drink. Jeremiah did so, but the Rechabites replied, "We will not drink wine, for Jonadab the son of Rechab, our father, commanded us, saying, "You shall not drink wine, you or your sons, forever." They said, "We have obeyed the voice of Jonadab the son of Rechab our father, in all that he commanded us, not to drink wine all our days, we, our wives, our sons, or our daughters…"

Verse 18: "Then Jeremiah said to the house of the Rechabites, 'Thus says the Lord of hosts, the God of Israel, "Because you have obeyed the command of Jonadab your father, kept all his commands, and done according to all that he commanded you; therefore thus says the Lord of hosts, the God of Israel, 'Jonadab the son of Rechab shall not lack a man to stand before me always.'"'"

Jonadab's commands were not purely moral or biblical commands; they were simply his personal instruction to his children and their descendants. Because of their strict obedience to his commands, God gave them one of the greatest blessings in the whole Bible: their line would last forever.

We would like to pose a question to our readers: *Is it well with you?* Consider this question carefully. "Well with you" doesn't mean you have everything you want. It means you have everything you need. It means having complete inner peace, joy, happiness, and the confidence of God's support in whatever you do. It means that even when things seem to be going badly for you, God comforts you and gives you grace. It means being spiritually happy.

> "Honor your father and your mother, as the Lord your God has commanded you, that your days may be prolonged, and that it may go well with you on the land which the Lord your God gives you." (Deuteronomy 5:16)

> "Honor your father and your mother, that your days may be prolonged in the land which the Lord your God gives you." (Exodus 20:12)

> "Children, obey your parents in the Lord, for this is right. Honor your father and mother, which is the first commandment with a promise: that it may be well with you and you may live long on the earth." (Ephesians 6:1-3)

When we honor our parents, God promises us His blessings on the rest of our lives. The fifth commandment promises that our years will be prolonged if we honor our parents. Actual physical length of life is mentioned in nearly every scriptural reference to the blessings of parental honor. And other things are promised. The book of Proverbs lists length of days and long life, spiritual peace, prosperity, happiness, wisdom and knowledge, honor and glory, spiritual safety, and success. God wants to bless His people with these things.

How do I honor my parents?

> "There is a generation that curseth their father, and doth not
> bless their mother." (Proverbs 30:11)

For girls like us who live in just such a generation, understanding
what actions are honoring or dishonoring can be difficult. Disrespect
has been redefined so that we can laugh at our parents under the
pretense of being affectionate and appreciative, not even realizing
just how confused we are. There *is* a biblical standard, though, which
needs to be rediscovered.

For a start, it's interesting to note that the above verse tells us
it's not only a sin to curse our fathers—it's a sin to "not bless" our
mothers! How often do you rise up and call your mother blessed,
like the children in Proverbs 31, saying, "Many daughters have done
nobly, but you excel them all"? To not do this for our mothers is
something very hideous to the Lord.

We are also commanded to obey our parents (Ephesians 6:1).
Obedience is more than outwardly obeying with a resentful,
grudging attitude. Obedience means inwardly obeying, from the
heart, with eagerness and cheerfulness. True obedience means
obeying even when it's hard. But obedience doesn't have to be
painful. When we have a deep, abiding inner reverence for our
parents and their wishes, it can become a joy to obey them with our
whole hearts. If we have a deep, abiding inner reverence for their
wisdom and instruction, we will actually seek out their guidance and
will consider their preferences as more important than our own. We
will go to our parents and ask them who it is they want us to spend
time with, and then obey them with all our hearts. We will ask them
what kind of clothes they want us to buy and what they want us to
look like, and we will follow their instruction wholeheartedly.

A saying that seems to have been long forgotten is, "Never keep secrets from your parents." If we want to have an honoring, obedient relationship with our parents, there is another thing we must do, aside from honoring and obeying. This is confiding—telling your parents everything. We know that we need to talk to God and tell God everything about us—including our difficulties, our troubles, our fears—in order to really know Him and have a good relationship with Him. If we want to obey our parents "as in the Lord," we should be aspiring to this kind of relationship with them.

We found a saying in an old book, *The King's Daughter*, which illustrates this point. "What is not fit for me to tell my mother is not fit for me to hear." We should follow the principle of not doing things or listening to things that we would be ashamed of if our parents could see us. That is true honor.

Ruth adds some insights:

There are several areas in which I have struggled with honoring my parents. I would like to briefly mention a few things that I have learned in some of these areas.

Ways in which I might honor my parents:

Obeying Immediately—My parents have a saying, "Slow obedience is no obedience." How true that is! Too many times I have taken my time responding to their call or doing as they have requested. This is not true obedience. If I am only "obeying" when I want to obey, I am not truly surrendering my will to theirs. To honor and obey them, I have learned that I must obey quickly with a submissive heart.

With a Joyful Heart—Recently I was reading Philippians 2, where it says, "…as ye have always obeyed, not as in my presence only, but now much more in my absence…do all things without murmurings and disputings: that ye may be blameless and harmless, the sons of God, without rebuke, in the midst of a crooked and perverse nation, among whom ye shine as lights in the world." It does not honor my parents when I murmur or complain about tasks that I have been given, nor does it honor Christ. As someone who desires to be a "light in the world," I seek to honor my parents and obey them cheerfully as unto the Lord. Colossians 3:17 has become one of my favorite verses and one that I often need to remember: "And whatsoever ye do in word or deed, do all in the name of the Lord Jesus, giving thanks to God and the Father by Him." And verse 23 says, "And whatsoever ye do, do it heartily, as to the Lord, and not unto men."

Honoring Them in Public—Many children are not being taught to speak respectfully to their parents. I find myself very disgusted when I hear a child demanding something of his parents, ignoring them, or being rebellious. I can imagine how embarrassed and heart-broken their parents must be! This has caused me to consider myself and how I speak of my own parents in the presence of others. Do I praise them? Or do I complain? What kind of testimony am I to them and to the Lord? In many ways we are, indeed, a testimony to them as parents, whether or not they have raised us in the nurture and admonition of the Lord. My mother has quoted 2 Corinthians 3:2 to us: "Ye are our epistle written in our hearts, known and read of all men"—for when others praise us, her children, they are often speaking of the way our parents have raised us, by God's grace, and we truly are a large part of our parents' reputation. When I obey them, praise them, and show righteous behavior, I am an honor to them.

Honoring Them in Private—In Ephesians 6:5-8 servants are told to be in obedience "to them that are your masters according to the flesh, with fear and trembling, in singleness of your heart, as unto

Christ; not with eyeservice, as menpleasers; but as the servants of Christ, doing the will of God from the heart; with good will doing service, as to the Lord, and not to men: knowing that whatsoever good thing any man doeth, the same shall he receive of the Lord, whether he be bond or free." This passage is very applicable to us, as well, as servants of Christ and one another. I am to do the will of God from the heart, not to please those who may be watching (although this may be an outworking of the service), but as unto the Lord, who is worthy of all of our praise. It is sometimes much easier to do a service in public where others might see and appreciate the deed, but we are told to serve as unto the Lord who sees all things. At home we have a tendency to grow indifferent, because we may get less attention for our accomplishments. I have learned that to honor the Lord and my parents, it is just as important, and even more so, to practice this at home where I can evaluate whether my motives are pure and if they are right. "Even a child is known by his doings, whether his work be pure, and whether it be right" Proverbs 20:11.

Giving Them My Heart—Sometimes honoring my father has been as simple as making something that he really enjoys or letting him know that I have confidence in him as the head of our family. My siblings and I enjoy making things that will please him—maybe fixing his favorite meals, encouraging him and standing beside him when he is standing alone, even simply praying for him. Proverbs 23:24-26 says, "The father of the righteous shall greatly rejoice: and he that begetteth a wise child shall have joy of him. Thy father and thy mother shall be glad, and she that bare thee shall rejoice. My son, give me thine heart, and let thine eyes observe my ways." My parents are delighted when their children do what is right, and it is a relief to them when they know that they have our hearts. We can seek to show this in many ways as we desire to honor and serve them.

Listening and Taking Interest—One way that I know I can honor my parents is by listening to them. Whether they are giving me instruction or counsel, reproving me, or telling me something of interest to them, I can honor them by showing interest in what they have to say. The book of Proverbs is full of verses which tell children to hear and keep the instruction of their parents. Proverbs 4:1 says, "Hear, ye children, the instruction of a father, and attend to know understanding." Proverbs 6:20 says, "My son, keep thy father's commandment, and forsake not the law of thy mother," and Proverbs 4:10 says, "Hear, O my son, and receive my sayings; and the years of thy life shall be many." Proverbs 15:5 even indicates that he who despises his father's correction is a fool. Thinking about these passages and many more has helped me to see ways in which I have dishonored my parents so that I may correct that and honor my parents better in the future.

I also want to be interested in the things they are interested in. I want to be a true helpmeet to my husband if I marry, and what an excellent opportunity I have to practice this with my own father! I also have the privilege of learning from my mother and being a servant to her. Lord willing, someday I will be a mother myself, and I will have not only benefited from these opportunities, but will, I hope, have honored my parents as I glean from their wisdom and help with their tasks. Eventually, I may be taking on the same responsibilities myself if I have the privilege of being a wife and mother—things such as running a household, training and teaching children, being the helpmeet to my husband—and I can glean much of this from my parents and meanwhile be a blessing to them.

Endeavoring to be Virtuous—This will honor my father and be a testimony to others. Just as it says in Proverbs 12:4 that "A virtuous woman is a crown to her husband" and that he can "safely trust in her" and "she will do him good and not evil all the days of her life" (Proverbs 31:11-12), so a faithful daughter will seek to do the same. One of the best examples I have had has been my own mother, who has honored both her own parents and her husband. I think of how she reverences her husband and realize that she is an excellent model to me of how I should honor my father and mother and how I desire to be a crown to my future husband some day as well.

I am very thankful to the Lord, Who, in His sovereignty, has given me a goodly heritage. Truly, "The glory of children are their fathers."

How can I be a good sister and build up my brothers and sisters?

As sad as this may sound, often the hardest people to get along with are our own family members. Think of the inter-familial relationships we see in the Bible: Cain and Abel, Jacob and Esau, Joseph and his brothers, David's sons…even if most of us haven't sold any little brothers into slavery in Egypt yet, it's clear that getting along all the time is something all siblings struggle with.

"Behold, how good and pleasant it is for brothers to dwell together in unity!" (Psalm 133:1)

It is likely that if we can learn to get along with our brothers and sisters, we can get along with anyone. Family life is where we practice Christian love and character.

Every time we are annoyed or provoked, God is testing us. We should learn to think of each trial as a moral test, which reveals where we really stand in our Christian walk. Do we pass our moral tests and refrain from exploding at our little brothers, or do we fail? These moral tests are an opportunity to mature in our godliness. We should be thankful for each one and make the most of it (James 1:2-4).

It is easy to think, when we are struggling, that the problems afflicting us are caused by the people around us, and that everything will be better when we get out of our families to get married. But our previous batting record will continue to haunt us, because the problems we really face are in our hearts. Until our hearts have changed, changing circumstances will do nothing for us. If we have trouble getting along with family members, it will be impossible for us to get along with our husbands.

But we need to do more than "get along." Jesus said, "A new commandment I give unto you, That ye love one another; as I have loved you, that ye also love one another. By this shall all men know that ye are my disciples, if ye have love one to another" (John 13:34, 35).

Is the way you treat the members of your family pleasing to God and edifying to the people around you? Family harmony is an important testimony, because people notice families, whether they are loving and harmonious, or hateful and quarrelsome. And daughters should take some of the responsibility for their family's shortcomings.

Always bear in mind that the behavior of just one person in a family can have a huge impact and influence on the whole mood of the family. When we're selfish and argumentative, the whole family is set back. It stops rising higher in godliness, and has to fight just to preserve its survival. Our time on earth is too short to spend in such a way, and this is why it is so important that we build each other up.

We need to think of increasing the standard of godliness in our homes as a kind of ministry. We can have an important role in the training of our siblings! We will never know how much influence we have, especially over the younger ones. We (the writers) are often horrified at how clearly our own shortcomings can be seen developing in our three younger brothers. They may not mean to imitate our failings, but we are the examples they see day after day. What kind of standard are we giving them?

Amy gives some practical advice on building relationships with very young siblings. (She has six under age eleven!)

Often we don't like the fact that we are copied in so many areas, but try to use it positively, and encourage them to be a godly example to their younger siblings. They will pick up on your attitudes towards your parents very quickly, so be careful to speak positively about your parents to them. Share with them your own struggles and victories, so they can pray for you and you for them. Be honest with them and they will be with you.

Do lots of special things with your brothers and sisters—they grow up fast and will remember what you did with them. You can have a far greater influence on them when they are your friends and enjoy being around you. Find out what they enjoy and join in sometimes! (Ask first of course.) My brother, 10, enjoys a good book, so I will often read him a chapter when he's in bed. This is a special time of one-on-one with him, and he often shares his heart with me and we can pray and talk about things together. The little girls love to dress up, and I often (though not as often as I used to or should!) dress up or just join in their imaginary game. Even pretending to order morning tea (Amy lives in New Zealand) via "McDonald's" in our kitchen, doesn't take much longer than a normal morning tea, but is special for them.

I am preaching to myself in all these things, but I have experienced the blessings of following these principles, as well as the consequences for not following them. May God bless you richly as you pour out your lives for your families, and thus for Him! "In as much as ye have done it unto the least of these my brethren, ye have done to me" (Matthew 25:40).

Let's move even further. How can we *actively* disciple our siblings?

When we all think of the family as a team and focus on building each other up and discipling and teaching each other the things we have learned, we aren't as tempted to squabble or fight for "our rights." Remember that your brothers and sisters will have an influence on society, whether for good or for evil. It would be a tragedy if you got married and moved away without making the most of your time with these developing people.

Our sisters provide a wonderful opportunity for us to put into practice the Titus 2 model of older women instructing the younger. If we can model all the characteristics described in the Bible to our sisters, it will be the most effective discipling we can ever do for them.

However, what we would like to focus on primarily is the relationships we have with our brothers. One of the greatest tragedies of our generation is the lack of godly men. It's easy for us, as women, to lament this lack and quickly point out the men's faults. We should really be asking ourselves just how much the failures of the men around us are a result of our failures as women. When men are weak and childish, refusing to grow up and take responsibility, it's often because they are afraid we or our society will resent them or shove them down. Being a man is not easy, and the way our generation glorifies feminism and mocks masculinity and fatherhood makes it even harder. Men, created as they were to need helpers, *need our help* in order to be *real* men.

We recently spoke at a Christian conference for girls. One of the other speakers was a psychologist who spent most of his session waving statistics which "prove" that girls are smarter than boys, more capable than boys, and more law-abiding than boys. He told us that boys flunk out of school, score low on IQ tests, and become criminals more often than girls. In fact, he said he couldn't really think of anything boys could do better than girls except commit suicide. He told us that boys are doing worse each generation, that their performance is plummeting, and he didn't know the reason. Basically, in trying to build the girls' "self-esteem," he was encouraging them to despise and belittle masculinity.

Though nothing can absolve boys from their individual responsibility before God to do right, we do believe that a society, and especially the influence of women, can assist in dragging men down by telling them from childhood that they're stupid, not good for anything but committing suicide, and that they belong in jail. And when girls mock and tease boys for being boys and having dumb "guy" traits, it makes boys ashamed of being boys and afraid to become men. In this respect, women are in large part responsible for the shortage of real men in our society.

Our society revels in dragging men down. If we have brothers, we need to remember that what they really are is men-in-development, who are having a fierce war waged against them. They are under constant assault from the media, re-written history books, psychological studies, political correctness, and many other weapons of the neo-Marxists. Our brothers need all the help and support they can get. They will grow up to be men, and God expects many things from men, such as maturity, responsibility, leadership, courage, and boldness. They will need to be the leaders, initiators, protectors, providers, prophets, priests, and kings to their wives and children. The way we treat our brothers can affect how they perceive masculinity, how they will view their wives, how they will treat their children, and what kind of stand they will take in our culture. Will we teach our brothers that they should get used to being bossed around by women, that their opinions don't matter, that their leadership is lousy and unwanted, that their protection is insulting and their presence is distasteful? Or do we teach them that they are created in God's image, to be the head, to have the love, help and support of women—ours first, and then their wives'? Do we teach them that we value their opinions, respect their leadership, and appreciate their protection? Do we help them become cultural leaders?

Kelly gives some advice:

Sisters, be a part of pointing your brother in a godly direction! Find ways you can help him! When it is appropriate, pull him aside and kindly whisper in his ear: "It's your job to open the door for these girls." Or say something that lets him know you care about the kind of man he becomes. After reading a book about someone, or even meeting someone, of godly character, point out to your brother specific characteristics that you find in this person.

I've often said things like the following to my brother, David: "Someday you can be a godly protector for your wife and children. If you practice now by being a protector to your sisters, you will be better able to do it when you are older!" You would not believe the support they feel from encouraging words like these. It means more than they know how to express in words that you take seriously their call as a man! It may not always be easy to find the time to do things like this, but be willing to go out of your way to find ways to encourage them. Find the time. You'll be glad you did.

Encourage in your brother a love for purity and grace. Give him such a love for the purity and grace that he sees in you that he has no desire for the "qualities" that our world offers. Keep in mind that the qualities he finds in you will be qualities he looks for someday in choosing a wife! If that fact doesn't make you rethink the kind of life you may be living, my dear sisters, your heart needs to be made right. Maybe there needs to be a time of repentance and confession before the Lord. This is important! It is serious! The way our lives are lived affects more than just us. The choices we make will forever affect the people in our lives. We shouldn't allow ourselves to be selfish. We can't afford to be.

One of the wonderful things about all of this is that not only are we encouraging, preparing, building up, and inspiring our brothers, but our own walk with the Lord will mature as well. Use this time to learn how to raise the sons you may have someday! Understand that there will be a need for you to do many of the same things for your husband, also! If you can learn now how to gently encourage and how to point in the right direction by your example, you will find it much easier later when you have a family of your own. If you were to remember only one thing from all that I have said, I would hope it would be this: We must understand that our time at home, as sisters and as daughters, is our training ground for becoming mothers and helpmeets for our husbands. It is so important that we not waste this season in our lives, because this season will affect us forever.

What hope for this kind of family reformation is there for girls who have no families at all?

For girls who either have no families or who have been rejected by their families, there is still plenty of hope. If you are one of those girls, it would be wise for you to seek out an alternate authority figure (we talked about this in more detail in Chapter Five) or, ideally, an entire alternate family that would take you in.

Whatever your situation is now, develop a vision for how you want your future family to be, and *do not compromise*. Resolve to give your daughters the opportunities you didn't have. Marry a man who will be to your daughters the kind of father you would have wanted. Be the kind of mother who can set an example to her daughters of what a real woman looks like. Resolve to establish a family that will be a "self-sufficient, fully functioning, economically viable agent for the dominion of God." If you are serious about reconstructing a biblical society, rediscovering biblical truths, and reestablishing a biblical model for the family, you cannot afford to make a careless decision. We young women must take this culture for Christ by rebuilding the biblical family—starting with our own.

CHAPTER FOURTEEN

FATHERS, DAUGHTERS, AND MARRIAGE

PREPARATION FOR A LIFE-LONG MINISTRY

Should I be thinking about marriage at all?

A surprising number of Christian young women and their fathers view marriage as a "detour" from Christian work and a "distraction" from serving God. We know many young women who have made commitments to stay unmarried until their late twenties, so that they can "serve God" until then. Nevertheless, most of these people recognize that eventual marriage is God's plan for their lives. Because they don't understand the original purpose of marriage, they see it as incompatible with Christian ministry and deduce that it must be a necessary evil.

This sort of thinking leads to the idea that thoughts and plans concerning marriage should be avoided until marriage inescapably smacks you in the face, because if you have to stop serving God once you're married, then you certainly don't want to waste one second thinking about or planning for it until it's too late to get away from it.

This is corrupted, pseudo-Christian thinking. God created marriage, but He didn't create it as an excuse for people to lay aside service to Him. Marriage is not about planning big weddings or playing house or just finding companionship. What did God create marriage to be?

> "So God created man in His own image, in the image of God created He him; male and female created He them. And God blessed them, and God said unto them, *Be fruitful, and multiply*, and *replenish the earth*, and *subdue* it: and *have dominion* over the fish of the sea, and over the fowl of the air, and over every living thing that moveth upon the earth." (Genesis 1:27, 28, emphases added)

Marriage is about dominion. It's about filling the earth and subduing it. Marriage is about two people of different abilities and roles becoming one flesh, sharing one life and one vision, so that the two will complement each other and complete each other. It's about restoring the rib to the side of the man so that the two are whole, finished, fulfilled. Only when they are united can the two represent the image and glory of God together. As a unit, the husband and wife can be *fully* effective, working together in a specially ordained dynamic life purpose—establishing the kingdom on God's terms for God's glory. Marriage isn't where your ministry stops so that you can play house and play family. Marriage is where your new ministry starts, where you become, in a sense, the queen of a little kingdom where you rule with your husband as God's vice-gerents,[1] working together extending the kingdom, subduing the earth, properly managing its resources, and discipling the nations.

---

1 This very important word and concept has almost been lost in the mists of antiquity, but deserves to be revived. A vice-gerent is someone who is to stand in the place of another authority with a specific purpose. Christians are God's vice-gerents on earth: "The heaven, even the heavens, are the Lord's: but the earth hath He given to the children of men." (Psalm 115:16).

"And Adam said, 'This is now bone of my bones, and flesh of my flesh: she shall be called Woman, because she was taken out of Man.' Therefore shall a man leave his father and his mother, and shall cleave unto his wife: and they shall be one flesh." (Genesis 2:23,24)

God created the man and the woman to be together. Together, they are an earthly image, a constant reminder, of the union of Christ and His Church, and will obey God's command to raise up godly seed (Malachi 2:15). When God created humankind, He created them male and female, and then and there established the institution of male-female lifelong unions and multi-generational dynasties. This is the heart of society. This is the heart of the Dominion Mandate. This is the heart of marriage as God created it.

I would love to get married and have children, but isn't it wrong to think about it too much?

Girls have told us that thinking about marriage encourages infatuation, daydreaming, broken hearts, and wasted time. But when we talk about planning for marriage, we don't mean fantasizing about our future weddings or future husbands. We're speaking of a mindset and the actions that go with it. Parents should help prepare their daughters for marriage to worthy husbands by helping them become worthy brides. Of the girls we know, the ones who have the mindset that God has ordained a husband for them spend far less time "thinking about boys" than the girls who aren't giving marriage a thought. Even if marriage doesn't appear to be on the horizon for you, your attitude toward it will affect your life now—whether you're five, fifteen, twenty-five, or thirty-five. We need to be thinking about and preparing for marriage. It's far too important for us to neglect. We read in Lamentations 1:9, "She has not considered her future; therefore, she has fallen astonishingly."[2]

Is remaining unmarried a legitimate choice?

The unmarried apostle Paul wrote, "For I would that all men were even as I myself. But every man hath his proper gift of God, one after this manner, and another after that" (1 Corinthians 7:7).

We also read in Matthew 19:10-12 that Jesus's disciples said to Him, " 'If the case of the man be so with his wife, it is not good to marry.' But He said unto them, 'All men cannot receive this saying, save they to whom it is given. For there are some eunuchs, which were so born from their mother's womb: and there are some eunuchs, which were made eunuchs of men: and there be eunuchs, which have made themselves eunuchs for the kingdom of heaven's sake. He that is able to receive it, let him receive it.' "

"Singleness" is a very important state. It is a calling God bestows for an important reason. However, it seems from what we've read in the Bible that it is a calling God bestows only on a very few people. The apostle Paul himself says, "Do we not have a right to take along a believing wife, even as the rest of the apostles, and the brothers of the Lord, and Cephas? Or do only Barnabas and I not have a right to refrain from working?" (1 Corinthians 9:5, 6) implying that he and Barnabas were the only apostles who had been called to remain unmarried. Second, it's important to note (from the verses above) that singleness is a *gift* or a *calling*, not a lifestyle option.

How does a girl know if she has the gift of singleness? Well, the truth is that we don't know. We wish we did because girls ask us

2   This verse taken from the New American Standard Bible ©1960, 1963, 1968, 1971, 1972, 1973, 1975, 1977, 1995 by The Lockman Foundation. Used by permission.

about this. We would like to imagine that if a girl has the desire to marry, she doesn't have the gift of singleness, and God will give her a husband. But it doesn't always work this way. We cannot make up our own theology based on our own imaginings.

In 1 Corinthians 7:26, Paul writes, "I suppose therefore that this is good for the present distress, I say, that it is good for a man so to be." (Literally, it is good for a man to remain as he is.) Some theologians believe he's referring to a specific crisis occurring during his times—the barbarous persecution of Christians under the Roman Empire. During such distress—when Christian men and women were in constant danger of being arrested and thrown to the lions, being scattered in persecutions and dispersions—marriage would have been, temporarily, extremely difficult. We also are living in a time of great distress, but the greatest crises facing us are very different from the afflictions of the Christians in Rome: the feminization of men and the masculinization of women; the mass murder of unborn children all over the world; and the systematic destruction of the biblical family.

It's important to understand this about our society. We read in 1 Chronicles 12:32 that the children of Issachar "were men that had understanding of the times, to know what Israel ought to do." Because they understood the times, they were able to make intelligent and successful strategies. When we understand the defining crises of our generation, we can think in terms of a comprehensive battle plan for reformation. And because one of the greatest needs of our generation is the rebuilding of the biblical family, one family at a time, it is vital that those who are called to marry do so, making wise choices in terms of spouses.

Marriage is and always has been the norm, though there are the exceptional few who are given the gift of singleness. Marriage is central to the first part of the Dominion Mandate: to be fruitful and multiply. We do not mean to undervalue the gift of singleness to those young women who have truly been blessed with it, but we do want to emphasize that we young women should not "choose" to take a gift which has not been offered, and in so doing, miss out on a great blessing God has been preparing for us.

CHAPTER FIFTEEN

FATHERS, DAUGHTERS, AND PURITY

A FATHER, THE GUARDIAN OF A MAIDEN'S HEART

How pure do I have to be before marriage?

Many teenaged girls have asked us, "How far is too far?" or "What is permissible?" when it comes to relating to young men they are not married to. But again, the question we should all ask is not, "What can we get away with?" but instead, "What standard of purity does God require?" If you think God's standard for purity is lax and loose, you're wrong. God's standard is this:

> "Husbands, love your wives, just as Christ loved the church and gave Himself up for her; that He might sanctify her, having cleansed her by the washing of water with the word, that He might present to Himself the church in all her glory, *having no spot or wrinkle or any such thing;* but that she should be *holy and blameless.*" (Ephesians 5:25-27, emphases added)

Because our future marriages represent the marriage of Christ to the Church, this means that as young women *we symbolize the Bride of Christ!* So the minimum requirement is this: that we have no spot or wrinkle or any such thing, but that we be holy and blameless. This is our standard.

How pure does the Church of Christ have to be? Christ's Church must be completely faithful to Him, completely devoted to Him, and should not allow herself to be courted by any false prophets who would try to steal her away. The Church of Christ should have no impure thoughts about being joined with anyone but Christ, or being joined with any ideas or theology aside from Christ's.

When Paul wrote to the church at Corinth, he said, "…for I betrothed you to one husband, that to Christ I might present you as a pure virgin" (2 Corinthians 11:2). The Church of Christ has to be pure, because she belongs to *one* Husband, and on the day that she is joined with Him, she must be able to present herself untarnished, unblemished, and saved exclusively for Him.

Like Christ's Church, a pure bride would be completely faithful to her own husband, both before and after marriage. Because we are supposed to be doing our husbands good and not evil *all* the days of our lives (Proverbs 31:12), one way we can do this is by letting our bodies, minds, emotions, and affections be devoted to our future husbands *before* marriage so that on the day we walk up the aisle to be joined with them, we are truly presenting ourselves to them "in all [our] glory, having no spot or wrinkle or any such thing; but…holy and blameless." Physical purity is an absolutely clear requirement of God's will for our lives.

Do we need to be more than physically pure?

God demands physical purity as a fundamental requirement of holiness. But His standard goes much further than this. To men, Christ said, "Whosoever looketh on a woman to lust after her hath committed adultery with her already in his heart" (Matthew 5:28). God demands purity of heart and mind also. Our hearts, like our bodies, must be saved exclusively for *one* man.

One girl asked us recently if it was wrong to have a crush on a boy, because the way she saw it, a girl can't control whether she has a crush or not. Our answer: your heart belongs to your future husband. To give it casually to someone else could be emotionally careless or impure. Unfortunately, this is easy to do, because God created males and females to be attractive to one another. This is why Proverbs 4:23 says, "Keep thy heart with all diligence; for out of it are the issues of life." It's not easy! It takes *active vigilance*. The definition of vigilance is, "Watchfully; with attention to danger and the means of safety."[1]

A girl can't necessarily help being *attracted* to a boy, or *tempted* to be infatuated, but she *can* help giving in to that temptation. Infatuation is an emotional state that involves giving free reign to our heart's imaginings and indulging in those fantasies. The real question is, "Can we resist our emotions, or do our emotions control us?" For some people, it *is* impossible to avoid having "crushes," because they let themselves be controlled by their emotions instead of godly discipline.

Our hearts are hard to control and guard, and at first it may seem impossible, but we can take strength in the verse, "I can do all things through Christ which strengtheneth me" (Philippians 4:13).

---

1   *Webster's 1828 Dictionary.*

If we strive to guard our hearts, even when it's seemingly impossible, God will reward our efforts. To think that God can't be in control in matters like these is to deny that He is all-powerful.

How can I stay pure?

Because girls have naturally vulnerable, easily-led hearts, keeping them totally pure and spotless and reserved for our future husbands is a gargantuan task. This is where our guardians and knights in shining armor come in! Our fathers are here to protect us—our hearts, souls, bodies, minds—they are to fight to defend the virtue of them all.

We should be so thankful when our fathers take an interest in our minds and souls to protect us. We should welcome the barriers they put up around certain books, magazines, movies, or even certain people. Rather than ever resent these protective measures as being "too strict," we need to recognize that our fathers do this to help preserve our purity, which we should be fighting to preserve ourselves.

One helpful restraint to keep our hearts from wanting to chase after relationships with young men is a strong, confiding relationship with our parents, and especially our fathers. In many cases we've heard of, a daughter's road to compromised purity (of many kinds) starts when she keeps a secret from her parents. This could be in the form of a secret correspondence or friendship, or even a secret interest in or infatuation with someone. One of our friends recently told us that when she finds herself thinking too much about a certain young man, she goes to her father and shares her heart with him, asking him to pray for her. She told us it's amazing what this has done for her relationship with her father, and also for protecting her heart.

A father can meet many of his daughter's natural desires for masculine love and companionship by giving his daughter the proper kinds of attention and affection. A daughter who has such a strong, loving relationship with her father will be far less likely to become entangled with young men. As many of our young heroines have put it, they keep their hearts pure by "entrusting them to their fathers," trusting their fathers to keep and guard and nurture their hearts until the time comes for their hearts to be given to their husbands. There is nothing mystical or super-spiritual about this. It's simple heart-management. To summarize, it should be repeated that we must first give our hearts to our Lord, and love Him with all our heart, soul, mind, and strength. This is primary. We shouldn't give our hearts to our husbands in the same way. And when we entrust affairs of our hearts to our fathers, we shouldn't give them our hearts in the same way we do to the Lord or our husbands—rather, we turn our hearts warmly to our father's instruction, involving him sensibly and closely in the safekeeping of our emotions.

But what if my father is neither affectionate nor attentive?

Talk patiently with your father. Work patiently to establish a relationship with him. From that relationship you may discover that he has resources of affection and attention he never showed you. If he never responds, don't make the mistake of leaning on a young man prematurely to provide what you think you need. Ask the Lord to give you the grace to wait until a good husband can be the one who loves you and generously wraps his protection and care around you. Remember during this time that the primary lover of your soul is the Lord Himself, and as you lean steadfastly on His faithfulness, you will always draw comfort from Him, before and after marriage.

How should a girl relate to young men?

It can help to keep an eternal perspective. God speaks about knowing individuals long before they are born.[2] He talks about planning kindnesses and blessings for them long before they are born, arranging their atonement and planning every one of their days, and even the good works they will do.[3] If He is this intimate with His children, he must take special joy in placing two *specific* parents together to bring these specific, eternal children into the world. What has God planned for your children? What husband does he have in mind to use as His instrument to bring these children into existence?

It's a mystery to us how God puts husbands together with wives. But His intentions should make us serious and cautious about those men we get close to.

Because God's plan is better than ours, and because He is sovereign, we don't have to be searching for husbands, worrying about being pretty enough or charming enough to attract one, or fretting over the prospect of dying old maids. He is in control! He knows what He is doing! " 'For I know the plans that I have for you,' declares the Lord, 'plans for welfare and not for calamity, to give you a future and a hope.' " (Jeremiah 29:11)[4]

When in the presence of young men, we should act as though *our husbands* might be in the room watching us. We should pray that no young men ever rob us of feelings we are saving for our husbands, and in the same way, we *must not* defraud other young men of what

---

2   Isaiah 46:9-12, Isaiah 48:5, Jeremiah 1:5, Psalm 139.

3   Ephesians 2:10; Ephesians 1:4, 5; 2 Thessalonians. 2:13; 1 Peter 1.

4   This verse taken from the New American Standard Bible © 1960, 1963, 1968, 1971, 1972, 1973, 1975, 1977, 1995 by The Lockman Foundation. Used by permission.

belongs to their wives, because God has chosen wives for them, too. It is almost as though they are already married, and this fact should affect the way we treat them, so that they will think of us "as sisters, with all purity" (1 Timothy 5:2).

John W. Thompson explains his views on why dating makes this difficult:

> Dating, even Christian dating, generally results in a series of emotional attachments or bonds with different dating partners. To express this in the language of romance, a young woman gives a piece of her heart to a young man when she becomes emotionally involved with him. By the time she meets the man she will marry, she will have only a fragment of her heart left to give. Even without going out on a date, a young woman can give pieces of her heart to several young men during her youth, so that by the time she marries, she is no longer a one-man woman (1 Tim. 5:9). Yet Paul's analogy of Christ and the Church in 2 Corinthians 11:2-3 explains that a pure maiden saves her love for one man only, not just physically but emotionally too. The goal is not just physical purity but emotional purity—only one romance for life![5]

This is why dating and putting ourselves in other romance-stimulating environments can never be an option for us. The real problem with dating isn't in the procedure, however people may define it. The real problem with dating is the philosophy behind it—as John W. Thompson calls it, the "dating spirit."

The dating spirit springs from the philosophy that we have to be romantically attractive and romantically available to a lot of men, and that they should be equally attractive and available to us, so that

---

[5] "God's Design for Scriptural Romance, Part II; Dealing With the Dating Dilemma," by John W. Thompson at www.patriarch.com.

we can "try each other out" and get emotional thrills out of each other's company. People with the dating spirit believe that romance is worth pursuing just for the fun of it, and that we can get out of any relationship as soon as it doesn't meet our wants, needs, and desires, or just becomes boring. The dating mindset is that we should get into relationships looking for romance instead of commitment.

Men with the dating spirit, regardless of whether or not they have made commitments not to "date," are interested in pleasure rather than purpose. They are looking for an emotional thrill on their own terms, rather than seeking wives and helpmeets who could be compatible life partners for them. Women with the dating spirit are looking for love, affection, protection, and assurance that they are attractive and desirable, outside of marriage. To sum up, the dating spirit seeks to please self rather than to please God, and pursues present pleasure rather than future blessings.

Disregarding God's principles always has its consequences, and Mr. Thompson explains that young men and women who indulge in the dating spirit suffer from hearts wounded by emotional scars, bitterness, and insecurity; consciences generally defiled and seared by impurity; and future marriages troubled by past emotional bonds, unrealistic standards of comparison, and appetite for variety and change.

Are these views about dating all just a bunch of rules and restrictions to get in the way of "innocent," girlish fun? No. God wants us to be happy, and He wants our marriages to be blessed. There are many reasons why He wants the relationship between you and your one and only to be untainted, pure, and beautiful.[6]

---

6   In talking candidly with older couples, those who entered marriage in purity continue to learn, year after year, about the associated blessings of a pure start. Couples who started their marriages on a compromised foundation learn many of the same lessons from a regretful perspective. God can heal scars masterfully, but

Can a girl whose purity has been compromised become pure again?

You may wish to earmark this answer and refer to it, or refer others to it, often. We hold up a high standard of purity in this book. It may frustrate some readers because, well, we live in such an impure world and we know it has rubbed off on us. We're embarrassed by that fact. We have reason to be ashamed of what we see around us. Every one of us has been defiled in some way by the crooked and perverse generation we were born into. None of us is as pure, mentally, as we could be or should be. Some girls who read this have had their physical purity compromised, either by their own foolishness or against their will. Our corrupt and predatory culture is a very unsafe place for the gentler sex, and the Lord Jesus Christ knows our predicament very well.

What did Jesus tell the woman taken in adultery? "Go your way, and sin no more." The same love that was extended to her has been extended to us by the same Savior. The forgiveness offered to us in Christ motivates us to pursue sanctification. This means we become set apart from our ugly culture and from what we once were, by the Lord's grace.

He knows we are not as righteous as He is. He knows we have reason for shame, so He gives us His righteousness so He can accept us as righteous and look at us as completely pure as He is. This is the essence of forgiveness in Christ, which makes us clean in God's sight. We need to learn to delight in this forgiveness.[7] It would be insulting to our Savior for us to morbidly sulk about our former impurity. We have been purified by Christ.

---

the consistent message from older couples is this: Build your relationship the Lord's way from the beginning.

7   The Apostle John tells us, "If we confess our sins, He is faithful and just to forgive us our sins, and to cleanse us from all unrighteousness" (1 John 1:9).

Think about your future, ladies, not your past. We have so much to look forward to thanks to the forgiveness given to us because of what of Jesus Christ did for us on the cross. He has replaced our impurity with His righteousness so that we can live forever in a place of no impurity. When we die we will be raised up in glory and recognized as beloved of our Father, *openly acknowledged as having no impurity.* We should live every day in the comforting assurance of this position and in a way that honors the Savior who bled and died to exalt us to such a place.

Once you understand your forgiveness in Christ, you will be able to think and act like a pure woman, and your future husband will be able to truly see you as such.

CHAPTER SIXTEEN

FATHERS, DAUGHTERS, AND SUITORS

THE GREATEST GIFT A FATHER WILL EVER GIVE AWAY

*If dating is unwise, then how should
we get to know possible spouses?*

John W. Thompson has examined this biblically:

> How did Christ betroth Himself to His bride? First, the
> Heavenly Father and Son together chose the bride (Ephesians.
> 1:4; Jn. 15:16). The Son was then sent to seek His bride (Luke
> 19:10). During this time He was in continuous communication
> with and submission to His Father (John. 5:30). At the time of
> betrothal, Christ paid the greatest bride price in history, His own
> precious blood (1 Peter 1:18-19). The bride (the church) has the
> choice to accept or reject the groom's offer of marriage (John
> 3:36). During betrothal the groom (Christ) is demonstrating
> His love for us through words, acts and gifts, and we grow
> to know and love Him more and more each day (Ephesians
> 3:17-19). Christ's love for His betrothed is a secure, permanent

relationship, unlike dating around (Hebrews. 13:5; Romans 8:37-39). During betrothal we cannot touch Him, but after He comes for us in marriage, we will (John 14:2-3). After our processional to heaven, our marriage to Christ will be celebrated with a great wedding feast (Revelation 19:7-9).[1]

A new movement is sweeping America and other Western nations. Or, rather, it is not *new* but is instead the *rediscovery* of family-centered marriage customs. There was no formal name for the practice, but it is widely becoming known today as "courtship." Even today there is no official definition for "courting," but the young people who prefer this practice to dating are creating a kind of movement with the following elements.

In a nutshell, the concept behind courtship is that marriage is important and permanent, and that making a good match requires discernment. Finding a mate should therefore be about purpose and not infatuation. Courtship is about working in submission to God to make a permanent marriage between two people God has prepared for each other for a special mission. Courtship means having a righteous standard and honorable intentions in every relationship, and not pursuing any romantic relationship with any person until, in God's good time, the bride and groom are both spiritually and practically ready for marriage and ready to covenant together.

Courtship means understanding that romantic attraction can be disorienting, and that serious couples need objectivity and third-party counsel to make such an important decision as marriage. Thus courtship means leaning on the guidance of your father and mother

---

1 "God's Design for Scriptural Romance, Part I; Number I: Rediscovering the Timeless Truths," by John W. Thompson at www.patriarch.com.

and heavenly Father to help you evaluate the suitors who take an interest in you.

Young couples committed to courtship don't want to pursue a relationship isolated from their families and the real world. In the dating environment, there can be a lot of posturing, showing off, and flirtatious manipulation of the other person's opinion—and even the other person's emotions. A courtship environment is usually in secure proximity to family and friends, in a real-world setting of real people who know all the real strengths and weaknesses of the two people who want real answers, not fairy tale fantasies. Those committed to courtship want to get to know potential spouses who want the truth. That truth is usually most evident in settings with minimum emotional dizziness and maximum input from the people who know both parties best.

But does courtship really work?

It has worked gloriously with many families and couples we know. These families approached it with the right heart attitude and perspective and kept the main end in view. It has even worked with girls whose immediate families refused to be involved, because the girls followed the principles of finding mature input and protection from other sources. We've heard a very few stories involving families who tried so hard to follow an arbitrary, complex courtship formula that things didn't go very smoothly, but it still worked better than the dating alternative.

How can I make courtship a possibility for my life?

Get your parents involved in your life and let them know what you're thinking about marriage, dating, and courtship.

But won't my parents think courtship is totally weird?

It's true the dating culture has taken over the West. But give your parents credit for warming to wisdom when they see it. To introduce your parents to courtship, start by showing your parents genuine interest in their advice. You're not asking them to "arrange" a marriage for you while you wait on the sidelines. You're asking them to share your life's greatest challenge with you as you cautiously work through it.

Before marriage, a woman is under the authority of her parents. A father has the authority to give his daughter in marriage (1 Corinthians 7:36-38). When a father gives his daughter in marriage, he is transferring his authority to another man. Most fathers either don't understand or are afraid of the magnitude of this responsibility, and it may be your task as a daughter to introduce these new ideas to him, slowly and respectfully. Make it clear how much you value his wishes and opinions.

Talking to your parents extensively about many things will be very important. Before a young woman can really enter into courtship, she needs to have a high level of communication and understanding with her parents. During courtship, they will be her advisors and confidantes more than ever, and it's important that they have the same goals and vision.

But if both sets of parents get involved, couldn't that be a real mess, especially if they don't totally agree on what courtship is?

Yes, it could make things complicated. This is why we don't define courtship as a formula with a set number of complicated rules. We try to emphasize the simplicity of the concept. Courtship is about discernment. It's about helping a young couple discover the truth about each other and each other's families before they make a permanent decision. It's about a young couple being mature enough to know they need some outside counsel when it comes to marriage.

Where is a good place to start with my parents?

At some point you will need to *establish a standard* with your parents of the character qualities you are looking for in a possible husband. What father would not want to add a few things to such a list? We recently sat down with our father to figure out the most basic essentials for any man to possess in order to be a candidate for either of us. Here is what we came up with:

Foremost, of course, the man must be regenerated.

Many Christians understand this requirement as the first. But few fathers know how to help their daughters determine if a young man is really a Christian. Lots of young men know how to talk the talk and look the part. Having "prayed a prayer" or "walked an aisle" does not make one a Christian. We know many young married women who have been shocked to discover their "Christian" beaux to be impostors—but only after the wedding. One groom was a leader of campus Bible studies for a parachurch organization.[2] Another groom was a superstar international preacher. Both turned out to be liars and outlaws. One of them is going to jail, if he doesn't die of AIDS first.

Where were the two dads before the weddings? Well, one father pleaded with his daughter not to marry the suitor, but she did anyway; the other father didn't think it was his place to get involved. He didn't warn his daughter even though he may have seen a few red flags. His silence was thus a careless endorsement of the "Christian"

---

2   A parachurch organization is a Christian group involved in outreach and discipleship but without scriptural church government.

leader. The following 23 "preferences" of ours may be of help to both girls and their fathers to discern the character of interested suitors.

He must be a mature Christian, who consistently demonstrates the fruit of the spirit.

Fake Christians can't consistently demonstrate the fruit of the spirit as it is described in Galatians 5 (love, joy, peace, patience, kindness, goodness, faithfulness, gentleness, and self-control).

He must be the kind of man whom I can respect and joyfully submit to.

In order for our marriage to be the most successful and productive, I must marry a man that I can entrust with the rest of my life. He will become my life's work. I intend to devote myself to the man I marry, obeying him in everything. I intend to devote my energies to building this man up and making him the best warrior for Christ that he can be.

He should have a vision for ministry to which I can devote my life.

This does not mean that the suitor will know exactly what he'll be doing for the rest of his life, but he will have a general understanding about the ways he can best serve God which is compatible with my understanding of how the kingdom of God is to be built. As co-laborers, husbands and wives must share a vision and work toward the same goal, in order to be the most productive for the kingdom of God. We've seen many husbands and wives with good intentions and good hearts, who have separately devoted themselves to individual ministries and aspired to different goals. Though they have in essence become "one flesh," they have different life-works. There will always be a limit to how much fruit their ministries can bear.

He will love God with all his heart, soul, mind, and strength.

There will be nothing that is more important to him than serving God. He will hate what is evil and love what is good. There will be no aspect of his character that contradicts what he professes. He won't be addicted to anything but kingdom business and will put no vile thing before his eyes. He won't be devoted to any particular TV show, comic strip, computer game, book, movie, hobby or even his job more than his family or his duties as Christ's ambassador.

He should love me, just as Christ loved the Church and gave Himself for her, but I want him to love Christ more than he does me.

He should treat me with honor and respect but should not be afraid to be the active head of the family.

I'm really looking for a man who is not afraid to lead in a strong, masculine way. I'll know a lot about this by the way he leads others spiritually within his current sphere of influence.

He should be respectful and considerate of all women in general.

He should be a protective, loving father to our children and will want as many as God is pleased to give us.

He should be a leader and not a follower and will speak out boldly for what is right.

So many men these days are happy to go with the flow and are afraid to do anything that might stand out or contradict what others are doing. They are consumed by the fear of man, afraid to be above average or high achievers. My husband should be a hero, a man of valor. He will want to do the most he can do for the kingdom of God, regardless of how anyone might think of him. Whatever he does, he will do it with all his heart and excel at it. He will have the mindset to do everything as if he is doing it for the Lord.

He should be devoted to prayer.

He should be habitually eager to learn from Scripture, to be challenged by Scripture, and to seek God through Scripture.

He will delight in meditating on God's Law, as King David did.

He should have a solid Christian worldview and the moral clarity and moral courage that go with it.

He will have the discernment to recognize the traditions of men, the elementary principles of the world, bad philosophy, and empty deception. He will not be taken captive by false doctrines but will consult Scripture before forming doctrinal judgments.

He should be able to understand and evaluate historical and current affairs with a thoroughly biblical perspective.

I want to marry someone who understands his times and times past. This could cover everything from politics to church history to economics. He should be able to look at a new bill being proposed and know what to think about it, or evaluate whether the cause of a war is biblical and just, or know whether an institution is going to advance or hinder the kingdom.

He should seek the companionship of wise men and limit his association with lesser men.

"Be not deceived: evil communications corrupt good manners" (1 Corinthians 15:33).

"He that walketh with wise men shall be wise: but a companion of fools shall be destroyed" (Proverbs 13:20).

He should be respected and esteemed wherever he goes—his character should be irreproachable.

If he is a courageous, righteous, non-compromising Christian, he will have enemies, but though they may plot against him, they won't be able to find fault with his character. In his manners and behavior it will be obvious that he is a representative of God.

He should be teachable and able to teach with humility.

He will be able to speak with authority and confidence. However, he will welcome correction and be willing to admit when he is wrong.

He should be well-educated in the right ways and for the right reasons, and will not place undue value on the world's academic credentials.

He will recognize that a godly education must be purpose-driven and practical, and he will not pursue academic achievement merely for the sake of worldly esteem. He should have an appreciation of history.

He should have a vision for his family that is multi-generational.

He will be thinking down a long track. Unlike many young men, the extent of his vision will go beyond "what I'm gonna do this weekend"—he will recognize that every decision he makes now will have consequences generations and centuries down the line. He will know that children are a blessing and will want a whole "quiver full" of them. Training them to be godly Christian warriors will be his primary work.

He should be able to fit in comfortably with my family and have a respectful relationship with my father.

If he doesn't fit in with my family, he probably won't be compatible with me either (this may not be the case for every girl, though). The more he likes and respects my dad, the more able I will be to respect him.

He should be a good steward of all that God has given him (e. g., time, money, spiritual gifts).

He will recognize that everything he has is God's. As a good steward, he will, for example, invest his time in worthy causes (1 Corinthians 3:10-15). He will make use of his God-given abilities and assets (Matthew 25:14-29). He doesn't have to be rich by any means, but he should demonstrate sound fiscal sense and business acumen. However, he will not be materialistic or a servant of Mammon.

He will have a respect for God-given authority.

He will be very respectful, especially to his parents, and consequently, it will be "well with him."

Of course, we understand that a perfect person does not exist in the world. As our final item, he will be aware of his faults and will have the humility to overcome them by God's grace.

The most important qualities to look for in a husband would be that he loves God more than anything and is humble and teachable. If a man had this, and not just the appearance of this, and was striving above all to become more Christ-like, it wouldn't really matter if he was a young work-in-progress. The best men are and always will be. We will all marry men who are works-in-progress. He might need the help of a really understanding wife to bring him to the level of the man described above, but not by cajoling. By her love and enthusiastic support, she could help him. In developing our standards, we need to keep foremost in our minds that our own character will need to grow in order for us to become worthy partners of such good men.

Are there really any young men out there who are even remotely close to your list?

Yes, we know of some, and we have some friends who have married some of them.

If a standard such as the one above is a topic of conversation between fathers and daughters, it becomes clear that both father and daughter would need to know a lot about any suitor in order to know if his character was genuine or artificial. The dad needs to know a lot about the suitor's heart before courtship can be authorized by the dad, and the daughter needs to take the opportunity during courtship to find out anything her father didn't.

What exactly is the courtship process?

There isn't an "exact" process, and we hope people won't take the following paragraphs and insist that they represent the true formula, because they don't. We'll try to describe some very general stages we have observed in some sensible relationships. These stages served both families very well.

Because there are no "official" customs, courtship works differently for every couple. Every family must determine its own standards and rules of conduct. Every family can establish its own preferred customs, which can be used by future generations. The four basic stages we have observed were followed by families who were novices at courtship. The process was sort of experimental but based on biblical principles. It's important to note that, during each stage, the relationship between the young man and young woman was clearly defined. There was no anxious speculating, "Does he love me? Does he love me not? What are his intentions toward me?" The whole process was honest, open, and progressive.

In an ideal courtship, the first stage appears to be *friendship*. Before there are any thoughts of matrimony, the young man and woman will just be friends. During informal friendship, they will have time to observe one another indifferently, simply as a brother and sister in Christ. Because it is up to men to initiate, the process will be described from the young man's perspective. If the young man, after he has gotten to know her from a brotherly perspective, thinks the young woman may be his intended bride, he discusses the wisdom of his opinion with his parents. He then approaches the girl's father without informing the girl about it. He will then seek the father's permission to get to know the daughter better *with marriage as the probable outcome.*

In the ideal situation, the father already knows the young man, because the two like-minded families will have known about one another and probably will have spent time together. But if the father does not know the young man, he needs to find out enough about him to know if marriage is even a likely possibility. Would his daughter like and respect this fellow? Does the young man come anywhere near his daughter's standards of character? If the young man obtains the approval of the father to begin courting, the daughter is consulted as to her wishes. If she is interested, the courtship begins when the girl's father gives the young man the go-ahead and some guidelines on his preferences on how the courtship should be handled. The father is still the daughter's protector at this point, and it is his duty to be especially protective of her heart at this critical moment in her life. In giving the young man permission to court, the father fully understands that marriage is the likely outcome. This means the father needs to know enough about the young man to approve of the marriage before permission to court is granted.

The purpose of the *courtship* period is for the young people and their families to objectively evaluate the situation and the young couple's compatibility with each other. At any point in the courtship, either the man or the lady can graciously bow out, if they have any reason to think the marriage might not work, with no hard feelings or broken hearts on either side. *Theoretically.*

Courtship makes a lot of sense because it takes into account the frailties of our hearts. But courtship doesn't fix frailties of heart. We can still find our emotions entangled and disheveled under the most protective, sensible scenarios, and some people who court let themselves become just as emotionally devastated as people who date, if the courtship is called off. We cannot make an idol of any method no matter how biblical it may be.

The design of courtship merely facilitates interaction between two frail people and two frail families, providing some very sensible safeguards. If the daughter discovers there are things about the young man she's not happy with, the father can then tactfully help the daughter end the courtship and redefine the relationship between the young man and his daughter. The couple is then back to the brother-sister *friendship* stage, and the father handled the hardest parts of the "breakup" process. This brings up an interesting observation. Breakups shouldn't be common. Courtship isn't just another version of dating. It's not supposed to represent a successive string of temporary trial relationships. This is why the courtship should not begin unless the couple is reasonably certain that marriage will be the outcome.

The ingredient that seems to make courtship work is emotional and spiritual maturity on everyone's part. It is personal discipline on the part of the couple that minimizes the risk of premature obsessions that may hurt future friendships if the courtship does not work out.

As long as the couple are communicating honestly with one another and looking at the situation without emotional entanglement, sexual tension, or moral shame, they will be able to evaluate their situation clearly and should be able to come to a sound conclusion within a few months. They will be spending time with family and friends, getting input from those closest to them. If the couple believes it's a match made in heaven, and if their parents and closest advisors see nothing to make them think otherwise, the couple then confidently come to a decision to marry. This is usually called the *betrothal* or *engagement* period. From examples we can see in Scripture, this was a binding commitment to marry, which was nearly as binding as marriage. It's our father's opinion that, generally, courtship should takes as long as it needs to, and that the engagement should be short.

What about physical romance?

John W. Thompson states that, "Physical romance is to be withheld until the wedding where the chaste couple experience their first embrace and kiss. This is why the traditional wedding ceremony includes a statement, 'You may now kiss the bride.' It hasn't happened before, at least in the familial order of things. The kiss was the symbol for sealing the new marriage covenant. Only by following the biblical pattern for relationships will romance be protected from the tarnish of impurity so that it remains beautiful rather than harmful to the new couple."[3]

The final stage is the *marriage*. This is when the father officially transfers his authority and protection to the young man, and gives away his daughter—as our father says, the most precious gift he could ever give.

Why do all these stages require so much caution?

Because young people are vulnerable. Our hearts and emotions are sensitive and need to be protected so that our judgment can be brought to bear on a decision that will affect us the rest of our lives. That's what the whole courtship process is about—helping young people marry without putting their hearts at ultra-high risk. Every story is as unique and varied as are the people committed to following courtship.

---

3   See "God's Design for Scriptural Romance Number VII: How to Marry: Courtship Questions," by John W. Thompson at www.patriarch.com.

My father disappeared when I was four years old. How could courtship work for me?

With alternate authorities who can provide wise input and counsel. This is also true for girls whose fathers are not affectionate or interested in their futures. This is sad because such situations are more the rule than the exception. Observe how courtship worked out for **Sarah Irene,** who didn't have a father involved, but stuck to her commitment to follow biblical principles whatever circumstances came her way.

> What a story we are about to tell! So unique and intricately woven are the details, that it could only have been planned and orchestrated by the hand of our loving Father, who both guided our steps as we lived life on separate coasts, and then ordained that our paths join together. I, (Sarah), will be the narrator, and Josh will add a few comments at the end.
>
> ### The Phone Call
>
> "Sarah? Hi, this is Mom. I know you're busy there right now but you need to find somewhere private to talk for a minute. There's something I need to tell you…"
>
> And that is how it all began. Little did I know that when I answered my cell phone from Colorado, my life was about to change drastically. I was, at the time, accompanying a friend on a two-week trip through a region of the United States where she served as Family Coordinator for a Christian ministry. The goal of the trip was to visit with and help answer questions for home-educating families who were using the ministry's curriculum, and it was in the middle of one of those meetings that my mom's call arrived.

As I stepped outside into the chilly winter air, I listened in disbelief as Mom told me that a young man had asked her about the possibility of "getting to know me" a little better. My disbelief turned to utter shock when she told me who it was that had called—a guy named Josh.

The Trip

The previous week, Mom, my brother Seth, and I had all participated in a historical tour of the Plymouth, Massachusetts area. Packed with site-seeing and excellent lectures on the different aspects of early Pilgrim life by various experts, we all had a wonderful time and made many new friends. Included among them was our team leader, a young man and Vision Forum employee by the name of Josh. Throughout the week we had had many opportunities to talk and interact with him and his brother Joel, and although by the end of the week my family had begun to suspect a little partiality toward me on his part, I was in denial.

After the week was over, we all went our separate ways, literally, at the airport. Seth flew back to Chicago where he worked, I grabbed my flight to Colorado where I met up with my friend Kara Lee for our two weeks of travel through her region, and Mom boarded a plane bound for Minneapolis where she would catch her connection to Washington. Much to Mom's surprise, she discovered that Josh was on her first flight and invited him to come back and visit once they had taken off. Unaware that Josh had asked my brother the previous day how to get permission to keep in touch with me (Seth hadn't had time to mention it to Mom before we left), Mom was in for a big surprise. Two hours later as they were landing in Minnesota, Mom and Josh parted...and the ball began to roll...

Let the Process Begin...

I met Josh's parents for the first time at a wedding in San Antonio that we were both attending. My friend Kara Lee was a bridesmaid, and this wedding "happened" to fall in the middle of my travels with her. We had planned to go to it long before I knew Josh existed, but it was a perfect opportunity for his parents to meet the "mystery girl" from Washington that Josh had told them about. Mom's first phone call to me about Josh had arrived just a few days before this, when she told me of Josh's interest and that she wanted me to meet his family while at this wedding. It definitely made for an interesting afternoon, and I will admit that, although the wedding was lovely, my mind was not really on the ceremony. I kept glancing around the room, trying to figure out who Josh's parents were...

Throughout the rest of my two-week trip, after several days of fasting and seeking the Lord's direction, Mom and Josh's parents began to visit over the phone and by e-mail as they tried to find a good place to start. There was so much to talk about, so much to be considered, and so much at stake. Both sides had been praying for years that God would prepare and preserve the spouse of His choice for their child's life, and all felt the weight of the decision that they were potentially making. After many hours on the phone and a couple of weeks of intense prayer, all felt a green light to go ahead, and our families planned to meet for the first time.

The Meeting

Josh's family arrived in Spokane, Washington on Thanksgiving, 2003, strangers to the Northwest, very unsure of what people from the "West Coast" were like, and about as nervous as we were! What an indescribable mix of feeling it was as we took them back to our home for dinner and the first round of "talks." The word "awkward" comes close to capturing the essence of that first evening.

The next few days we spent with them were indeed ordained of and blessed by the Lord as our families got to know each other through various activities together, and Josh and I were given the chance to compare our beliefs, convictions, backgrounds, etc., as we and our parents spent literally hours talking through and about many, many different topics. Looking back on it now, I can see at least part of why God planned this into the process, for it enabled Josh and me, who both tend to be people-pleasers, to be honest with each other as we answered questions and discussed issues. Had I known him better at this point, it would have been far more difficult to be as open with my answers, because I would have cared more about his opinion of me. It also helped that our parents were in on the discussions, because although we may have been able hide our "real" selves from each other, we could not do that in front of those who knew us best!

At the end of that visit, we all felt that God was continuing to give us the go-ahead, and our "courtship" officially began. Josh headed back home to San Antonio, Texas, and we agreed to keep in touch through phone calls and e-mail.

Goin' Courtin'

Over the course of the next several weeks and months, Josh and I continued to get to know one another through our many conversations, letters, and emails. We swapped childhood stories, questions about likes and dislikes, and discussed all kinds of wacky things, all the while gaining a greater understanding of and appreciation for each other. I traveled to Texas for about a week and a half in December to visit his family, meet his friends, and do a little sight-seeing around the San Antonio area after my Mom and brother arrived toward the end of my trip. Josh then came to Washington over the New Year to go skiing with us and spend a little more time in "God's Country," as Seth lovingly calls it.

As time progressed, I found myself more and more pre-occupied with thoughts of a certain Texan, a bittersweet revelation as I realized that I would need to, more than ever, keep my heart and mind focused on God's direction. We both agreed that we wanted God's will for our lives ultimately, whether that in the end meant we were together or apart, but as time went on, the struggle to keep my will under the protection and wisdom of God and my Mom increased. At one point, our dedication to this principle was tested when we experienced a serious "speed bump" in the process. As I faced the possibility of "losing" my relationship with Josh, God gave me the opportunity to place my own "Isaac" on the altar just as Abraham did, and although there were many tears, God's grace prevailed, and I experienced both the freedom of a burden lifted and indescribable joy when God chose to give him back to me. I had a whole new appreciation for him after that and a deeper level of communication with the Lord.

The Proposal

Josh and I continued to communicate throughout the first few months of this year, with another trip for me to Texas taking place in February. With each passing day, I realized more and more how much I admired Josh and enjoyed his company. I began to pray earnestly that God would give me clear direction through His Word, my Mom, and His Spirit as to what His will was for me.

At about this time, plans were made for both Seth and Josh
to come to Washington for several days so we could all go to the
Oregon Coast. A favorite place of our family's over the years, we
wanted Josh to experience the Pacific and to share in many of
the special memories that the area held for us. Seth was to arrive
on Thursday, March 13, and Josh was scheduled to come in on
Friday. Little did I know that I was in for a big surprise.

All went according to plans on Thursday as we picked Seth
up from the airport and then headed out to run a few errands
before ending the evening at Seth's favorite restaurant for
dinner. When we arrived, we were escorted back to our table
but…something was wrong. There was already someone sitting
there! As we neared the table, the "mystery person" stood up,
and my heart hit the ceiling. It was Josh! Mom and Seth both
congratulated themselves on their successful secrecy and then
headed off to another part of the restaurant. I sat down across
from Josh, still in utter disbelief, but as I did so, noticed that the
table had been beautifully decorated and a large bouquet of roses
that bore my name accompanied it. He explained it all with the
reasoning that he had wanted to have a nice dinner with me, as it
had been a while since our last visit. And I bought it…

We chit-chatted for a long time, catching up on all that had
happened since we had last talked, ate dinner, and then talked some
more. It was at this point, when the dishes had been cleared, that I
was given my first indication that something was out of the ordinary.
Josh pulled out a letter and asked me to read it. I opened the short
note that basically said he had something he wanted to show me
and instructed me to look up at him when I finished reading. As my
eyes very slowly raised to meet his, he began to tell me how much
he'd enjoyed getting to know me and how God had given both him
and his parents peace and direction about the timing of this…and

I heard no more. I knew what was coming. Josh came around to my side of the table, got down on one knee, and asked me to marry him. I think you can guess what my answer was.

Conclusion

Thursday, March 13th became a very special day in my life for two reasons, as I later realized. First and foremost, because it was the day that I said "yes" to the most incredible guy I've ever known. Second, because it was the one-year anniversary of a very special event in my life. The previous year, I had attended a writing conference at which Vision Forum's founder, Doug Phillips, was speaking. Each of his sessions had great impact on me, but God used one in particular to solidify His calling on my life to be "just" a wife and mother, and to set me free from the guilt I had felt for many years over not having a world-impacting "career." I recorded these events in my journal along with a prayer that God would give me a husband who had this same mindset, and as I looked back on the date of that entry, I realized that it occurred on March 13, 2002…and God answered that prayer exactly one year later.

And now, my friends, you know the rest. I married the most wonderful man on August 2, 2003. He is all that I have ever prayed for and more than I hoped for, and is the greatest earthly gift God has seen fit to give me.

Josh Writes:

As Sarah has explained for you our story, I hope you are struck by the fact that the blessing of this relationship has come to us through the goodness of our Heavenly Father. I was impressed with Sarah from the very first back in Plymouth last October, and never doubted that she was a wonderful, beautiful, godly young lady, and I saw Jesus reflected in her. And through the many letters, e-mails, phone calls, and across the tens of thousands of miles traveled to spend time with each other (figured at over 30,000!), that fact was more clearly demonstrated to me. But, above all, Sarah and I both wanted what the Lord had in store for us. That is all that really mattered, and that was my constant prayer as the relationship developed.

It was really hard to keep that focus, especially since we had such good times together, whether visiting the Alamo, skiing in Canada, meeting all my co-workers and local friends, and taking trips to the Oregon coast. We loved to talk on the phone together, to spend time praying and talking about what the Lord was teaching us, and just simple things like sharing thoughts while doing chores were now tons of fun. Sarah quickly came to occupy a large part of my thoughts, and life suddenly became a little more complicated, in a good way. Well, as the Lord continued to guide our steps and finally made it clear to me that Sarah was the girl to be my wife, it was a great adventure to be able to plan the surprise on that memorable night in March. The initial shock on her face when she saw me there at the table, to the surprise and tearful "yes!" that came shortly thereafter when I popped the question, are moments that will always live in my memory (as well as the nervousness preceding her "yes!") Such a strange chain of events over the past six months had led to an exciting culmination.

I am so very grateful to the Lord for the incredible way in which He brought us together and the joy over the wonderful girl He has given me to be my helpmeet and companion in life. Our goal and prayer is that together, by His grace, we might glorify our Savior in our new marriage and be a blessing to others as well. Little did I imagine back in October, when the trip in New

England was winding down, that I would ever see her again, much less have her agree to marry me, but I am so glad she did! Together, we give praise to Him who orchestrated the events in our lives, as I look forward to living life with the woman of my dreams.

I want to get married now, but God isn't bringing me a husband. Why?

We need to wait on God's timing. God is kind to His people and blesses them for their righteousness. We have many friends who wanted to get married early, but now are so thankful that God waited on bringing their husbands…usually because these young woman had moral battles to fight, personal issues to sort through, families to help, and feminist hearts to tame. If He had blessed them in marriage when they originally expected it, their marriages might have been ruined. He knows what He is doing!

God wants you to learn to rely on Him as your true source of contentment and happiness. Contentment has nothing to do with our circumstances—only with the state of our hearts. If you are not content without a husband, you would never be content with one.

One young heroine, **Amber Dawn**, traveled the path of discovering contentment as a daughter at home under the headship of her father, waiting on the Lord's timing for marriage. Embracing God's call, she let Him teach her the real meaning of being at peace with His will for her life, and now, at age 23, she shares with us what that meaning is:

"…For I have learned, in whatsoever state I am, therewith to be content." (Philippians 4:11b)

The *1828 Noah Webster Dictionary* defines content(ment) as: "to satisfy the mind; to make quiet, so as to stop complaint or opposition; to appease; to make easy in any situation; a resting or satisfaction of mind without disquiet; acquiescence."

Contentment can be one of life's biggest challenges, yet it is exceedingly worth striving for. It affects every area of our lives—our attitudes, the way we talk, how we carry ourselves, finding pleasure in even the simplest things in life and peace with what we already have, having a joyful spirit, and the list could go on.

"But godliness with contentment is great gain. For we brought nothing into this world, and it is certain we can carry nothing out." (1 Timothy 6:6-7)

The foundation of contentment rests in finding completion and fulfillment in Jesus Christ as our Lord and Savior, without which, we will always fail to find the joy and peace of contentment.

Because of our sinful nature, discontentment and dissatisfaction are prevalent and present themselves as battles to be fought. It is part of man to want more, have more, or be more than what he already has, is, or wants to be. Hence the saying that "the grass is always greener on the other side of the fence." Without Christ as the center of our lives, mankind is always discontent with his current surroundings; always stretching his neck out as far as he can through the fence to taste of the grass that is just beyond his reach. This weakness in us has a great deal to do with why the Lord gave us the tenth commandment: "Thou shalt not covet thy neighbor's house...wife, manservant, nor his maidservant, nor his ox, nor his donkey, nor any thing that is thy neighbor's" (Exodus 20:17).

Jesus instructs us to lay up treasures in Heaven and to not worry about the things of this world, for He shall supply in His perfect timing (Matthew 6:19-20, 24-33; Psalm 37:3-5). This applies to every area of life: maidenhood, marriage, children, money, our hopes and desires, and even simply just living each day with joyfulness and gladness in the fact that the Lord is the Supreme Provider. Do we trust the Lord to supply all of our needs? Do we trust Him to fulfill the desires of our hearts and His plan for our future? "But my God shall supply all your need according to His riches in glory by Christ Jesus" (Philippians 4:19).

Being content is an act of resolve. It is something that is worked at, learned, and acquired with dedication and commitment. It is a conscious effort made to forget self and rest in God's perfect will and plan—for everything works for good to those who are in Christ Jesus (Romans 8:28). It is the quieting of the mind from care and worry about the things that are just beyond our reach. If it is something that would be beneficial to us, the Lord will provide, in His time.

One area of contentment that is often not realized is contentment during suffering. The Lord doesn't promise us a care-free life on earth without any pain or suffering or persecution; but He does promise to sustain us through those times of trial if we are faithful to take up our cross and follow after Him (Luke 9:23). Even Job, in his greatest hour of sadness and heartache, trusted the Lord's plan and called upon His name—"The Lord gave, and the Lord hath taken away; blessed be the name of the Lord" (Job 1:21b).

Through trials we are made stronger in Christ and shall abound in joy (1 Peter 1:6-9; Romans 5:1-5). "Beloved, think it not strange concerning the fiery trial which is to try you, as though some strange thing happened unto you: but rejoice, inasmuch as ye are partakers of Christ's sufferings; that, when His glory shall be revealed, ye may be glad also with exceeding joy" (1Peter 4:12-13).

When we surrender our self-will and allow the Lord to lead our plans, desires, and aspirations, contentment is bound to follow.

I've found that this is particularly true in waiting on the Lord to bring a godly spouse in His perfect time. Finding contentment in even this area of life is refreshing, rewarding, and freeing. When we think, "If I only had a husband, children, my own home (you fill in the blank), then I would be content,"—beware! If we are not content without a husband, etc., we will not be content with one. We should not expect him, or any other person or object, to make us content. If we expect others to fulfill our needs, we place a great burden upon their shoulders and put them into a place that only the Lord can fill and complete. Wait on the Lord, be of good cheer, have faith, and He shall bring it to pass.

Jesus Christ is The Beginning and The End. May we make Him number one in every area of our lives, keeping our eyes and hearts focused on Him, daily praising Him for every little blessing which He has bestowed upon us, and being satisfied with what they happen to be. Then all of life shall be joy and contentment, having found complete rest in Christ.

Contentment founded on Christ is worth striving for and successfully obtaining.

"But seek first the kingdom of God, and His righteousness... take therefore no thought for the morrow, for the morrow shall take thought for the things of itself." (Matthew 6:33a, 34a)

Our unmarried years are a blessing from God. "The unmarried woman careth for the things of the Lord, that she may be holy both in body and in spirit: but she that is married careth for the things of the world, how she may please her husband. And this I speak for your own profit; not that I may cast a snare upon you, but for that which is comely, and that ye may attend upon the Lord without distraction" (1 Corinthians 7:34, 35).

Married years are an important time for bearing important fruit. So are unmarried (maiden) years. Both belong to God and should be dedicated to His service. Because of this, it is up to Him to decide when we stop serving Him in one way and start serving Him in another, to bear a different kind of fruit. We must not try to put restrictions on God or disregard His timing. It's not up to us to make up detailed, rigid agendas for our lives, dictating when and where we will serve God/marry/have children/die. Our attitudes toward our future should be as that of submissive, humble Mary, the most blessed woman in the world, who said, "Behold the handmaiden of the Lord; be it unto me according to Thy word" (Luke 1:38).

CHAPTER SEVENTEEN

FATHERS, DAUGHTERS, AND "MISSIONS WORK"

A PROTECTED WOMAN'S MINISTRY

If the unmarried women are to be "concerned with the things of the Lord," should I devote these years to a very spiritual cause, like a missions organization?

Our whole lives belong to God. All the years of our lives should be devoted to the very greatest cause: making disciples of all the nations, teaching them to observe all of God's commands, and filling and subduing the earth. Every Christian is called to this work. If the word "missionary" means a Christian with a cause, a purpose, a mission from God, then every Christian is called to be a missionary.

We must understand our lives have been bought with a price. Our lives belong to Jesus Christ and we must sacrifice our own agendas and ambitions in order to execute our mission in the way God commands. Though all Christians have been assigned this mission, they can't accomplish it just any way they feel like. God's work must be done God's way.

So what is God's way for young women? First, we need to remember that God is not silent on this issue. His word is full of examples showing exactly what role women play in taking dominion, reaching out to the poor and needy, preaching the gospel, and making disciples. One thing we *never* see in the Bible is women working in missions organizations or any first-century equivalent. What those godly women of the early Church *did* do was serve in *their homes, families, communities, and churches*, and they had a powerful witness *serving God His way*.

We have a friend who has a wonderful, willing heart for serving God. Unfortunately, she has been enticed into a mode of "service" that doesn't really use her God-given role in a way that will give Him the most glory. Our friend was led to believe that her late teens and early twenties were somehow owed to a "really important" Christian organization, which operates largely on the labor of young volunteers— mostly women. How is her time used by this organization? She spends eight hours a day vacuuming the carpets. That is her only responsibility. She has made a commitment not to leave this "important" work she is doing, even to get married, until she is twenty-five. We believe her situation is tragic, because the "best years" of her life are not being invested in the highest calling God designed for her. We also believe this situation is tragic for another reason. *Every time Christians compromise, the kingdom falters, because the Lordship of Christ is not properly honored.*[1] When we compromise, we are trying to go about doing God's work in our way, and it's never as effective as God's way.

We do not imply that janitorial work is ignoble. Any work done in faith has its nobility. We do not imply that the Christian organization

---

1   This in no way implies that God's will can be thwarted by man's negligence. We simply suggest that kingdoms stand as subjects stand together doing duties required of the King.

does unimportant work. Any organization that takes even one glass of water to the thirsty is significant. The question here is not one of whether or not such work needs to be done, but of *whom* God commands to be engaged in the work and within what sphere. We simply argue that the home is so much more valuable than our wayward, self-centered generation realizes. The Christian home should be a beacon for the gospel in a culture that is quickly self-destructing.

But I always thought that missions-type activity was somehow more "spiritual" than other Christian activities. If I really want to serve God to my utmost, shouldn't I become a missionary and serve on the missions field?

You need to understand that you and every other Christian have been called to be a missionary, according to our previous definition, and you are supposed to serve God every day of your life. It's a mistake to think that the only worthy mission fields are third-world countries. The entire earth is our mission field. Christians need to serve wherever they are, with the same sacrifice, resolve, selflessness, and commitment as the most noble missionary in Africa. This means you should be a missionary *right now*, wherever you are.

So what about short-term foreign missions trips? A girl from my youth group went on a missions trip and came back really changed for the better because her eyes were opened up for the first time. Isn't it a hugely beneficial experience for us and the people we minister to?

Many young people are changed for the better because they've been challenged by lessons from the real world—lessons they should have been receiving at home and at church but apparently were not given. There is no doubt that missions trips can illuminate the shortsightedness of any number of young people playing missionary. But one passport and one plane ticket does not qualify a blind person to lead others out of great darkness. According to the leader of one international Christian resource agency, though mission trips can be interesting "field trips" to the young people on them, they are not helpful to the people they are supposed to be helping. He reports that the short-term missions trips confuse and discourage those who are visited, especially those in third world countries. He wishes American youth groups would stop sending people out to do "missions" activities.

Jennie writes about how a short-term missions trip proved more revealing than she had expected:

> When I was 15, I went to Mexico on a two-week "mission" trip. I teamed up with about a dozen other people from various churches in my home state, and our objective was to visit a very poor section of the Yucatan Peninsula. While there, we would be painting the pastor's house and all of the chairs for the church sanctuary. We also took suitcases of clothing to give to the people in the church. For ten days, our team painted everything in sight. I spent a great deal of time playing with the children in the church, trying out my very limited Spanish as I attempted to be a part of their lives in a meaningful way. Only one woman in our group spoke Spanish fluently, so she did the translating for us. The warm and friendly members of the church made us meals every day, and we had fun learning to sing some of their praise songs. Every night we slept in hammocks, just as our hosts did. While the experience was definitely an enjoyable one for me, I have to say that my eyes were opened in a way that I utterly did not expect.
>
> At the end of ten days of work, our group headed to Cancun for "debriefing." We spent three days on the beach, staying in

a very nice tourist resort. We took sight-seeing excursions to visit some Mayan ruins and basically did the American tour-group thing. While we were on the beach, soaking up the sun, I overheard some conversations between our group leaders about one of the families in the church we had just "helped." I had grown very fond of the children in that particular family and could not help pricking up my ears at the sound of their names. It turned out that the parents were deeply in debt and wanted help from the "rich Americans," since their church had no way to get them out of their trouble. Our group leaders expressed their consternation at being presented with needs that went deeper than paint and fellowship and agreed they could offer no help to the family, lest everyone else in the church feel left out. I pretended I had not heard any of this conversation, but it left my brain in a whirl.

In my 15-year-old mind, going on a mission trip was supposed to be a way to serve the Body of Christ in another country. All of us cheerful, hardworking Americans flew in and got an entire church painted and looking beautiful. We sang songs and played games. We hugged the elderly and kissed the children. But with a sickening feeling in my stomach, I suddenly came face to face with the fact that everything we had done was, at best, cosmetic. We had not brought any scriptural teaching to people who really needed to know how to live the gospel in their country. We had come in with our rich clothes, shoes, watches, and hair dryers, thinking we could minister to people whose real dream was to leave Mexico and move to the United States. This became doubly apparent to me when the family in question suddenly showed up in Cancun the next day. They acted like they had just come because they wanted to see us again before we left, but I overheard our group leaders talking animatedly about how the father had asked our team leader for money. I continued to pretend I knew nothing about the whole situation and just acted happy to see my favorite family again. The children played with us on the beach, and we said sorrowful good-byes at the airport the next day. But I left Mexico very sobered up. I realized that what we had done could not be termed "missions" work at all. What these people needed was a faithful, biblical pastor who could lead their church into the "meat" of the gospel, teaching them how to manage their limited finances and to serve Christ even out of their lack. This was a church starving for solid biblical teaching, and all we had done was to paint their chairs and walls.

Of course, this is not the report I gave to my home church when I got back. I shared all of the fun and all of the photographs I took. I described the sweet children and the delicious meals. I talked about the joy of the singing during the Mexican church services. I wanted my home church to feel they had done well in sending me to minister in another country. But, deep down, I knew that we had made very little difference. The paint would fade. The songs would fade from memory. But a hundred Mexican Christians would still struggle to serve Christ in their impoverished country. They didn't need short-term "missionaries" at all—they needed faithful "fellow workers" in the gospel who would be a part of their work and members of their church all the time. I saw that the problem of short-term missions was that it tended to give a short-term view of the work of the Church. We cannot just blow in from out of town and "fix" things in ten days. When Paul and his fellow missionaries traveled to share the gospel, they stayed with the people to whom they ministered for long periods of time. They showed the local church body how to effectively minister Christ within their own communities. After he was imprisoned, Paul kept in touch through his letters of exhortation. But all of the work was long-term—not built around quick fixes. It involved building relationships to a degree that cannot be done through short-term missionary projects.

How many of us are frustrated at the lack of joy or faithfulness or growth in the Lord within our own local church bodies? The answer to this problem is staring us in the face: our own churches and communities are our "mission field!" Let me tell you from experience that it is much harder to faithfully and consistently demonstrate hospitality and love and to serve the members of our own local church than it is to escape overseas for a couple of weeks and see "instant" results. The work of building the Body of Christ is not easy or glamorous, but it must be done. It is best done with patience over the long haul. If we want to see genuine community and faithfulness within our own church body, we need to be a vital part of that body—just as we need to be faithful members of our own families. Galatians 6:9-10 says, "And let us not grow weary while doing good, for in due season we shall reap if we do not lose heart. Therefore, as we have opportunity, let us do good to all, especially to those who are of the household of faith." The work of building Christ's kingdom can be wearying, but we shall reap if we obey Him and faithfully serve in the sphere to which He has called us.

Leaving the sphere of our greatest influence and effectiveness to follow teen trends has not been a fruitful investment of time or resources. Focusing on the superficial, cosmetic needs only discourages the needy and confuses those who think they are helping. The real crying needs of the third world are complex and controversial—nothing that can be fixed by a group of teenagers on a "missionary" tourist excursion. And the biblical solutions are consequently being neglected because this superficial activity is hyped as "God's will." Even secularists can see the folly of this kind of international humanitarianism. Author P.J. O'Rourke commented on the hype generated by an African charity rock concert.

[S]ay some, [it] sets a good example for today's selfish youth, reminding them to be socially concerned. Nonsense. The circus atmosphere of the Live Aid concerts makes the world's problems seem easy and fun to solve and implies that the solutions are naturally uncontroversial.[2]

The circus atmosphere of many short-term missions trips has not led Christianity toward more fruitfulness, but it has reinforced the pragmatic[3] trends of evangelicalism, which are redefining Christianity as experience-oriented or entertainment-oriented. The Faith is being advertised as an amusement-ride thrill. This only distorts the life-and-death seriousness of the Christian life. As Jennie pointed out, the need is for comprehensive shepherding through churches and biblically qualified leadership. It is in this sphere that the fundamental needs can be met and root problems alleviated.

But what about long-term work by women who are really committed to helping the countries they serve in? Surely this is a very important, fruitful work. Doesn't God call some women to devote their lives to foreign missions?

God does use women for His glory on foreign missions fields, but there is something we need to understand. *Never in Scripture do we see an example of women being called or commissioned or sent out*

2   P.J. O'Rourke, Give War a Chance (New York: Atlantic Monthly Press, 1992), p. 101.

3   In *Ashamed of the Gospel*, pastor John MacArthur stated, "Pragmatism is the notion that meaning or worth is determined by practical consequences. The belief that usefulness is the standard of what is good. To a pragmatist, if a technique or course of action has a desired effect it is good. If it doesn't seem to work, then it must be wrong." In modern missions, pragmatism often elevates traditions of men to a position of superiority over scriptural examples.

as missionaries—only men. "Believing wives" go along with their husbands (1 Corinthians 9:5), but they aren't sent out alone.

Let's take a look at what the women of the early Church were doing, that the apostle Paul praised them as "fellow workers in the gospel" (Philippians 4:3):

> "I commend unto you Phoebe our sister, which is a servant of the church which is at Cenchrea: That ye receive her in the Lord, as becometh saints, and that ye assist her in whatsoever business she hath need of you: for she hath been a succourer [helper] of many, and of myself also." (Romans 16:1,2)

> "Greet Priscilla and Aquila my helpers in Christ Jesus: Who have for my life laid down their own necks…Likewise greet the church that is in their house." (Romans 16:3-5)

> "Greet Mary, who bestowed much labour on us." (Romans 16:6)

These women weren't going to the far ends of the earth on their own. They were serving in their local churches, helping their husbands and the godly men of the church. We believe the Bible teaches that this is how women are supposed to conduct "missions" activities. It's not simply because women are less capable than men to carry the gospel around the world on their own, or because women "aren't allowed" this kind of "freedom." It's because women are so valuable in their primary sphere of influence. Helping godly men is a mission God created woman to accomplish. She and her role were made for each other, so to speak.

We are aware that this may be one of the most radical points we make in this book. We are aware that many Christians have a great respect for women such as Amy Carmichael and Mary Slessor and use them as examples to prove that God does call women to the missions field on their own. We need to be very cautious in the way we treat real-life examples, careful that we don't hold up real, fallible people as the infallible standard. We should give godly people honor for the worthy things they did and learn from their examples. But we should recognize that these godly women do not in fact feature in the Bible, and their examples can't be used as a scriptural precept. Just because a godly person did a good deed in a certain way doesn't mean that it was *God's way* of getting that deed done. Throughout the Bible we see examples of God bringing good out of situations that weren't ideal. He illustrated His sovereign power through Pharaoh's stubbornness. He brought glory to Himself through Joseph's jealous brothers.

He advanced military victories for Israel through Rahab, a prostitute. But does this mean that Christian women should willfully make mistakes and hope that the end will justify the means?

We do not mean to criticize any well-meaning missionary woman. Our purpose in writing this is to stress that we must study Scripture, trusting only Scripture, to tell us exactly how God wants *us* to live. Are we willing to follow *Him*, instead of our human heroes and heroines? Or will we instead stubbornly follow our own ideas of what is "right" and "spiritual"?

Are you saying there is a "wrong way to do right?"

There can be. When the Israelites were traveling with the Ark of the Covenant during David's reign (2 Samuel 6:3-7), they pragmatically updated its prescribed mode of transportation. God had commanded that it be carried on poles supported by the priests' shoulders. In this instance, the Ark was loaded onto a modern oxcart. As the procession went along, the oxen stumbled and the Ark slipped. A well-meaning young man named Uzzah put out his hand to steady the Ark, despite God's command that it never be touched. Did God reward Uzzah's zeal? No. Uzzah had tried to do "right" in his own way instead of God's way. God struck him dead.

Well-meaning Sarah wanted to see God's promise to her and Abraham fulfilled. She decided to make it happen her way instead of waiting for God to do it His way (Genesis 16). She trusted in her own understanding of how Abraham should father a son, instead of trusting that God's way and God's timing are always best. Blessings did not ensue.

Okay, so it's not purely biblical for women to become overseas missionaries on their own, but I feel like God is calling me to the mission field. Doesn't the revelation God gives me over-rule anything in Scripture?

No. His revelation is Scripture, not the imagination of your heart. Proverbs 28:26 says, "He that trusteth in his own heart is a fool: but whoso walketh wisely, he shall be delivered." Our hearts can be desperately selfish and darkly deceitful. When Jeremiah thundered against people who dealt treacherously against the Lord, he was talking about "hearing" words from God which were nothing more that the "imaginations of the heart." In Chapter 11 he says, "They did not obey or incline their ear, but everyone followed the dictates of his evil heart." This is what brought such terrible judgment on God's chosen people. Even the prophets and the priests were false. Jeremiah said, "They speak a vision of their own heart, not from the mouth of the Lord. They are prophets of the deceit of their own heart" (Jeremiah 23:26). This is why we must stick to the revelation of Scripture.

"Son of man, prophesy against the prophets of Israel that prophesy, and say thou unto them that prophesy out of their own hearts, Hear ye the word of the Lord; Thus saith the Lord God; Woe unto the foolish prophets, that follow their own spirit, and have seen nothing! They have seen vanity and lying divination, saying, The Lord saith: and the Lord hath not sent them: and they have made others to hope that they would confirm the word. Have ye not seen a vain vision, and have ye not spoken a lying divination, whereas ye say, The Lord saith it; albeit I have not spoken? Therefore thus saith the Lord God; Because ye have spoken vanity, and seen lies, therefore, behold, I am against you, saith the Lord God. And mine hand shall be upon the prophets that see vanity, and that divine lies: they shall not be in the assembly of my people, neither shall they be written in the writing of the house of Israel, neither shall they enter into the land of Israel; and ye shall know that I am the Lord God… Likewise, thou son of man, set thy face against the daughters of thy people, which prophesy out of their own heart; and prophesy thou against them…" (Ezekiel 13:2-9,17)

So what is God's way for women to help the needy, minister to the blind, and spread the gospel?

First we need to explore God's design for doing His work. Though people may invent "more modern" or "more trendy" or "more effective" ways of doing evangelism and ministry, man's most clever pragmatism is always inferior to God's design. The question to ask is, "What is the biblical method for expanding the kingdom of God, and how can I demonstrate faithfulness to that method?"

As part of God's design, He created and gave specific roles and duties to three institutions—the Family, the Church, and the State. He ordained the State to bear the sword and suppress evil by protecting the law-abiding. The Family is to be fruitful, multiply, and exercise responsible dominion. *The Church* is the institution that was designed to extend the reconciling gospel into new regions, providing support and discipleship as a family of families, who best represent the wonders of God's order to societies in need of redemption. *Churches, as they multiply and expand in orderly growth, are the primary biblical missions agencies.*

The Church Militant—the worldwide body of believers which make up local churches—is the agency through which God advances Christ's kingdom, knitting together the gifts of men, women, children, and families into powerful weapons wielded for His glory. Local assemblies of believers become the agents for equipping the saints, shepherding families to be the light and salt of the gospel in their communities, discipling individuals, training leaders, ministering to the needy, visiting orphans and widows in their distress, and giving the right help to the poor in the right way. The Church is the agency that carries the apostolic duties and responsibilities of exhortation, discipline, nurture. This is why the Church must itself be missionary.

Independent missionaries and modern missions organizations that operate outside church authority appear to be outside kingdom architecture. Their work does not actually strengthen or expand the kingdom on God's terms.

Then why are so many women finding fulfillment and purpose in missions work?

Because they are bearing some fruit. Even when we attempt to serve God in ignorance, immaturity, or for misguided motives, we find joy in bearing even a very small amount of fruit. But we learn in John 15 that the Lord wants us to abide in Him so as to bear much fruit. Jesus said,

"I am the true vine, and my Father is the husbandman. Every branch in me that beareth not fruit he taketh away: and every branch that beareth fruit, he purgeth it, that it may bring forth more fruit. Now ye are clean through the word which I have spoken unto you. Abide in me, and I in you. As the branch cannot bear fruit of itself, except it abide in the vine; no more can ye, except ye abide in me. I am the vine, ye are the branches: He that abideth in me, and I in him, the same bringeth forth much fruit: for without me ye can do nothing. If a man abide not in me, he is cast forth as a branch, and is withered; and men gather them, and cast them into the fire, and they are burned. If ye abide in me, and my words abide in you, ye shall ask what ye will, and it shall be done unto you. Herein is my Father glorified, that ye bear much fruit; so shall ye be my disciples. As the Father hath loved me, so have I loved you: continue ye in my love. If ye keep my commandments, ye shall abide in my love; even as I have kept my Father's commandments, and abide in his love. These things have I spoken unto you, that my joy might remain in you, and that your joy might be full." (John 15:1-11)

His will for us is that we bear a lot of fruit by keeping His commandments and abiding in His love. If we're bearing any fruit, our Heavenly Father prunes us so we bear more. He often purges or prunes people by convicting them and turning them back toward commandments that have been long misplaced or forgotten, so that they can recover those ways and methods that are *most* fruitful.

Without analyzing or criticizing the modern missions movement, we would like to suggest that no Christian can bear much fruit outside of the methods recorded in the Word of God. A little fruit? Yes, and we praise God for it. Much fruit? No. Would the well-intentioned missions movement have started outside the Church if the word of God had been abiding richly in the Church? Probably not. Will well-intentioned women bear more fruit if they return to those scriptural roles and tasks God custom-designed for their utmost fruitfulness and complete spiritual joy? We think so.

Because we're living in a time when our society and our churches are so far from God's design, wouldn't it be permissible to work in less-than-biblical organizations? At least they seem to be getting things done.

This is the big temptation. Missions organizations are indeed doing the great bulk of the hard, sacrificial, and emergency work worldwide. But remember what happens when Christians compromise: our King is not comprehensively honored and the advancing kingdom falters. No pragmatic substitute should ever be endorsed over the order God intended. Christ is the King and we're the subjects. We're not supposed to ignore His commands and follow other peoples' inventions as to how we live as Christians. We abide in His love by abiding in his commandments.

Faithfulness to God's commandments is a big recurring theme of this book. Young women are influential. Our actions will influence the direction of culture for generations. We can compromise spiritually and get comfortable in today's compromised evangelical culture, or we can help move our entire culture back in a good direction if we begin to follow seemingly insignificant biblical patterns of living and thinking. We must stop "getting it wrong" by following the practices of an apostate age. Our churches are weak, and our families are fragile. Yes, there are strong-hearted Christian people who want to do well in spite of this. But look at what happens when those serious Christians devote their time, talents, and resources to pursuits outside the framework of God's best design: the Church remains in weakness, and families remain fragile. The kingdom does not advance on God's terms.

In terms of missions activities, are there not many things that could be done right on the home front in our suffering communities, which are drowning in unbelief? If churches and families routinely involved young people in the tasks of reaching out to the less fortunate, there would be much less blindness on the part of so many spoiled Westerners, who only see the spiritually needy in regions safely removed from the harsh realities of their own neighborhoods.

But aren't the two of you serving as independent missionaries in a foreign country?

Well, it's true that we live on the other side of the world from where we were born. But "foreign" is a relative term and does not mean we are part of the missions culture. We live at home, where our father and mother and brothers are. Yes, we have the opportunity to minister to people from diverse international backgrounds. This does not mean we're part of the missions culture. We do what we do for our Lord's kingdom through our father's guidance within our family and our church, not a short-term missions project.

But if I turn my attention to my own home and church and community, what about the crying needs in Asia and Africa?

Did you know there are teenaged girls from Christian homes in Asia and Africa who are asking the same thing about pagan America? There are Christian girls in Asia who think they will be more fruitful on "foreign" soil than they will be at home. We will be giving copies of this book to them.

Is it heartless to be unconcerned about needs far away? We must not be unconcerned, but we must remember that we cannot fight every battle. We must fight the desperate battles at hand. In the first century A.D., Paul saw the needs in Asia, but the Lord Himself forbade Paul to go there. During the years we turn our hearts to home, there still may be ways we can meet emergency needs in places away from our immediate community.

Here's how we handle this very dilemma. We know many places we could serve desperate people in desperate situations all over the world. For example, there are young girls our age dying every night under the rigors of forced prostitution in Thailand. Their own fathers sold them into slavery. We know of a rescue operation that gets these girls out before they die. This operation could use our presence. Would we like to go and help? Of course we would want to help save any lives we could. We would also like to see this operation supervised and strengthened by local church authority, which simply isn't there yet. In the meantime, we are working to build up our own local church authority and our own integrity by fulfilling our biblical duties in our home and community. We pray for our friends in Thailand and we send them funds that can sustain them until their situation is on more biblical footing. This is how we handle a complex need during an historic period of transition.[4] Let's work to see a successful transition by strengthening the families and churches in our own area, starting with our own.

---

4 We believe we should work toward a cultural transition that can move families and churches from dysfunctional status toward consistent biblical fidelity. This transition will not be brought about by feminine manipulation, nagging, or organizing, but by God's supernatural blessing as more and more girls and women begin personally and privately obeying what they see in Scripture.

If we could see today's situation with mature spiritual eyes we would see just how desperate are the needs in our own back yard. And not just with the destitute. Apostasy is a desperate condition that must be addressed. Apostate families and churches require the kind of repair that can only be done as average people obey simple commands of Scripture. As we stop compromising and start obeying, we will see the transition back to biblical methodology become a reality.

In a less-than-perfect church, what can I do to minister to the needy?

No church will ever be perfect. Because at the moment our churches are *seriously* less than perfect, there is a *lot* for willing, hard-working young women to do. Most churches and communities are desperately needy.

If you want to be involved in missions work, start where you are and begin thinking like a missionary. Locate the pressing needs. Find the lost and then biblical ways in which to reach them. Before the days of widespread missions organizations in the 19th century, and before the days of government welfare in the 20th, families served as the providers of evangelism and outreach to the poor, the lost, and the needy. Fathers took initiative to provide not only for their own households, but others. The members of his household, often the women, acted on the father's wishes in his name and provided relief. This kind of generosity and munificence marked a man as a leader, and his influence in the community grew with his maturity and reputation as a protector and provider. Imagine the kind of influence your family can have on the direction of society and culture when your father's well-earned stature as a town father is recognized. Family members who work together, doing God's work together, will become tomorrow's leaders. Together they will begin to reverse the problems girls face as they look at their options. Girls will begin to increase the extent of the influence they can have through their families.

These are a few specific things the women in the Bible did to serve those around them:

Teaching and discipling younger women to be keepers at home, submissive wives, loving mothers, modest, and good (Titus 2:3-5); helping to provide and care for widows in their immediate family (Ruth, I Timothy 5:16); creating garments and other necessities for the poor and visiting the sick (Acts 9:36-39, Matthew 25:35-40); giving to the needs of the Church (Matthew 27:55, Luke 21:2-4, Romans 16:1-2); talking about the things of God in the home to instruct fellow Christians (2 Timothy 1:5); extending hospitality to saints and strangers alike (Genesis 18:6, Genesis 24:15-20, I Samuel 25:14-42, I Kings 17:8-24, II Kings 4:8-38, Matthew 8:14-15, Acts 16:14-15, Romans 12:13, I Timothy 5:10, Hebrews 13:2, I Peter 4:9, 3 John 1:8).

But what can young women do when the whole culture is in a weakened, dysfunctional state? What if our fathers, pastors and even mission societies are all more interested in the weak alternatives to God's order? What if they don't like God's design?

This makes it very difficult for young girls, especially when they want to do the right thing by honoring and obeying those in authority over them. This is why it is so important to study and then begin to appeal to those authorities from the position of having blameless lives.

We know now what happens when daughters humble themselves and then begin to be strong in those biblical patterns within their control—like, for example, showing our interest in the great potential of the home. It is a powerful thing when daughters show serious interest in their fathers' role as the head of the home. What if we all showed a greater willingness to serve our fathers and all their interests, especially those spiritual interests few people ever cared for?

We have seen that when girls do this, they discover more biblical paths toward community evangelism and opportunities for helping the poor. It is not long before fathers begin to see the wisdom in walking in those paths rather than in the counterfeit ways that take their daughters far from productive homes. Will all fathers walk in the wisdom that is revealed to them? Maybe not all. But maybe yours will.

Do you think girls who are involved in certain missions or ministry work should leave that work and try to be more productive at home?

Erica gives her perspective:

There is a worldwide movement within the Church that promotes the idea that a majority of Christian women, especially single women, should be involved with ministries based outside of their homes. Unfortunately, this idea has numerous roots in feminism. Without realizing it, many dear sisters have combined feministic ideology with their Christianity. Worthy pastors and other spiritual leaders, using fragments of Scripture, have instructed them that a decision to leave their families at home while they "follow God's will" is noble, good, and even sacrificial. These women and girls deny their God-given role and instead turn to embrace the position of their counterpart, the men of our societies. The result is a global Christian community made up of domineering women who wonder why there are so few godly male leaders around. I was one of those young ladies. If the above statements had been addressed to me a couple of years ago, I would have recoiled at the allegation that I had feministic tendencies. It wasn't until I was convicted by the truth that my heart began to change. Proverbs 27:5, 6 says, "Open rebuke is better than love carefully concealed. Faithful are the wounds of a friend, but the kisses of an enemy are deceitful." I write in the spirit of Ephesians 4:15. The words I share with you are not meant to condemn or belittle. Rather, I urge you to read this and prayerfully seek application for your life.

I want to open with a question: "Does the principle of having ministry-at-home (vs. ministry-outside-the-home) apply to all girls?" It would be wrong for me to make a blanket statement and say that all Christian women are called to ministry exclusively within their home...forever...no exceptions. It would be equally wrong for me to say that most Christian women are called to ministry outside of their homes. In Titus 2, Paul writes, "...admonish the younger women to love their husbands, to love their children, to be discreet, chaste, homemakers, good, obedient to their own husbands, that the word of God may not be blasphemed." This verse speaks of a woman who is content ministering within her home to her family. This is not a popular passage of Scripture within the Body of Christ today. One thing we ladies need to grasp is that our cultures usually don't reflect God's best for us. And in our efforts to attain His best, we have often, like Eve, caved in to temptation and attempted to "become like God," creating ideas and convictions which have very little, if any, scriptural basis. We must retrain our minds and hearts to follow not what the majority says (even the Christian majority), but what the Holy Scriptures instruct.

For example, if God wanted the majority of His daughters to be about His business in ministries based outside of the home, don't you think He would have included many examples of that in the Bible? Instead, we see time and time again faithful wives, daughters, and servant girls in submission to male authority, which was usually their husband, father/father figure, or master. Even single women were able to have wonderful ministries from their homes (Acts 9:36-41, 16:14, 15).

Often Christians confuse achievement or prosperity with being in line with God's perfect will for one's life. Although these two can go hand in hand, it is not true that just because you are doing well in life, you are in the center of God's will. Oswald Chambers said in *My Utmost for His Highest*, "It is the things that are right and noble and good from the natural standpoint that keep us from God's best." My heart is grieved when I think of Christian brothers and sisters who are very "successful" and yet at heart they are discontent and miserable, because they have settled for mere good instead of striving for God's best. Having experienced this myself only makes the observation more difficult. I am so thankful for the grace of God continually at work in my life.

At the age of 16 I left home to do full-time ministry work with a United States pro-life group. The group's mission was to polarize the issue of abortion, or, in other words, make people decide which "choice" they really supported, life or death. I knew that the work I was doing was "good." After all, I was in a ministry that brought the reality of abortion to the people of the USA. I really thought this was where God wanted me, but somewhere, in my heart, there was a yearning for so much more. I found myself making the 3-hour trip home almost every weekend to go and see my family. Once I got there, it was difficult to leave. I wanted to be home. My little brothers and sisters would beg me to stay. It was hard to explain that I was following my "duty to God." Or was I?

At this point in time, I hit rock bottom. I remember being on my bedroom floor in my apartment, sobbing. I lay there and cried out to God, "O Lord, please show me Your will for my life so I can follow it. I want to do what You want me to do. If I am in the center of Your will, then why am I so miserable?" No answer. I continued to call out to my Savior, pleading with Him to show me the path I should take. As I cried myself to sleep, a command came to my mind, "Seek Me."

The life application of this command came through a slow and tedious process. And trust me, I am still working on it! In my finite thinking, I had come to believe that seeking God was confined within Bible studies, church attendance, theological discussions, etc. My patient Teacher began to show me that to seek Him I must know Him. To know Him, I must follow in His life steps. I really began to pray to God, asking for wisdom and guidance in every decision I made. I did my best to submit myself to Christ's authority over every area of my life. I immersed myself in the Word of God, asking for discernment and ways that I could exercise in my own life the concepts I was learning through Scripture. Through a variety of sources (i.e., Scripture, sermons on tape, articles, books, etc.), the Lord showed me that I needed to return to my father's home. Above all of them was the Holy Spirit-driven conviction and scriptural confirmation that going home was right.

Once home, my parents and I began to discuss what God's will for my life might be. I was back under my father's roof, now what? Through the Word, He reminded me to seek Him:

"Be still and know that I am God..." (Psalm 46:10)

"I waited patiently for the Lord; and He inclined to me, and heard my cry." (Psalm 40:1)

"Trust in the Lord with all your heart, lean not on your own understanding; in all your ways acknowledge Him, and He shall direct your paths." (Proverbs 3:5,6)

The Lord wants us to be still before Him, learning patience and allowing Him to work through us, tuning our ears to His call on our lives as He molds us into His image.

Now that I have recognized the high calling of serving in my home, each day is looked at as having the utmost potential. I am learning to take joy in serving my father and mother and to honor them in all I do. As I learn to disciple my brothers and sisters, I know that it will have an eternal effect. I have my bad days, for sure (just ask my five siblings!), but I strive to be aware of areas that need improvement and begin afresh right away. Most of my time is spent at home cleaning, cooking, and caring for children. On the surface, this looks like a life of monotonous drudgery, but that is far from the truth. In fact, this time is incredibly precious! What other way would I be able to spend hours on end with my little sisters at my side, teaching them how to become godly and proper young ladies? If I were outside our home, would I be able to regularly participate in my younger brothers' chivalrous adventures in our woods? My service is not limited to my family, either. Because I have not committed my time to outside ministry, I am available to help others in addition to my household. I am so thankful for my father, who allows me to serve others in this capacity. These blessed opportunities confirm in my heart that I am more productive for God's kingdom now than before. All honor and praise be to God, Who has brought me truly home!

I will say that the act of returning home can be much easier when your parents, especially your father, agree with you. When I first returned home, it took a while for my father to understand my convictions. I came to realize that my presentation of my newfound beliefs was not as respectful as it should be. As we learned to communicate better, our relationship deepened, and I am happy to say that we get along better now than ever before!

When we ladies choose to "turn to the ancient paths," we will see an awakening within the Bride of Christ. May we never forget Who has called us, and let us always strive for greatness! I will close with a verse of encouragement and instruction.

"When You said, 'Seek My face,' my heart said to You, 'Your face, Lord, will I seek'...I would have lost heart, unless I had believed that I would see the goodness of the Lord in the land of the living. Wait on the Lord; be of good courage and He shall strengthen your heart; wait I say on the Lord" (Psalms 27:8,13,14)!

To God be the Glory!

But what about Jesus's remark that anyone who is unwilling to leave father, mother, sisters, brothers, etc. is not worthy to follow Him? If Jesus calls me to do something for Him, am I not obligated to leave my family behind?

We need to understand the context of this verse. At first, becoming a Christian convert meant leaving the religion of the Pharisees and the oral traditions of a tight religious community. Converts found opposition and rejection among the other Jews, even within their own families, and then Gentile converts did too. What we believe Jesus is saying here is this: we are supposed to love Him more than we love any of these things, and we must be willing to leave everything dear to us, in order to follow Him. We must leave situations that will stand in the way of obeying Him and following Him. We can't become so comfortable in our homes, communities, and countries that we are unwilling to leave those for His sake—or we are unworthy of Him.

The principle applies to Christians today as much as to the first converts. If your family is pagan and tells you that you cannot follow Christ, and you cannot appeal to them, the answer is clear: you must follow the Lord instead of family members. Christ is not necessarily commanding physical departure from families (this verse also mentions leaving wives and children, but we know from Scripture that a believing husband can't abandon his unbelieving wife, and if he does not provide for these, he is called "worse than an infidel"). He is certainly not commanding that we separate ourselves from families who are following after Him. Those families are not going to hinder the gospel; they will promote it and live it *as a family*.

But there may come a time when a Christian has to separate herself, physically, from her family. If a girl is in an unbelieving family that doesn't welcome or allow her sanctifying influence, she may well have to leave her family in order to follow Christ. As we have stated before, she needs to seek first the godly advice and then protection of a substitute authority. It would be safer if she could be taken in by and become part of another godly family, serving and ministering to them and their church, until she is married. We know of several families with young children who have been happy to take in such young ladies and consider their presence in their busy homes a real Godsend.

Though the young woman wouldn't be at home with her *biological family*, she would be able to use her God-given role and duties within the sphere she is created to glorify God in best: the home.

So being in our homes counts as ministry?

Not if you're lazy. But if you are serving diligently, you are ministering. And if you are ministering, you are helping your home become the powerful influence it was meant to be. It is a tool for reaching out. It can be a center for extremely fruitful ministry. Focusing ministry to others from the home does not mean, of course, that a woman rarely sets foot outside the house. It doesn't even mean that all ministry has to be strictly home-centered, even though it should primarily be done *from* the home. A woman's home is her headquarters, and from it she can extend her influence and benevolence to others in all places. But some of the greatest victories for the kingdom take place *within households*.

There are some who think the work that goes on in the churches is somehow more "spiritual" than ministry conducted from the home. However, Scott Brown, the director of the National Center for Family-Integrated Churches, says quite the opposite has been true:

> The home in the New Testament was the center of spiritual activity. Even a casual reading of the New Testament reveals that the home was a haven for prayer, healing, biblical teaching, breaking of bread, hospitality, ministry to the sick, and happy, genuine relationships. In short, it was a place to display the truth, justice, mercy, and goodness of God. …In the early Church, the work of evangelism and equipping was regularly staged in the context of a home. The home was the cradle of the Church. In contrast, in the modern Church, the ministry of the home has been transported to the church facility. In fact, most pastors do not think you are involved in "ministry" unless it is on their turf.

Ministry in the home has been devalued at the expense of the family, fragmenting ministries of the local churches.[5]

The widow of Zarepheth, the Shunammite, Mary and Martha, Dorcas, Lydia, and Phoebe were all commended for opening their homes to people and for their gracious hospitality. New Testament examples of spiritual activity taking place in homes and households include Acts 2:46-47; Matthew 9:10-13; Matthew 8:14-15; Luke 7:6, 10; Luke 7:36-38; Acts 5:41-42; Acts 10:30-32; Acts 11:11-14; Acts 16:31-34; Romans 16:5; Romans 12:13; I Peter 4:9; Hebrews 13:1-2; I Timothy 3:2; and I Timothy 5:10.

Even unusual biblical examples, like those of Rahab and Jael, illustrate how women can do great deeds in their homes (Rahab opened her family's home to the Israelite spies—Jael was practicing hospitality in her tent!) Had these women been strapping on armor and battle gear, and gone to seek glory and fame in the more "obvious" way, they might have missed out on the opportunity to do the *greatest* good for God's nation. God can provide us incredible opportunities to serve Him when we are in our homes, ready and willing to serve Him there.

Crystal tells about a few ministry projects she has done at home:

> I helped edit a book for Christian young women, published a newsletter encouraging young women in godliness, and assisted a few families who owned home businesses at their booths at homeschool conferences, among other things. Really and truly, I sought none of these jobs or ministries. In each instance, my parents or I were approached about them, or the Lord just laid them in my lap.

---

5 Scott Brown, "Restoring the Household for Equipping and Evangelism," June 7, 2004.

If you *really* want to serve God with your whole being, He will bring the opportunities, no matter where you are.

What does a family hospitality ministry look like? How does it work?

Our mother, a modern-day heroine of the faith, understood the importance of keeping the home, and the magnitude of everything involved in that. She made her home and its inhabitants her life's work. But she did not let her work stop at keeping us clothed and fed and the dishes washed; she made homemaking an art form, and her home a work of art. At one time in our childhood, we lived temporarily in a small, charmless house. But despite the limitations, our mother made this home so pleasant and cozy that we still remember it with our fondest childhood memories.

In fact, we children weren't the only people who loved being in that home. Our house was a favorite place of many of our friends, who came to visit all the time. They were attracted to it because of its hospitable warmth and the pleasant family atmosphere that our mother took pains to develop. Ever since, we have loved demonstrating hospitality, considering it an art form, but even more importantly, as one of the greatest ministries that a family can have. Demonstrating hospitality so well as to attract people to your home can be used as a tool and opportunity for discipleship—something that the whole family can contribute to.

Our father, who worked as a political consultant at that time, looked on our home as his favorite lecturing ground. He would invite people from all social backgrounds and fields, of all ages and interests, in groups and individually, into our home for meals, Bible studies, one-on-one mentoring, lectures, political meetings, business meetings, and the list goes on and on. Our home seemed like the focal point for everything interesting that was going on. We attribute this to our mother's gracious hospitality, since she could make any person from any strata of society feel welcome and comfortable.

We considered it a privilege to help her clean and decorate the house and cook for guests—we knew what an important work it was, and how much it was appreciated by the people we welcomed into our home. Even at young ages, we knew the home was not simply our own refuge from the world—a place to sit back and block the world out—but one of our most important mission fields for discipling and shepherding people. Recently a friend of ours told us, "One of the things I love about your home is that you all seem to genuinely want me to come here and take up all your time. I've had other families invite me over for a meal, and they're really nice and hospitable, but after a certain amount of time is over, they make it clear that the visit is over, and that I'm intruding on their time and on their lives. Your family seems so eager to give me your whole day, to talk to me about anything and help me with anything. That really means a lot to me."

Our ministry of hospitality to young women is a large part of our family's legacy. If it wasn't for our mother's example of whole-hearted ministry from home, our father's courageous teaching, and needy, appreciative young women like this, we never would have written this book.

CHAPTER EIGHTEEN

FATHERS AND DAUGHTERS OF DESTINY

BECOMING A WOMAN OF VISION

The future is bright for today's young women. How can we say this, in light of all the problems afflicting the girls of this generation? We have not glossed over the fact that Western women have suffered more in the past 60 years than during many periods of Western history. We have done our best to address the heartbreaking trials girls are facing right now—their compromised circumstances, their enemies, their temptations, the ungodly influences surrounding them. But our book's overall message is one of hope.

Many young women look at their options and feel only despair, and look only for survival tips and quick emergency fixes to their problems. Girls such as these may find the solutions and strategies we offer in this book impossibly naïve and idealistic. We do want to acknowledge the emergency needs of today's daughters, and most of all we want to explain biblical solutions which will prove to be long-term.

The future *is* bright, because young women all over the world are just starting to realize that they can have an influence for good when they start changing their lives and choosing the less-walked path toward honor and protection. They are starting to change history just by looking for the simple commands of Scripture, to obey them, verse by verse.

We don't want to make any wild promises here. We can't promise that God will turn your father into a man of vision and faith who will lead and protect his daughter. We can't promise that your family will become an example of unity and a powerhouse for reformation. We can't even promise that your parents won't reject you if you pick up any of the ideas in this book. We can't promise that you will meet Prince Charming and have a fairy tale life. We can't promise that God will spare our nations the judgments they deserve for their disobedience.

But we can tell you what God promises:

> "Blessed is every one that feareth the Lord; that walketh in His ways. For thou shalt eat the labour of thine hands: happy shalt thou be, and it shall be well with thee." (Psalm 128:1, 2)

> "And we know that all things work together for good to them that love God, to them who are the called according to His purpose." (Romans 8:28)

> "For the Lord God is a sun and shield: the Lord will give grace and glory: no good thing will He withhold from them that walk uprightly. O Lord of hosts, blessed is the man that trusteth in Thee." (Psalm 84:11, 12)

Like the Proverbs 31 woman, we can truly smile at the future, because we have blessings in store for us. Those who fear and obey God are promised such things as wisdom, peace, happiness, full lives, straight paths, prosperity, favor, and good repute in the sight of God and man, and "a hope and a future."[1]

What will your hope and future be? Most young women, even most Christians, don't give their futures much thought. We want instant gratification and immediate personal fulfillment. We want immediate results, and we want them now!

Working toward and looking forward to the personal blessings we will see in our lifetimes is a good start, but we should think further, about the consequences our deeds will have on the rest of the world, now and after we're gone. How is your obedience to Scripture affecting the world? The Bible tells us that God rewards righteousness not only with *personal* blessings, but also with blessings on a person's church, family, government, and entire nation.

When our fathers have our devotion, our help, and our prayers, they can grow as men of God. As they lead and raise the standard for righteousness in their own families, their families stand out as lights. Daughters, by learning to act like godly women, give the entire culture an example of womanliness which needs to be revived. They encourage our society to rethink its view of the value of women. They inspire the men around them to become valorous, chivalrous, and masculine. By striving above all to obey God, they invite Him to shower our land with His greatest blessings.

We aren't trying to work you up into a feministic, "girl-power" frenzy. What we want to do here is encourage you to be grateful to God for giving you your womanhood, your role, and your mission field, to take hold of these firmly and rejoice in them.

---

1   Psalm 111:10, Psalm 29:11, Psalm 21:6, Psalm 92:10-14, Proverbs 3:6, Psalm 35:27, Proverbs 3:4, Jeremiah 29:11.

We stated at the beginning of this book that this was not a survival guide. We hope by now to have given you a small glimpse of a vision—a vision of Victory through Virtuous Womanhood. We will now unveil womanhood's final secret weapon in the battle for progressive dominion: *mother*hood. Our posterity. The legacy we will pass on to our children.

Woman's hope and future is fulfilled through *motherhood,* one of the greatest blessings God gives women. One of the ways God bestows blessings on women is through children. And not just 2.2 or 2.5 children, but many children. We should seek to deserve this kind of blessing: "And they blessed Rebekah, and said unto her, Thou art our sister, be thou the mother of thousands of millions, and let thy seed possess the gate of those which hate them" (Genesis 24:60).

Yes, children are a *blessing* from God. "Lo, children are an heritage of the Lord: and the fruit of the womb is his reward. As arrows are in the hand of a mighty man; so are children of the youth. Happy is the man that hath his quiver full of them: they shall not be ashamed, but they shall speak with the enemies in the gate" (Psalm 127:3-5).

We should aspire to be like the wife in Psalm 128:3: "Thy wife shall be as a fruitful vine by the sides of thine house: thy children like olive plants round about thy table."

Too many women forget that the hand that rocks the cradle really does rule the world. As Christian women, we should pray that God would bless the fruit of the womb and grant us a full quiver. We should study and prepare to raise them to be exemplary, effective Christian warriors. We should think ahead, not only to our children but to our grandchildren and great-grandchildren, aspiring to be a mother of thousands of millions, and aspiring to see our children possess the gates of their enemies for the glory of God. This is the vision of Victory through Virtuous Womanhood.

You have but one lifetime to spend in our Lord's service. How you spend these years of your life will touch the course of history and change it forever. Fourteen young women, contributors to this work, rose above their inherently sinful feminist natures, through God's grace, and became heroines of the faith. They did this by repenting, then putting their hands to the plow, not looking back.

Now is the time to take your stand. Are you ready to become a heroine of the faith?

> "Choose this day whom you will serve...but as for me and my house, we will serve the Lord." (Joshua 24:15)

APPENDIX A

ADVICE TO FATHERS:
AN INTERVIEW WITH GEOFFREY BOTKIN
BY ANNA SOFIA AND ELIZABETH BOTKIN

*D*addy, *what are some of the most important things you think dads need to hear?*

GB: About their duties to their daughters?

A&EB: *Yes.*

GB: Traditionally, dads would hear about those things when very young, in their homes, where their own fathers would be training them to care for their sisters and mother in preparation for being the leader of their own family some day. Adult men would traditionally hear these duties reinforced in church, proclaimed without apology by church officers and modeled by all the men of the church.

A&EB: *Right. That's traditionally. But what about today?*

GB: Many of today's dads don't go to church. And the ones who do aren't hearing these things, because many pastors are afraid to teach them. The new tradition doesn't say much about duty of any sort. Church has become a place for religious self-fulfillment. Many male churchgoers go today for some sort of therapy, or feeling. Not to learn how to be men.

Before I go further I should clarify the importance of the Church. If I ever sound critical of the Church, I am critical only of the Church's enemies, those people within the Church and outside of it who force the Church off of her foundations and redefine its purpose. The Church is a vital part of Christ's kingdom. Men must be champions of the Church's purity and important stature in society.

My big complaint about the modern Church is the weak new pragmatic traditions that creep in and rob the Church of her glory. One of the worst of these trends transforms Christian men into wimps. Many of today's teachings turn male moral cowardice into some kind of Christian virtue of modern delicacy. Maturity has been redefined into sophisticated selfishness. Women of the Church want their part of the trend. They insist they are entitled to roles of authority. Men politely shrink away. With nothing left to do in feminized churches, they don't lead and rarely participate.

A&EB: *Is this the main reason men are so uninvolved in church?*

GB: The main reason probably goes back to the flawed structure of the modern Church, which is not biblical. With the "senior pastor" or "celebrity pastor" model, men are not needed for anything but check-writing. And driving kids to youth group. It is actually in the pastor's interest to keep men invisible, immature, and disenfranchised from church leadership. It is men who started this tradition, and it is men who sustain this by their silence and ambivalence.

A&EB: *And you believe men should be working to recover the good traditions. The older traditions.*

GB: Yes. With all their strength. With all their resolve. With all their masculinity. We should defend the Bride of Christ. Whatever happened to the doctrine once known as the priesthood of every believer? Not long ago, all the men helped with church affairs and church expansion. All fathers were the spiritual leaders at home. Men can and should begin exercising this kind of courage as boys. Once they become fathers, they should be so motivated by the desire to protect the future for their wives and children that they work even harder.

A&EB: *But if the churches are too weak to tell them or show how to do this…*

GB: Then fathers need to take a lesson from the great Reformation. God's commandments are available in their personal Bibles, which fathers must start reading on their own. Then, obedience to Scripture must be modeled even in the face of ridicule. And even in the face of state threats and social stigma. This is difficult, I know. It's especially tragic when a man wants to do something valuable in God's service, consults the church and is told to lower his aspirations, and to limit his spiritual initiative to service as Sunday parking attendant. That hardly advances the kingdom of God.

A&EB: *You're saying mature fatherhood advances the kingdom of God.*

GB: It advances it, sustains it, glorifies it, and illustrates several important aspects of the kingdom and the character of the King.

A&EB: *So why do fathers not want to rise to the glorious calling God has appointed them to?*

GB: Well, deep down, many fathers really want to. If young men could see mature fatherhood modeled in their homes, all of them would dearly aspire to follow in their dads' footsteps.

A&EB: *Most of today's fathers have not seen biblical fatherhood. How about grandfathers?*

GB: Very few men born since 1945 have seen biblical family life and functional family life.

A&EB: *Why is this?*

GB: The predominant Christian worldview of the 19th Century was replaced with a dark and pessimistic one in the 20th. This steered the entire culture, not just the family, into spiritual blindness. Because of spiritual blindness, men think and act as slaves of a world system that locks them into blind conformity and chronic cowardice. It's very hard to see one's way out of this system, but many men repent of gross negligence once they see a picture of godly masculinity, and they turn their hearts toward their children.

A&EB: *Talk some more about turning hearts to children. Is this the first step in becoming the fathers they were meant to be?*

GB: For many fathers, this step of repentance has been the first step. They see eternity. They see the souls of their children. This new concern gives them new sight, new vision. They can see the weakness of the chains that have kept them tied down in fear for so long, and then they begin leading. Simply stepping out of that darkness and opening up Scripture is a step of leadership. Once they start reading Scripture daily to their children, everything changes.

A&EB: *The fathers become leaders?*

GB: The entire family changes and can begin leading other families. The sons become more serious about being real men. God commands us in Colossians 2:8 to be free men. We can't be free when we're deceived. Deception keeps us in captivity to false ideas. We are warned in that verse about being taken captive to philosophy and empty deception, according to the elementary principles of the world and the traditions of men. Today we're all captive to some extent, because we do not live in Christian societies that encourage biblical thinking and living. But this is no excuse to live in ways contrary to our Creator's will. We must think like the Lord, then act like him.

Tomorrow, if the government announced, "The newest scientific research shows that the best dads and the most compliant dads must all place their daughters in state-run orphanages at age six months," dads had better check this against the guidelines of Scripture to see if this is consistent with mature fatherhood or a betrayal of their high office. Dads have a duty to find out how the world's traditions have infected everything we do, and then start doing things differently. The goal is not to be different, the goal is to be sanctified, to be holy, to be set apart to advance the Lord's business on His terms.

A&EB: *In what areas have today's fathers been most deceived?*

GB: For Americans who profess to be Christians, the list is as long as their daughters' sorrows are deep. That's a long list. The biggest area of deception is in the realm of covenant duty.

A&EB: *Can we make a list of the deceptions? How about "the top ten lies that rule the lives of modern fathers?" A list like this would be welcome to many fathers. Or would it?*

GB: It would be welcome to many. To others who are even mildly deceived, their response will be angry hostility to such a list. This is the nature of deception. If you publish this list, many of your critics will say, "These things are not lies, or transgressions, or problems. We can be Christians and still think like everyone else thinks. We have Christian liberty to live the way everyone else is living, and this list smacks of legalism."

A&EB: *In our book we define legalism as the fleshly pursuit of man's moralism in hopes of earning salvation. Joyful obedience to all of God's precepts is the response of the grateful believer who has been saved by grace through faith.*

GB: Well put. Careful conformity to God's standards for righteous living is not legalism but faithful maturity. Accusations of "legalism" are the first defense of the man (or woman) who is ashamed and reluctant to repent. Are you sure you want to publish such a controversial list?

A&EB: *What is your advice, Daddy?*

GB: Good answer! I'll give you an abbreviated list that's not too… dangerous. I'll share it in love, and you can print it in love. When the critics land on you with boots and spurs, I'll protect you. Ready?

A&EB: *Ready.*

GB: This is controversial territory. Maybe we'll go with this one for your first book: "The top ten empty deceptions that keep today's Christian fathers from turning their hearts to the duties they owe their daughters, denying daughters the richness of life they might otherwise experience."

A&EB: *Okay.*

GB: *Deception 1:* "I belong to myself."

With this attitude men turn their hearts inward toward pathological selfishness. They look out for "number one." They become withdrawn, distant, defensive, and abdicate faithfulness in even small matters, as their families become typically dysfunctional. Once dads shift their thinking into this self-preservation mode, moral cowardice replaces all fatherly initiative. Because the Lordship of Christ is nothing more than a catch-phrase, the authority and protection offered by Christ is not real to them at all. Neither is the authority and protection the father might have offered his daughter. Because his life is not driven by his duties to his Lord and King, the deceived dad does nothing to bring the world under Christ's dominion. Rather, he exists as an opportunistic slave of the world to get all that he can from it. His theology becomes antinomian, which means he believes he can decide for himself what is lawful and unlawful. He does what is right in his own eyes and simply wants others to leave him alone. This is a very dangerous outlaw mentality.

Solution 1: Repent privately and then confess your faults to your family. Give your heart fully to the Lordship of Christ and turn your heart fully to your daughter. Lose your life in the duties you owe the kingdom of God by building your family on God's terms. Read the Bible to your family daily so you can all be reoriented together.

Deception 2: "All I need to know I learned from the schoolyard."

When in the narrow "self-preservation mode," the modern father is voluntarily ignorant. He learned about survival from streetwise peers who are also victims of a corrupt and feminized culture. He is stubbornly devoted to this law of the jungle. Why should he expose himself to more of the disgrace he already feels being a married male? Especially if he is a Christian father? After all, the Christian stigma is an embarrassing one these days. Dad doesn't want to know much lest he discover what God truly expects of a Christian man. He doesn't study the Bible. He rarely reads it. When he does, it is to find justification for what he is doing, not to discover his marching orders.

Solution 2: Ask God to forgive you for your willful scriptural illiteracy. Ask Him to teach you from the Word, then study it carefully every morning. Explain what you learn to your family.

Deception 3: "Success is everything."

By this most fathers mean, "Failure, as defined by the world, is my worst nightmare." Because of spiritual blindness, dads don't know there are far worse nightmares than this. Thus fathers fear their contemporaries, and they are scared of state authorities, unwilling to challenge the opinion of either. This leads to doing everything the world's way, bowing to every statist bureaucracy, and even thinking in conformity with the state, making scientific pragmatism an authoritative voice in decisions. Success at any cost means moral cowardice at every turn. What do daughters learn from this example? "I guess I've really got to go easy on the Christian stuff or I'll be stigmatized and won't get ahead or find happiness." This can lead daughters into idolatry, which they come to think is acceptable. Mammon and the pop culture become central in their lives.

Solution 3: Reevaluate every official obligation and every financial transaction in light of kingdom requirements. View unlawful state requirements as judgments on your disobedience and ask God to lift them and put all your affairs, especially your material affairs, under His lordship. Make every decision on principle, not according to pragmatism. Make whatever changes you need to make with courage and decisiveness.

Deception 4. "Daughters are a big expense and big inconvenience if they are born at the wrong time."

Even Christian men have been taken captive by the idea that children are a curse and that debt is a blessing, when the opposite is true. So dads aggressively limit the blessings of God (babies), especially during the first years of aggressive, selfish consumerism that makes for the "solid" evangelical marriage. Incalculable numbers of daughters and sons have been killed by secretive evangelical abortions and abortifacient birth control practices. Evangelicals have redefined marriage along worldly lines.

Solution 4: Remember that good providers provide what God counts as blessings, not what they world insists are entitlements. Believe God when he says children are a blessing and that he is a faithful provider.

Never cut off the offspring God calls holy—bring your daughters up with the aspiration that marriage can advance the kingdom of God and that children are of measureless worth to God and all fathers.

Deception 5: "You can't hold onto 'em forever!"

By this deception fathers relinquish responsibility for their daughters at younger and younger ages. Fathers are supposed to hold onto their daughters until the daughter is given in marriage to a responsible husband. Deceived dads use Deception 5 to unnecessarily expose their daughters to the dangers of ruthless day care environments, false religious instruction in government classrooms, the company of wayward peers, unsafe employment experiences, oppressive personal debt, and one of the worst environments of all: the college campus.

Solution 5: Understand your duty to provide religious instruction to your daughter, to protect her mind and body with the highest standards of purity, and train her for a fruitful, successful marriage. Don't delegate any responsibility you are supposed to keep for yourself. Resourceful fathers can provide everything a daughter needs, including higher education, under the shelter of the paternal roof.

Deception 6: "The 'attitude thing' will fix itself."

Every father has periodic difficulty and disciplinary challenges with a daughter's behavior, emotions, attitudes, and conduct. Fathers are quick to withdraw and not deal with problems biblically, because today's psychologists offer the ideal excuse: toxic behavior will heal itself, and parents should not worry about rebellion. Daughters at every age need godly discipline, just as fathers do. It is the father's duty to provide it for the daughter without compromise. Sin must be justly dealt with. Immediately. Fathers have a duty to fix patterns of misconduct when daughters are young. This is God's prescription for peace and the delightful father-daughter relationship.

Solution 6: Spank her firmly and calmly when she's young, for active and passive disobedience, and she will love you for it all her life.

Deception 7: "She's got to have a college degree from a state-approved school."

Why do modern fathers believe such nonsense when they know colleges no longer offer higher learning? Any father who has attended college knows about academic corruption, classroom dishonesty, and campus moral degeneracy. Why does a young girl need college? To be initiated into modern degeneracy? To become acceptable to the state? To be sorted by the state for service to the state? For the defiling experience of enduring the politics of a modern bureaucracy? In order to develop disciplines she never was encouraged to get at home? Because she has no other options for spending her time more productively? Because she needs to become a wage slave at a place that only hires people with questionably-obtained bachelor's degrees? So she can get a job later in life when her deadbeat husband refuses to work, or leaves her for a younger woman?

Yes, these are some of the faulty reasons many deceived dads have in mind as part of a young lady's educational upbringing. And these things are all good reasons *if* the girl is to be abandoned by her father to a life working in a corrupt bureaucracy, and *if* she is incorrigibly undisciplined and unresponsive to her father, and *if* she is incapable of working with her father, and *if* her father will not protect her from dangerous suitors.

Many college girls come from just such a tragic father-daughter relationship. Dad has been negligent in everything except helping her get her student loan, so she can be flung into the world in four years saddled with debt on top of her other weaknesses and vulnerabilities.

Solution 7: Protect your daughter properly when she is young, providing her freedom and training suitable to high calling, and she will not need a state credential to be educated or successful when she is 20 years old. Success in the real world of family living is no longer tied to a bachelor's degree.

Deception 8: "But my daughter needs the entire school experience in order to be a survivor like me, and to fit unobtrusively into today's modern world."

If daughters get schooling rather than education, they will turn out deceived, a chip off the old man's block, and they will be just as trapped in the ways of blind conformity as their cowardly fathers— in the permanent underclass.

In the words of public school teacher John Taylor Gatto, "Look...at the seven lessons of schoolteaching: confusion, class position, indifference, emotional and intellectual dependency, conditional self-esteem, surveillance—all of these things are prime training for permanent underclasses, people deprived forever of finding the center of their own special genius. Such a curriculum produces physical, moral, and intellectual paralysis, and no curriculum of content will be sufficient to reverse its hideous effects."

Solution 8: If you want to get the very most out of the short time you will have with your daughter before she marries, and if you want a close, joyful, relationship in which you can watch her develop her highest and best talents to their fullest extent, make home education a priority and sacrifice whatever worldly success you must in order to succeed at home, with your family.

Deception 9: "Close relationships with women are impossible, even with wives and daughters, because men and women are so different. We really don't need each other that much."

It is true that women do not need cowardly men, and have little desire to know them. But women do need the protection and intimacy of men who are courageous leaders and fearless protectors. Men can learn about the intricacies of the woman's heart by learning to understand their wives, caring for them and letting their wives draw close to them in respect. Daughters will respond with their hearts also, and ever more deeply as the father's heart is turned toward them and the health of their very souls. Men and women were designed to need each other and to function best when the relationship is spiritually close.

Solution 9: Don't believe the modern assessments of human relationships. We are made in God's image and have potentials that have been barely explored, especially in the father-daughter relationship. Love your wife in an understanding way and your daughter in a compassionate way, and respond to your daughter when she attempts to communicate with you.

Deception 10: "Love and marriage is a 'Cupid thing.' Chemistry and all that. Dads have to stay out of the way and let Cupid get his shot."

Most dads are stupefied when it comes to a daughter's relationships with boys. This is one of the more blinding deceptions of our time. The time just prior to marriage is the time in a girl's life when she needs the protection, advice, guidance, and blessing of her father more than at any other time. Marriage is the biggest practical decision she will make, and it is only cowardice that motivates fathers to excuse themselves from involvement.

Solution 10: Raise your daughter from a young age to have high standards of purity and high standards for suitors based on your own example in the home. When she is ready for marriage, thanks to your conscientious training, she will know how crucial is the choice of a man who will become her life's work. She will know about her own weaknesses and be as careful as she can be and lean on you heavily for your advice. If you are wise, you will do everything you can to help her meet a man of the caliber she will want, and deserve, and can grow old with.

A&EB: *How strict will you be with our suitors on the bride price issue?*

GB: That will depend on the suitor.

A&EB: *Can you tell our readers a little about the biblical bride price?*

GB: Well, it takes a history lesson. I'll keep it simple and brief. Families have always cared for themselves and their communities better than governments can. Before today's inferior days of forced wealth redistribution and impersonal retirement homes, sons and their wives would care for the sons' elderly parents. Sons also carried on the family legacy. All this was part of duty, passed down through generations. Daughters would marry outside the family and advance their husbands' estates. Because daughters didn't have the same responsibilities as sons, they did not formally inherit, but they did receive dowries from loving fathers *because daughters were not inferior to sons.* Sons received the inheritance, which was the foundation for furthering the family estate and providing for the elderly.

The bride price was usually the amount of a dowry, probably about three years' wages. Noble suitors would give the bride price to the girl's father and the father would give it to the girl as her dowry.

The bride price tradition benefited every culture that practiced it. Without the tradition, daughters were a financial liability to families and came to be viewed as inferior to sons. Sometimes daughters were murdered at birth. Those who weren't would have been unpopular with brothers because their dowries diminished the inheritance available to sons. Girls with dowries attracted plenty of worthless suitors who wanted the dowry more than the daughter, and the institutions of family and marriage were weakened.

With the bride price tradition, both institutions are strengthened over many generations. Good daughters attract worthy suitors who have proven themselves good, productive servants. By giving the bride price to the girl's father, suitors also prove they understand the father's authority over the daughter and their subordination to God's order and the father's authority. By giving the gift to the daughter, the father signifies his obligations to succeeding generations.

A&EB: *Can the bride price be something other than money?*

GB: I hope no father reading this turns the bride price tradition into an impossibly legalistic formula with dollars and cents attached to it. There is wisdom in all things endorsed or commanded by God, and we will benefit if we discover the principles embedded here. What are you looking for in a husband?

A&EB: *Well, among other things on our "list," we want men who are humble, mature, responsible, full of character, in submission to Christ and His order, including their authorities and ours.*

GB: You have just described spiritual capital. The bride price tradition will help you evaluate a young suitor and will show you whether he is rich in spiritual capital or so impoverished that he would make a miserable husband. A wealth of virtue may not be reflected in a young man's bank account. David was a poor shepherd boy. But he was rich in faith and courage and brought King Saul the head of Goliath as a bride price. Spiritual capital is a lot more important to me than a young man's bank account, and I'm thankful it is to you, too.

A&EB: *Let's get back to your list of deceptions. Have you known a lot of men who have repented in the ways you suggest above?*

GB: Many. Probably hundreds. And I'm old enough now to have seen the happy fruit they enjoy in being fathers and grandfathers whose daughters are grounded in the real liberty of solid family life. I also know many men who refused to do those simple things, then lost daughters, sons, and even wives to the world. These men have outward trappings of success, and that's what they chose over the better part. Today they see, with bitter regret, the folly of their decisions and the worthlessness of mammon.

A&EB: *How would you summarize your main message to men of the 21st century?*

GB: Men will always be leaders, whether they rise up and lead in the right direction or shrink back and lead in the wrong direction. Men cannot escape their role in God's order any more than women can. If men stand up and act like men according to a biblical definition, families, churches, and societies become functional instead of dysfunctional.

All men must start leading spiritually in their homes, their churches, and their communities. They need to discern what traditions should be established and maintained. They need to get started building firm foundations and customs—the institutions of civil society.

What has amazed me about good masculine leadership is this: some of the weakest, most unassuming men can rise up out of their cowardice and lethargy and become very effective champions of biblical leadership. It's not that hard. It's not that complicated. Taking the first simple steps of leading is the tough part, and then it gets easier from there. Biblical literacy is not that great a challenge. Mastering important doctrines is not that tough if one is willing to go beyond today's evangelical pabulum. Even leading publicly, in the roles of statesmen, is not that hard for a man who denies his fears and seizes the grand momentum of Western civilization.

A&EB: *What is the grand momentum of Western civilization?*

GB: Multigenerational sanctification. That means young people tried to understand what God had accomplished for and through the previous generation, and then to build on that foundation. Each generation tried to go beyond the previous in terms of personal holiness and biblical fidelity.

But let me be clear about the traditions of the West. Whether a tradition is old or new doesn't have anything to do with its value. Fidelity to scriptural truth is what matters. There are some old traditions that can be left in the ash heap of history. There are others that are godly and helpful that must be recovered. And there are new ones that can be started by resourceful, brave men. Discerning these differences is just one responsibility of wise leadership.

A&EB: *What were some of the biblical traditions men once understood and sustained?*

GB: In a general sense, after the Reformation, good men were more free to be Christian gentlemen in public. Concepts like duty and responsibility tended to be lived-out along biblical lines. Men knew where their duties and responsibilities lay. They knew it was up to them to strengthen their own backbones so they could in turn provide character to their communities, churches, and governments.

European nations were monarchies in those days. Subjects of European kings seemed to understand what it meant to be a subject of the King of kings. All men had a duty to honor Christ in thought, word, and action. At all times. A definition of manhood was being communicated to boys that suggested that real men honor Christ privately and publicly—that real men are family men—that real men face the problems of life in faith—that real men know how to live and how to die for the glory of God.

A&EB: *What were men like in those days? In everyday life?*

GB: Wow. What a great question. I wish I knew exactly what men were like. Have any of us "moderns" ever known a man who matched the stature and character of those men? Maybe not. But we fathers can aspire to that for ourselves and steer our sons in that direction.

I don't want your readers to misunderstand. God always has His dedicated enemies among men and women, and there were some clever rebels in the 17th and 18th centuries. But they had to be careful in revealing their rebellion because the culture was so comprehensively Christian. What did that mean for the average man? Someone said recently that even the average unregenerate fellow, meaning an unbeliever of those days, thought and acted with a solidly Christian worldview. His outward actions were consistent with biblical morality. They also pointed out that today's average believer lives and acts with a thoroughly pagan worldview. This is the big difference in pre-modern and post-Christian cultures. The men think and act differently.

As I read literature from the days of the Christian West, it appears that a large segment of the male population worked hard to be proper and civil at all times. They carried themselves with a dignity that becomes a man made in the image of God, and consistent with the humble character of their Savior. They saw it as a duty not only to possess exemplary manners and morals, but to improve themselves and their sons so that society could become more civilized with each passing generation. They knew they were building something important. They knew their building blocks were the commands of the King of kings. They seemed to understand the kingdom of God and why it was important for God's will to be done on earth as it is in heaven. The men seemed to understand that the family and the Church were vital institutions that needed to be sustained according to God's blueprint.

Fathers of that time seemed to know their assignment from God and didn't run away from it. It wasn't a grief to them. They found pleasure in being family men. They were thrilled by the kisses of their children, the hugs of their wives, by good food and drink. They reveled in good, hard work, in protecting and providing.

A&EB: *So family was more important then? To fathers?*

GB: In the thinking of virtually all young men and young women it was central to the work of building every institution of the kingdom of God.

A&EB: *And this is why God's sworn enemies, like Marx, wanted to destroy the family.*

GB: Exactly. No family…no kingdom of God. Weak family… kingdom of God in serious retreat.

A&EB: *And, no father…no family.*

GB: Dead right. That is what the Frankfurt School revolutionaries understood so well. The family can be destroyed by destroying the authority of the patriarchal father. Wilhelm Reich put it this way: "We must dethrone the patriarchal power in men."

A&EB: *How did the family become so dysfunctional? Is the Frankfurt School to blame?*

GB: Technically and scripturally, the buck always stops with Christian men, because we have the duty to protect society and the family. Christian men, primarily pastors, are to blame. Having said that, the Frankfurt School faculty saw the weakness of the Church and capitalized on it.

A&EB: *So they were capitalists all along? (laughter)*

GB: Actually, these socialists *were* masterful capitalists in the intellectual capital they deployed across the West. These neo-Marxists of the 1920s influenced the schools and media of the entire Western world so that the plague of anti-Christian and anti-family dogma would become universal by 1970. Their ideas are the root and branch of every deception I listed above. Thanks to the Frankfurt curriculum, everyone now "knows" that dads are the original oppressors and villains. The anti-family worldview has achieved dominion. But it would be wrong to place all the blame on the Comintern.[1] Their ideas attained dominion because the Christians relinquished dominion seventy years before the Comintern organized its comprehensive cartels. Today's widespread masculine cowardice spread across the West in the mid-nineteenth century in shameful voluntary retreat. Cowardice didn't spread into the pulpits. I'm afraid it started in the pulpits and spread outward from there.

A&EB: *Would you say there is a lot of Marxism in modern churches?*

GB: There is a lot of Marxist thinking everywhere in Western society because it is now the dominant worldview. Few church leaders know how to recognize it and refute it.

A&EB: *What does the Marxist worldview look like?*

GB: Many men who think like Marxists don't realize they do. Many pastors are insulted by the suggestion they might be Marxist. But then they express hostility to the suggestion that they need to conform their thinking to an unmoving biblical standard. This in itself is a Marxist

---

1   The Comintern is the nickname of the Communist Internationale, the organization charged by Lenin with the international expansion of the Communist revolution. The most influential Frankfurt School faculty members and founders were Comintern agents.

hostility to higher law, and it's reflected in the way they run their churches. Instead of preaching from a firm standard, they are more inclined to take a poll and give congregations what they want to hear.

If Christians depart from biblical theologies regarding God, man, and good and evil, then the pragmatic arguments of Marxism make sense. This is where Christians have stumbled into faulty thinking that leads to more faulty thinking. Marxism teaches that evil comes from environments, not wicked hearts. Marx wanted to destabilize society by starting fights between poor and rich. He heaped abuse on corrupt religion and tyrannical families and greedy property owners. He then taught that powerful socialist governments can solve huge problems and engineer evil out of society, especially as wealth is redistributed. Mixed-up pastors buy into these arguments and pass them on in the name of justice and compassion for the little guy.

Thus, vast numbers of church-goers now think that secularism in governments is religiously neutral; that arbitrary "neutral" governments can manage modern affairs better than Christian ones; that the government has a duty to license the church and marriage and to intervene in society by redistributing wealth and providing answers and resources for every problem. These church-goers also believe the government has a duty to school all children and prepare them to fit into the national economy; that the government should tax property, tax income, tax inheritance; that families and churches should conform themselves to the wishes of government and the changing nature of society; that men and women should both pull their weight in the workforce; and that everyone should trust experts who are certified by the government to engineer society to new levels of efficiency and modernity.

I've talked to some pastors who actually believe the government knows more about loving the unfortunate than God does. They have much more faith in government pronouncements than they do in the Word of God.

A&EB: *What is the Marxist view of the Church?*

GB: Today, Marxists look on the Church with a sophisticated pity. They think the poor, foolish Christians who keep it alive should just let it die; that Christians should stop believing such nonsense and conform themselves to the objective realities of modern secularism. Sometimes it seems that church leaders believe this too.

This comes out as church leaders teach inevitable surrender. What men of the Church get from this is a fear of responsibility and leadership; a fear of taking and holding dominion. This is what frustrates me about the false teachers in today's seminaries and churches. They bend over backward to find suggestions in Scripture that Christians are not meant to exercise dominion in the interests of the crown rights of Jesus Christ.

As an alternate theology, evangelical doctrine has now been refocused on a very small part of the human heart. It once spoke to every area of culture and society. Christianity once called men to meaningful lives of victory and gallantry. Now it offers men the excuses they need to retreat stylishly into oblivion. Participation in churches now requires getting in touch with one's feelings. All but the weakest of men now feel strangely uncomfortable in today's touchy-feely, emotion-driven, socially irrelevant churches. But that's another topic and another tragedy.

A&EB: *What can families do if both the churches and the fathers are weak?*

GB: Here's the short answer. Men should begin by reforming themselves, and then trying to help their churches. They must not be arrogantly divisive in their churches, and there are proper ways to leave and start other churches if that becomes necessary.[2]

But it is not a good solution to simply remain in a weak church without doing anything. Environments that perpetuate passivity are extremely unhealthy for men and their families. Churches must inspire men to pursue patriarchal leadership.

A&EB: *What is the main message of the weak church?*

GB: It is identical to the message they received in the government classrooms of the 20th century: "Sit down, be quiet, and feel guilty, because you have a masculine urge to stand up and get out of this inhuman environment."

And so modern men do grow up feeling guilty about being men. They are timid about showing any masculine traits of leadership and responsibility. Thus, many men are afraid to marry because of the responsibilities they would face and the leadership they would have to demonstrate. Those who do marry and have children seem to feel it would be wrong to *lead* their wives and families.

The course they follow is to settle into the role modern society tells them they are suited for: "dopey dad," the henpecked wage-slave who exists to be exploited by his kids while he tries to keep his sanity. His sanctuary is the pursuit of perpetual childishness. He can be a dull sports fan or maybe a hobby nut, as long as he keeps his head down and his opinions to himself. He's learned to be the "good" dad, the invisible dad. How many of today's young women have grown up with fathers like this?

---

2   Guidance is available at www.visionforum.org and the National Center for Family-Integrated Churches.

A&EB: *Among our acquaintances, maybe eighty percent. No, probably more like sixty because so many dads just pack up and leave.*

GB: The sad thing is that the sixty percent are the fortunate girls—those who have survived the abortion culture—or those whose fathers haven't totally abandoned them when they deserted the family to run away from responsibility.

A&EB: *Right. At least thirty percent of the young women in this city have grown up not knowing their fathers. What else can you tell the good fathers, and the more involved dads?*

GB: Contrary to popular thinking, being a disengaged or invisible dad is not "good fatherhood." Masculinity is not a problem to be overcome by therapy. Being a pushover dad is not responsible fatherhood. Spoiling daughters by withholding discipline harms them almost as much as giving in to their childish manipulations. Encouraging them to fit passively or popularly into a corrupt society is not loving them, and neither is having low expectations for them.

Too many fathers are resigned to the destruction of their daughters because we live in a destructive culture, and the "experts" continue to tell fathers that there's nothing they can do and there is nothing they may do to guide or nurture their girls. Problems of character are supposed to fix themselves as the girls leave home. Falling into danger or folly is something that just happens, and fathers must not interfere in their daughter's finding her place in the world.

Consequently, fathers think both they and their daughters are doing well if the daughter isn't on drugs, pregnant, or diseased by age 20. Fathers can and must think much more constructively about their daughters.

A&EB: *How can fathers involve their daughters more in their work and vision?*

GB: First, the fathers need to articulate a vision, and they can do this in stages for girls who are very young. You knew when you were five, six, and seven how important our home was in helping people. As you helped in the home, you knew you were important to the overall vision. Little by little you learned that your mother and I were discipling others in much the same way we were discipling you. I was able to show you how valuable you were in helping us show hospitality to others. You came to learn that everything you did to help was highly important to the overall mission. Watching the baby, changing a diaper, or sweeping the kitchen floor were jobs that had eternal value, because it helped your father and mother spend more time with the people they were trying to help. I made sure you knew this. When people's souls are changed so that they think differently and act differently, history changes. The consequences are eternal because souls are eternal.

Our constant stream of guests would not have been possible without your sharing the load. The best part about it was the way you helped. Having a house full of people became a way of life, and you served those people, whether high estate or low estate, whether the guests were planned or spur-of-the-moment, with the same attitude you always served your parents.

One day a famous journalist and his wife were at our home on business. As they were leaving, we asked them to stay and join us for dinner, and they watched you children with great fascination, especially when you quietly cleared the table. They were captivated. "May I take your plate, Mrs. ____?"

They asked later, "What makes your children so...um...how do you get them to do the right things before you even ask?" Two years later this family came to us for help and advice when they were having serious difficulty with their teenagers.

Anna Sofia, here's another story. You were five or six. I never told you the ending of this story. One night we were entertaining a very important travel-weary political leader. He would be staying overnight, so he and I were in the living room, talking on and on. You came over, untied my shoes and slipped them off, as you often have. You then went over to our guest and said, "Mr. ____, would you like for me to untie your shoes?"

Several years later he said to me, "You know when I decided we should have more children? It was that night your sweet little daughter helped me with my shoes!"

One simple act of hospitality had eternal consequences. How many hundreds or thousands of souls were affected by that one evening?

The point of these stories is that you understood one of the simpler parts of your father's vision: love people, be kind to them, and take care of them according to our family's traditions of bringing them into our home, and learning from how your parents disciple them.

Simply helping enthusiastically is a very powerful testimony. It is a reflection of God's order. This is why the home is such an important center of evangelism and discipleship. Families can illustrate many aspects of the kingdom of God. When you were 8 and 10, an important foreign dignitary and his wife stayed in our home several days to meet with your father, and they observed our family closely. Later, when we were in their country, all nine of us, this Member of Parliament gave me the key to his home, saying, "We'll be away for a few weeks, just make yourselves comfortable and get to know our region, and help yourself to my library." This would not have been possible without the reputation you children earned for yourselves earlier, distinguishing yourselves with conduct that was pure and right.

A&EB: *I think the whole time we were in that beautiful home we only broke one thing, even with five growing boys in the house. It was a coffee mug.*

GB: And I'm the one who broke it. Anyway, you helped me tremendously by mastering the little things, and over the years the Lord has expanded your father's vision and your abilities to help.

A&EB: *Like with your speeches and messages.*

GB: Yes. Your research help to me is very valuable.

As is your help with media projects. When you were 12 and 14 you helped tremendously with the marketing of one TV series by creating the content of those educational activity workbooks. Because you had been faithful with little things, I could entrust you with tasks that were completely foreign to you. You were not intimidated by the impossible or unusual because you had been tackling new challenges with good attitudes from a young age. And in working together every year, we grow closer together.

A&EB: *What if fathers have no specific tasks their daughters can help them with?*

GB: Fathers should work hard to let their daughters know about every interest and concern. Their daughters may find creative ways they can help. But fathers need to be leading their girls, not the other way around.

If a father cannot involve the girls in his business in any way, they may need to get into different businesses. I've had fathers tell me, "But if I did that I would lose all the momentum I've built up in my current business." Yes, but if you don't you may lose your daughters. To many men, their businesses are more important than their daughters. This is because their hearts are turned toward their businesses and themselves and not toward their daughters.

Sometimes this means fathers should start a smaller business. Perhaps the daughters could supply such intensive new momentum that the financial tradeoff becomes positive in a short time. But a man's vision should extend so far beyond his own earning power for one generation that he sees vast amounts of spiritual capital in his girls. They are valuable.

Sometimes fathers can stay in big business and bring their daughters in to help them directly. When you were 14 and 16, I was not ashamed to bring you into the boardroom of the company at which I was CEO, to take minutes and serve as trusted personal assistants. In fact, there were professional reasons to display your professional conduct to the lawyers and accountants, as well as the senior company managers, who profited by your example. I needed to disciple many of them by upscaling their professionalism. What better way than to bring in professionals who are adequately trained?

A&EB: *You recommend fathers working closely with sons too, don't you?*

GB: Of course. It is imperative for fathers to bring their sons alongside them in their work.

A&EB: *If fathers have done this for sons in a very masculine business, how can daughters help?*

GB: If there are no positions appropriate for daughters, fathers can develop other interests or start other businesses that are more suitable for daughters. Endorsing this book project is one example. I wanted to steer your attention to this topic at this point in your lives for your benefit. At the same time, you're assisting me in communicating specialized truth to people who must receive it. I'm very concerned for so many good young daughters being neglected and abandoned by their fathers, and we can work together on this project to help each other as well as thousands of readers.

I'm trying to find things for you to do that will perfect and complete your training while at the same time strengthen the estate we have begun to build together. This book will yield all kinds of benefits. Mostly spiritual, but even some financial benefits. Disciplined daughters can possibly work on many different projects simultaneously.

A&EB: *How can fathers work to be developing their own vision?*

GB: As I've stated, faithful obedience in little things can move the Lord to show a man bigger things. Men need to start obeying what they know, little by little. They need to visualize their daughters as mothers and grandmothers with millions of descendants.

With this perspective on the long term, dads can see the short term better. Dads only have a very few short years to give daughters an important cause to live for, and to prepare them for a future that can be a lot more than just survival in an uncivil society. Fathers, you can help your daughter find lifelong purpose, happiness, and meaningfulness in her God-ordained role that can completely realign society on constructive terms.

A&EB: *So what must today's fathers do first?*

GB: Recover this vision by acting it out, even in the small ways they may presently understand it. Be men at all times. Lead spiritually, as patriarchs, beginning in the home and working out from there. In connection to their daughters, fathers must develop a vision for what a daughter means in the grand order of God's design.

The father is placed over the daughter to be her guard, her protector, and her provider, to represent God to her in the generous ways He loves her and blesses her. The father must see just how much influence the daughter possesses in her role as a virtuous woman. She can make her father and his estate powerful and influential. When she marries, she will jointly rule and run a new estate, which might grow vastly influential over centuries as her descendants build on every influence she personally builds into her family.

So what does this vision mean practically? The dad seizes the short time he has with his daughter to prepare her for great things. He protects her diligently from anything that would compromise her future. He trains her very faithfully to be a good helper to a husband she will live with for more years than she spends with her father. The father does not send her away, unprotected. He gets her ready to be given away to another honorable man, and when the time comes, he needs to do that joyfully.

It also means that this very process of fathering inspires the daughter with great appreciation. She knows she is valued. Highly valued. She knows she is an integral part to a grand decree ordained by God himself. She is valued enough by her father to be given purpose and causes worth living for, and not just when she meets some young knight in shining armor. The daughter is given causes to live for in her youth. She is given a dad who will protect her and provide her opportunities for great influence whether she meets a good husband or not. She is valuable to her father and her family at every age. She is treated as though she is worthy of a superior husband. She is trained to be worthy of him. With the view of future marriage in mind, the father can help the daughter get closer to the reality of meeting a real knight in shining armor who will fully appreciate all the vision, and all the ability, and all the character that has been built into the maiden by a conscientious father. This suitor will value the investment of the father and become the new protector of the lady as the father joyfully transfers his God-given authority to this groom on the wedding day.

A&EB: *If the father doesn't have this vision, is there anything the daughter can do to help him get it?*

GB: Be sure to write a chapter about this in your book. It would involve the daughter's humble appeal to her father, giving him her heart, submitting to him to win him, serving him as self-training for marriage, and finding new things about him to honor. *[Editor: see Chapter Four of this book.]*

Let me say a word about what she should *not* do. Many girls think they have good relationships with their dads if they can tease, cajole, and manipulate their fathers as lovable but clueless sugar-daddies. This does not develop the relationship in the direction it should go, but tends to drive the dad deeper into the manipulated-follower role instead of the resourceful-leader role. Most girls who perpetuate this kind of shallow relationship do it to extort things from their fathers they shouldn't have.

There is an important place for humor, wit, and fun, but it should be built on a dignified relationship which the girls build by highly respectful interaction.

Fathers should never reward a daughter's guile, even when it seems good-natured. But fathers should respond generously and attentively to a daughter's respectful conduct, her appeals for guidance, and her quest for spiritual intimacy.

Dads, when a girl offers you her heart, take it and cherish it as if it was worth more than the crown jewels. It is.

A&EB: *Should girls show their fathers this interview?*

GB: Yes, at the right time, it may awaken something noble, but lecturing one's father is not the way to get him to learn or embrace his basic duties. A daughter, by humbly modeling her own duties to her father, will begin to show him the priceless asset he has in his daughter. Most men recognize and protect the value of their assets and will begin turning attention to girls who show themselves to be more valuable than rubies.

A&EB: *Okay. What if the father is noble and the daughter is an accomplished rebel?*

GB: Most fathers will know that the reason for this is their own negligence. This is the dad's fault, even though the girl is fully responsible for her own sin. Every cute little girl comes into the world as a rebel, but parents can guide little terrors into paths of outward righteousness at young ages. This teaches them about their need for salvation and inward righteousness.

Perfecting rebellion into an advanced art form also requires some discipling, and this is easy to find in any corner of Western society. Bad company is available. Fathers who fail to protect their daughters from the anti-family ideas girls can pick up from friends, media, school, or other bad company will find themselves with corrupted daughters who are very hard to win back.

Fathers must understand that the world's ideal father is not a biblical father. The hands-off father thinks neglect and abandonment are parenting skills, because this is what he is taught by the pop experts. He's supposed to spoil his girl, and then tell her, "Here's the world, Sweetie. Take every opportunity to enjoy yourself completely. You survive by being tough, masculine, popular, and, most of all, by fitting in. And, of course, I'll be cool and not interfere in any of your affairs."

Can you tell me what this kind of fathering has done to some of your friends?

A&EB: *First, it makes them confused. Their dads appear to be "good" dads. But the girls are uncomfortable because they know something is wrong. It makes them cynical, bitter, distrustful, and angry. After a few years of vulnerability, usually at college, they tend to regard their fathers as betrayers.*

GB: For good reason. Their fathers have betrayed them to be exploited by a predatory society. Many girls then also develop a blind rage against God's authority, because their fathers have represented an authority that has deserted them in their frailty. This exasperates girls, especially when dads say, "Go out and be independent, but if I want to boss you around sometimes, you'd better remember my authority."

This provokes young women to wrath, because they know it's wrong for a father to both demand respect for his authority and to abdicate it simultaneously.

I've seen girls develop personalities of giddy insolence, despicable contemptuousness, and a jubilant arrogance toward all authority. It comes out in their dress, their preferred celebrity idols, in their music, and in the cultures they create when they set up house in their private bedrooms, apartments, or dorm rooms.

A&EB: *So what kind of home should fathers provide their daughters?*

GB: A safe home. A meaningful home. An industrious home. One that conscientiously resembles the order God has designed. The dad should work to eliminate any hostility toward God's order in his home and in the minds of his family. He should identify every instance of hostility in the modern world and show his daughter how to live in antithesis. That means living in precisely the opposite ways to the world's chaotic disorder in order to restore God's order.

326

A&EB: *Can you give a quick summary of a dad's main responsibilities to his daughter?*

GB: Fathers are charged by God to be the honorable protectors and defenders of a daughter's mind, soul, body, honor, purity, character, and reputation.

A dad is also the provider of vision for kingdom responsibilities. He needs to explain to the daughter all her responsibilities for her youth and adulthood.

Dads must also provide the inheritance of life, moral duty, material wealth, religious education, discipline, standards of purity, and standards of virtue so she knows what virtuous girlhood and virtuous womanhood look like so that daughters can delight in the fact that they are women.

Fathers must represent God to daughters, because daughters are commanded to give hearts to fathers. From this they learn to give their hearts to their heavenly Father and to their husbands.

It's a scary job dads have. Women are uniquely valuable, and fathers must communicate the magnificence of womanhood to the girl. When under God's protection, girls attain great superiority of righteous influence, honor, strength, private and public respect, regal power, dignity, poise, refinement, wisdom, and grace of body and soul.

A father is to train his daughter to delight in the work God has called her to do:

To enlarge the boundaries of Christ's kingdom and subdue the earth for His glory.

A father is to train his daughter to be humble enough to work in intimate partnership with others to accomplish this, including her future husband.

The father-daughter relationship is crucial to God's design. It is primarily where girls learn God's ways and how to stay on track. It is a critical component in the high calling of women: finding complete fulfillment, strength, and purpose in femininity. It helps in the Lord's business of subduing cultures for His glory through the agency of the family. It helps in preparing girls to be able to give their hearts to God and to their husbands. It helps in preparing girls for their most important mission in life. Thank you, girls, for putting this book together. I am very thankful for you both.

APPENDIX B

THE NATURE OF MILITANT FEMINISM

"The most merciful thing a large family can do to one of its infant members is to kill it." (Margaret Sanger, founder of Planned Parenthood, in *Women and the New Race*, p. 67.)

"In order to raise children with equality, we must take them away from families and communally raise them." (Dr. Mary Jo Bane, feminist and assistant professor of education at Wellesley College, and associate director of the school's Center for Research on Women.)

"The nuclear family must be destroyed, and people must find better ways of living together. ...Whatever its ultimate meaning, the break-up of families now is an objectively revolutionary process...

"Families have supported oppression by separating people into small, isolated units, unable to join together to fight for common interests..." ("Functions of the Family," Linda Gordon, *WOMEN: A Journal of Liberation*, Fall 1969.)

"Marriage has existed for the benefit of men; and has been a legally sanctioned method of control over women…We must work to destroy it. The end of the institution of marriage is a necessary condition for the liberation of women. Therefore it is important for us to encourage women to leave their husbands and not to live individually with men." ("The Declaration of Feminism," November 1971.)

"Since marriage constitutes slavery for women, it is clear that the women's movement must concentrate on attacking this institution. Freedom for women cannot be won without the abolition of marriage." (Sheila Cronan.)

"[M]ost mother-women give up whatever ghost of a unique and human self they may have when they 'marry' and raise children." (Phyllis Chesler, *Women and Madness*, p. 294.)

"The cultural institutions which embody and enforce those interlocked aberrations—for instance, law, art, religion, nation-states, the family, tribe, or commune based on father-right—these institutions are real and they must be destroyed." (Andrea Dworkin.)

"No Socialist republic can operate successfully and maintain its ideals unless the practice of birth control is encouraged to a marked and efficient degree." (Margaret Sanger, founder of Planned Parenthood and member of the Woman's Committee of the New York Socialist Party, in her book *Women and the New Race.*)

"…Women's liberation, if not the most extreme then certainly the most influential neo-Marxist movement in America, has done to the American home what communism did to the Russian

economy, and most of the ruin is irreversible. By defining
between men and women in terms of power and competition
instead of reciprocity and cooperation, the movement tore apart
the most basic and fragile contract in human society, the unit
from which all other social institutions draw their strength."
(Harvard professor Ruth Wisse.)

"Marx was on to something more profound than he knew
when he observed that the family contained within itself in
embryo all the antagonisms that later develop on a wider scale
within the society and the state...[U]nless revolution uproots
the basic organization, the biological family...the tapeworm of
exploitation will never be annihilated." (Shulamith Firestone in
her 1970 tract "The Dialectic of Sex.")

"Feminism is not just an issue or a group of issues...It is the
cutting edge of a revolution in cultural and moral values. ...The
objective of every feminist reform, from legal abortion...to
child-care programs, is to undermine traditional family values..."
(Feminist revolutionary Ellen Willis in the November 14, 1981
issue of *The Nation*.)

"...No woman should have to deny herself any opportunities
because of her special responsibilities to her children. ...Families
will be finally destroyed only when a revolutionary social and
economic organization permits people's needs for love and
security to be met in ways that do not impose divisions of labor,
or any external roles, at all." ("Functions of the Family," Linda
Gordon, *WOMEN: A Journal of Liberation*, Fall 1969.)

"Only when manhood is dead—and it will perish when ravaged
femininity no longer sustains it—only then will we know what it is
to be free." (Andrea Dworkin, "The Root Cause," speech delivered

Sept. 26, 1975 at the Massachusetts Institute of Technology, Cambridge, published in *Our Blood*, Chapter 9, 1976.)

"...[I]t is important for us to encourage women to leave their husbands and not to live individually with men...All of history must be re-written in terms of oppression of women." ("The Declaration of Feminism," November 1971.)

"We can't destroy the inequities between men and women until we destroy marriage." (*Sisterhood is Powerful*, Robin Morgan (ed.), 1970, p. 537.)

"Being a housewife is an illegitimate profession...The choice to serve and be protected and plan towards being a family-maker is a choice that shouldn't be. The heart of radical feminism is to change that." (Vivian Gornick, University of Illinois, *The Daily Illini*, April 25, 1981.)

"No woman should be authorized to stay at home to raise her children. Society should be totally different. Women should not have that choice, precisely because if there is such a choice, too many women will make that one." (Simone de Beauvoir, in her famous 1974 interview in *The Saturday Review*.)

"We must go back to ancient female religions like witchcraft." ("The Declaration of Feminism," November 1971.)

"By the year 2000 we will, I hope, raise our children to believe in human potential, not God." (Gloria Steinem, editor of *Ms.Magazine*.)

"The care of children...is infinitely better left to the best trained practitioners of both sexes who have chosen it as a vocation... [This] would further undermine family structure while contributing to the freedom of women." (Kate Millet, *Sexual Politics*, pp. 178-179.)

"Our culture, including all that we are taught in schools and universities, is so infused with patriarchal thinking that it must be torn up root and branch if genuine change is to occur. Everything must go—even the allegedly universal disciplines of logic, mathematics, and science, and the intellectual values of objectivity, clarity, and precision on which the former depend." (Daphne Patai and Noretta Koertge, *Professing Feminism: Cautionary Tales from the Strange World of Women's Studies*, New York, Basic Books, 1994, p. 116.)[1]

---

1 The above quotes collected and posted by Bill Wood, www.fathersforlife.org, used by permission.

www.visionarydaughters.com